DEVELOPING
ACADEMIC READING
SKILLS

DEVELOPING ACADEMIC READING SKILLS

Laura Donahue Latulippe

*Director, Career English Language Center
for International Students,
Western Michigan University*

Prentice-Hall, Inc.
Englewood Cliffs, New Jersey 07632

Library of Congress Cataloging-in-Publication Data

LATULIPPE, LAURA DONAHUE
  Developing academic reading skills.

  1. College readers. I. Title.
PE1122.L34 1987   428.6   86-16905
ISBN 0-13-204157-X

Editorial/production supervision
and interior design by Eva Jaunzems
Cover design by Wanda Lubelska
Manufacturing buyer: Carol Bystrom

© 1987 by Prentice-Hall
A Division of Simon & Schuster, Inc.
Englewood Cliffs, New Jersey 07632

Printed in the United States of America

10 9 8 7 6 5 4 3 2

ISBN   0-13-204157-X   01

Prentice-Hall International (UK) Limited, *London*
Prentice-Hall of Australia Pty. Limited, *Sydney*
Prentice-Hall of Canada Inc., *Toronto*
Prentice-Hall Hisponoamericana, S.A., *Mexico*
Prentice-Hall of India Private Limited, *New Delhi*
Prentice-Hall of Japan, Inc., *Tokyo*
Prentice-Hall of Southeast Asia Pte. Ltd., *Singapore*
Editora Prentice-Hall do Brasil, Ltda., *Rio de Janeiro*
Whitehall Books Limited, *Wellington, New Zealand*

To my parents,
Wilbur A. Donahue and Hazel Donahue Schoning

Contents

7

More Reading Social Science • 232

8

Reading an Experiment Report • 271

Appendix: Affixes and Stems • 298

Preface

Developing Academic Reading Skills is intended for advanced students attending one of the many intensive English programs in the United States or international students who have already been admitted to a college or university, but who are taking English as a Second Language (ESL) to assist them with university study.

This book is designed to be used as part of a comprehensive reading program to prepare international students for the various types of academic reading they will encounter in an average American university or community college. Seven readings are taken from typical university-level texts in computer science, environmental science, business, and social science; a short report is also included (Chapter Eight) to show the type of journal article that students might read in the course of their research. The text teaches, provides practice in, and tests the reading skills necessary for academic success: word attack, identifying main ideas, relating main and supporting ideas, recognizing the function of a text, scanning, understanding reference words, using context clues, understanding logical transitions, understanding the author's plan, making inferences, distinguishing fact from theory, synthesizing the text with prior experience, and drawing conclusions. Once these skills have been introduced, they are practiced and reviewed to assure that the student masters them thoroughly.

By placing international students in reading situations similar to those they will encounter in a university, showing them how to cope with these situations, and giving them practice in doing so, *Developing Academic Reading Skills* should significantly ease students' transition from the ESL classroom to the university classroom.

L.D.L.

ACKNOWLEDGMENTS

I wish to thank Jane Hudson, Michael Latulippe, Mary Lu Light, Marilyn Van Hare, and my husband, Dale, for their help in editing my work and for their constant support of my efforts.

1

Reading
Computer Science

Punched card sorter installed at the U.S. Census Bureau during the 1890's

VOCABULARY PREPARATION

With each course you take in the university, you will find that there will be a list of basic words that occur again and again in both your textbook and the course lectures. These words should be very familiar to you in all their forms so that you can use them correctly as you write and speak. You also need to thoroughly understand the various definitions of each word and be familiar with appropriate synonyms that an author might use instead of repeating these words in the text. In each unit of this book you will work with the basic words for the textbook chapter you are reading.

In order to know a word well, you should:

1. Learn its various forms (verb, adjective, adverb, noun).
2. Recognize the correct definition according to context.
3. Learn the words that are related to it because they come from the same stem (or root).
4. Learn synonyms (words that mean the same thing) and antonyms (words that have the opposite meaning) of the word.

As an illustration, let's look at the word *import*. *Import* can be either a verb or a noun. (Japan <u>imports</u> large amounts of oil in order to keep its society running, but oil is only one of the <u>imports</u> that are necessary to this country's economy.)

The Random House Dictionary of the English Language (New York: Random House, 1969) defines "import" in the following way:

> **import** – v.t. 1. to bring in (merchandise, commodities, etc.) from a foreign country for sale, use, processing, or re-export. 2. to bring or introduce from one use, connection, or relation to another (*foreign bodies imported into the blood; foodstuffs imported from the farm*). 3. to convey as meaning or information, as by words, statements, actions, etc. (*her words imported a change of attitude*). 4. to involve as a necessary circumstance; imply (*religion imports belief*). 5. (Rare) to be of consequence or importance; concern.
> v.i. 6. to be of consequence or importance; matter.
> n. 7. that which is imported from abroad; an imported commodity or article. 8. the act of importing or bringing in; importation, as goods from abroad (*the import of foreign cars*). 9. meaning; implication; purport (*he felt the import of her words*). 10. consequence or importance (*matters of great import*).

These are the meanings for *import*; however, the word has other forms as well. The adjective for definition 7 is *importable*, and the adjective for definition 10 is *important*. There are two other nouns in this group of related words (*importer*, one who imports something; and *importability*, the ability to be imported), and we can speak of *imported* goods, taking the past participle form of the verb and using it as an adjective.

Finally, words that relate to a word because they have a similar meaning (synonyms) or an opposite meaning (antonyms) should be learned with the word. Authors will substitute synonyms for the words they originally use in order to provide variety, so the reader must be able to recognize these substitutions.

SKIMMING

Before you read each chapter in a textbook, you should skim the whole chapter to get a general impression of what you will be reading and to introduce yourself to important vocabulary used by the author. Getting a general impression before you read helps you anticipate (guess ahead) what you will read in each section of the chapter and recall what you already know about the subject. Remembering what you already know about the subject will help you guess the general meaning of passages that are not completely clear to you and help you organize the ideas of that chapter in your mind. As you skim, you will notice words that appear again and again in the text. These are the basic words that you must look up in a dictionary if they are not familiar to you. Finally, as you skim, you will become aware of the author's method of organization, which will help you locate the answers to questions quickly and find information you need to prepare the answers to essay exams.

These are the steps that you should follow to skim a chapter:

STEP 1: Read the main title of the chapter and all of the headings (titles for the sections of the chapter). Notice how these titles relate to one another. For example, are the headings steps in a process, categories into which the title can be divided, chronological events, or some other classification?

STEP 2: Examine pictures, charts, and other illustrations in the chapter to get information about the chapter's contents.

STEP 3: Find the names of the people mentioned in the chapter and try to determine who they are.

    a. Look for clues in the passage that will tell you something about the people. For example:

       "Although a number of people contributed to their development, Blaise Pascal (French mathematician and philosopher) and Wilhelm von Leibniz (German mathematician, philosopher, and diplomat) usually are singled out as pioneers."

    b. Look in the footnotes at the end of the chapter (or at the bottom of the

Exercise 1: Basic Vocabulary Chart

The basic vocabulary for this unit may already be familiar to you. The purpose of this chart is to give you the opportunity to become thoroughly acquainted with these basic words as well as to learn unfamiliar but related words. Use your English-to-English dictionary to help you complete this chart. Put the chart on a separate sheet of paper so that you will have room to write all of the appropriate definitions and related words.

Word	Part of Speech	Meaning (as used in indicated paragraph)	Related Words	Synonyms
device (4)	noun	*A thing that is made, usually for a particular purpose; an invention or contrivance, esp. a mechanical or electrical one.*	*deviceful—adj. devicefully— adv. devicefulness— n.*	*gadget*
process (6)	noun			
automate (9)	verb			
calculate (19)	verb			
accuracy (26)	noun			
conceive (35)	verb			
memory (41)	noun			

In addition to the different forms (parts of speech) of a word, there are often other related words (words that come from the same root or stem). *Import* comes from the root *port*, which means "to carry." *Im-* is a prefix (a word part added before the stem of a word to change its meaning) that is added to *port* to change its meaning from "to carry" to "to carry into." If we change the prefix to *ex-* the word (*export*) means "to carry out." Other words that are related to *import* include *transport* (to carry across), *report* (to carry back), *porter* (a person who carries luggage at a hotel or train station), and *deport* (to carry off, to expel from the country).

There are, then, two ways to find related words: first, you can find all of the other forms of the same word (noun, verb, and so on); then, you can find the words that come from the same stem or root (a list of common stems and their meanings can be found in the appendix of this book on page 300).

Finally, words that relate to a word because they have a similar meaning (synonyms) or an opposite meaning (antonyms) should be learned with the word. Authors will substitute synonyms for the words they originally use in order to provide variety, so the reader must be able to recognize these substitutions.

SKIMMING

Before you read each chapter in a textbook, you should skim the whole chapter to get a general impression of what you will be reading and to introduce yourself to important vocabulary used by the author. Getting a general impression before you read helps you anticipate (guess ahead) what you will read in each section of the chapter and recall what you already know about the subject. Remembering what you already know about the subject will help you guess the general meaning of passages that are not completely clear to you and help you organize the ideas of that chapter in your mind. As you skim, you will notice words that appear again and again in the text. These are the basic words that you must look up in a dictionary if they are not familiar to you. Finally, as you skim, you will become aware of the author's method of organization, which will help you locate the answers to questions quickly and find information you need to prepare the answers to essay exams.

These are the steps that you should follow to skim a chapter:

STEP 1: Read the main title of the chapter and all of the headings (titles for the sections of the chapter). Notice how these titles relate to one another. For example, are the headings steps in a process, categories into which the title can be divided, chronological events, or some other classification?

STEP 2: Examine pictures, charts, and other illustrations in the chapter to get information about the chapter's contents.

STEP 3: Find the names of the people mentioned in the chapter and try to determine who they are.

    a. Look for clues in the passage that will tell you something about the people. For example:

      "Although a number of people contributed to their development, Blaise Pascal (French mathematician and philosopher) and Wilhelm von Leibniz (German mathematician, philosopher, and diplomat) usually are singled out as pioneers."

    b. Look in the footnotes at the end of the chapter (or at the bottom of the page) if there is a raised footnote number at the end of the sentence containing the name. Here is an example of a footnote:

"In 1957 Murdock compiled data on some 565 societies."[1] (This sentence is part of the chapter reading.)

[1]G. P. Murdock, "World Ethnographic Sample," *American Anthropologist*, 59 (1957), 686.

(This is found at the end of the chapter or at the bottom of the page.)

The tiny *1* after the quotation from the chapter reading tells you that there is more information about this subject at the bottom of the page or at the end of the chapter. You can find the footnote by looking in these places for the same small number. The footnote will either give you information that the author didn't wish to include in the main text of the chapter, or it will tell you what source (book, magazine) this information came from. The example above tells you that G. P. Murdock (obviously an anthropologist) published an article called "World Ethnographic Sample" in volume 59 of a magazine called *American Anthropologist*. This volume was published in 1957, and the article is located on page 686.

c. If there is no footnote and no other clue, that person may be so well known in the author's culture that the author assumes all readers will know the name. You can find general information about famous people in a good English-to-English dictionary or an encyclopedia.

d. Finally, if all else fails, ask a classmate or your instructor.

STEP 4: Look at all italicized words and phrases (words and phrases in special print, such as *The Jacquard Loom*). Try to determine the author's reason for italicizing them. For example, they may be headings, important vocabulary words for which you should know the dictionary definition, important ideas that the author wants to make sure you don't miss, or words that have a special meaning in this passage that is different from their usual use.

STEP 5: Look at the review questions and the bibliography at the end of the chapter (if the chapter has them), to get more information about the chapter.

STEP 6: Rapidly read the first and last paragraph of the chapter and the first sentence of each paragraph. Don't worry about the words that you don't know. You are just trying to get an overall idea about the contents of the chapter so that you will know what to expect as you read.

STEP 7: Write a few sentences explaining what you think this chapter is all about.

Exercise 2: Skimming Practice

The chapter you are going to read in this unit is taken from a textbook called *The Mind Tool: Computers and Their Impact on Society* by Neil Graham. It is the first chapter of the book. Other chapters in the same section of the book discuss computer hardware, computer software, computer programming and how a computer works.

Begin your reading of this chapter by using the skimming steps. As you complete each step, answer the questions that follow it. (The chapter begins on page 9.)

STEP 1: Read the main title of the chapter and all of the headings. Notice how they relate to one another.

    a. What are the machines that came before the computer and had an influence on its development?

    b. Who are the people who are important in the early development of the computer?

    c. What are the names of the computer discussed in this chapter?

    d. How many generations of computers have there been, according to this chapter?

STEP 2: Examine pictures, charts, and other illustrations in the chapter to get information about the chapter's contents.

    a. Who were the following people?
1. Blaise Pascal
2. Gottfried Wilhelm von Leibniz
3. Charles Babbage
4. Herman Hollerith

    b. Why is the Selective Sequence Electronic Calculator important?

    c. Why is the Tabulating Machine Company important?

    d. How is *binary notation* used today?

STEP 3: Find the names of people, organizations, and so on (proper names) in the chapter and try to determine who or what they are.

    a. Use clues in the reading to determine who the following people are:
1. Jacquard
2. Herschel
3. Lady Lovelace
4. Augustus de Morgan
5. John W. Mauchly
6. John von Neumann
7. Howard Aiken

    b. Lord Byron and Tennyson are mentioned in this chapter, but there is no clue given as to who they are. The author of this chapter assumes the reader is familiar with English literature. Use a dictionary or encyclopedia to find out who these men were.

STEP 4: Look at all of the italicized words and phrases. Be aware of the author's reasons for italicizing them. The author uses italics in this chapter for some subtitles and for some important terms defined in the chapter. By looking for these italicized words and phrases you should be able to quickly find the answers to the following questions.

    a. What do the abacus, mechanical calculators, and the Jacquard loom have to do with this chapter on computers?

    b. What is *binary notation*?

    c. What is another name for the von Neumann machine?

    d. What is the relationship between *core memory* and *high-speed memory*?

STEP 5: Look at the review questions and bibliography at the end of the chapter to get more information about the chapter.

"For Further Reading" (page 19) is a list of books and magazine articles that can give you more information about the subjects discussed in this chapter.

The first entry is a magazine article. Notice the parts of the entry:

    Gleiser, Molly (author). "Lady Lovelace and the Difference Engine." (article) *Computer Decisions* (magazine), May 1975 (issue), pp. 38–41 (pages).

The second entry is a book. Notice the parts of this entry:

    Goldstein, Herman H. (author). *The Computer from Pascal to von Neumann* (title). Princeton: Princeton University Press (location and name of publisher), 1972 (year of publication).

    a. In what magazine is "Origins of the Binary Code" found?

    b. Which publisher published the book *Charles Babbage and His Calculating Engines*?

    c. In what issue of *Byte* is "A Short History of Computing" found?

STEP 6: Rapidly read the first and last paragraphs of the chapter and the first sentence of each paragraph.

STEP 7: In a sentence or two, explain what you think this chapter is about. (*You may answer orally or quickly write the answer that you would give orally.*)

FIRST READING

Quickly read the chapter "The Development of Computers" from *The Mind Tool* (pp. 9–20) in order to answer the following questions. You will read the chapter more thoroughly later, but for now, just read for the answers.

    1. What is the difference between the traditional tools of communication and the "mind tools" discussed in this chapter?

2. In what way did the Jacquard loom differ from the other information-processing machines that were forerunners of the computer?

3. What kind of a man was Charles Babbage?

4. What was Babbage trying to do when he invented the Difference Engine?

5. Why did he abandon this idea?

6. What role did Lady Lovelace play in the development of the computer?

7. Why was the Analytical Engine never completed?

8. Why did the Harvard Mark I become obsolete so quickly?

9. How did EDVAC differ from ENIAC?

10. What are the distinguishing characteristics of each of the computer generations?

The Development of Computers

Neil Graham

1   Tools are any objects other than the parts of our own bodies that we use to help us do our work. Technology is nothing more than the use of tools. When you use a screwdriver, a hammer, or an axe, you are using technology just as much as when you use an automobile, a television set, or a computer.

2   We tend to think of technology as a human invention. But the reverse is closer to the truth. Stone tools found along with fossils shown that our ape-like ancestors were already putting technology to use. Anthropologists speculate that using tools may have helped these creatures evolve into human beings; in a tool-using society, manual dexterity and intelligence count for more than brute strength. The clever rather than the strong inherited the earth.

3   Most of the tools we have invented have aided our bodies rather than our minds. These tools help us lift and move and cut and shape. Only quite recently, for the most part, have we developed tools to aid our minds as well.

4   The tools of communication, from pencil and paper to television, are designed to serve our minds. These devices transmit information or preserve it, but they do not modify it in any way. (If the information is modified, this is considered a defect rather than a virtue, as when a defective radio distorts the music we're trying to hear.) Important as these tools of communication are, however, they are not our concern here.

5   Instead, our interest lies with machines that classify and modify information rather than merely transmitting it or preserving it. The machines that do this are the computers and the calculators, the mind tools referred to in the title of the book.

A Chinese abacus. The Japanese abacus uses one less bead both above and below the divider.

PREHISTORY

6   The widespread use of machines for information processing is a modern development. But simple examples of information-processing machines can be traced back to ancient times. The following are some of the more important forerunners of the computer.

7   ***The Abacus***   The abacus is the counting frame that was the most widely used device for doing arithmetic in ancient times and whose use persisted into modern times in the Orient. Early versions of the abacus consisted of a board with grooves in which pebbles could slide. The Latin word for *pebble* is *calculus*, from which we get the words *abacus* and *calculate*.

8   ***Mechanical Calculators***   In the seventeenth century, calculators more sophisticated than the abacus began to appear. Although a number of people contributed to their development, Blaise Pascal (French mathematician and philosopher) and Wilhelm von Leibniz (German mathematician, philosopher, and diplomat) usually are singled out as pioneers. The calculators Pascal and Leibniz built were unreliable, since the mechanical technology of the time was not capable of manufacturing the parts with sufficient precision. As manufacturing techniques improved, mechanical calculators eventually were perfected; they were used widely until they were replaced by electronic calculators in recent times.

9   ***The Jacquard Loom***   Until modern times, most information-processing machines were designed to do arithmetic. An outstanding exception, however, was Jacquard's automated loom, a machine designed not for hard figures but beautiful patterns. A Jacquard loom weaves cloth containing a decorative pattern; the woven pattern is controlled by punched cards. Changing the punched cards changes the pattern the loom weaves. Jacquard looms came into widespread

BLAISE PASCAL.

Blaise Pascal (1623-62), who built one of the first mechanical calculators.

Gottfried Wilhelm von Leibniz (1646-1716), who built the first mechanical calculator that could multiply and divide as well as add and subtract.

use in the early nineteenth century, and their descendants are still used today. The Jacquard loom is the ancestor not only of modern automated machine tools but of the player piano as well.

THE ANALYTICAL ENGINE

10 When was the automatic computer invented? In the 1930s or the 1940s? If you think that, you are only off by a hundred years. A computer that was completely modern in conception was designed in the 1830s. But, as with the calculators of Pascal and Leibniz, the mechanical technology of the time was not prepared to realize the conception.

11 *Charles Babbage* The inventor of that nineteenth-century computer was a figure far more common in fiction than in real life—an eccentric mathematician. Most mathematicians live personal lives not too much different from anyone

else's. They just happen to do mathematics instead of driving trucks or running stores or filling teeth. But Charles Babbage was the exception.

12   For instance, all his life, Babbage waged a vigorous campaign against London organ grinders. He blamed the noise they made for the loss of a quarter of his working power. Nor was Babbage satisfied with writing anti-organ-grinder letters to newspapers and members of Parliament. He personally hauled individual offenders before magistrates (and became furious when the magistrates declined to throw the offenders in jail).

13   Or consider this. Babbage took issue with Tennyson's poem "Vision of Sin," which contains this couplet:

Every minute dies a man,
Every minute one is born.

Babbage pointed out (correctly) that if this were true, the population of the earth would remain constant. In a letter to the poet, Babbage suggested a revision:

Every moment dies a man,
And one and a sixteenth is born.

Babbage emphasized that one and a sixteenth was not exact, but he thought that it would be "good enough for poetry."

14   Yet, despite his eccentricities, Babbage was a genius. He was a prolific inventor, whose inventions include the ophthalmoscope for examining the retina of the eye, the skeleton key, the locomotive "cow catcher," and the speedometer. He also pioneered operations research, the science of how to carry out business and industrial operations as efficiently as possible.

15   Babbage was a fellow of the Royal Society and held the chair of Lucasian Professor of Mathematics at Cambridge University (the same chair once held by Isaac Newton, the most famous British scientist).

16   **The Difference Engine** The mathematical tables of the nineteenth century were full of mistakes. Even when the tables had been calculated correctly, printers' errors introduced many mistakes. And since people who published new tables often copied from existing ones, the same errors cropped up in table after table.

17   According to one story, Babbage was lamenting about the errors in some tables to his friend Herschel, a noted astronomer. "I wish to God these calculations had been executed by steam." Babbage said. "It is quite possible," Herschel responded.

18   (At that time, steam was a new and largely unexplored source of energy. Just as we might wonder today whether or not something could be done by

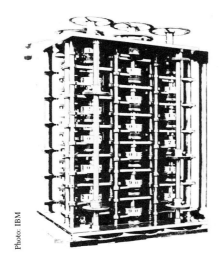

Photo: IBM

Charles Babbage's Difference Engine, a 19th century computer designed to compute mathematical tables. Babbage never completed the machine.

electricity, in the early nineteenth century it was natural to wonder whether or not it could be done by steam.)

19 Babbage set out to build a machine that not only would calculate the entries in the tables but would print them automatically as well. He called this machine the *Difference Engine*, since it worked by solving what mathematicians call "difference equations." Nevertheless, the name is misleading, since the machine constructed tables by means of repeated additions, not subtractions.

20 (The word *engine*, by the way, comes from the same root as *ingenious*. Originally it referred to a clever invention. Only later did it come to mean a source of power.)

21 In 1823, Babbage obtained a government grant to build the Difference Engine. He ran into difficulties, however, and eventually abandoned the project. In 1854, a Swedish printer built a working Difference Engine based on Babbage's ideas.

22 **The Analytical Engine**   One of Babbage's reasons for abandoning the Difference Engine was that he had been struck by a much better idea. Inspired by Jacquard's punched-card-controlled loom, Babbage wanted to build a punched-card-controlled calculator. Babbage called his proposed automatic calculator the *Analytical Engine*.

23 The Difference Engine could only compute tables (and only those tables that could be computed by successive additions). But the Analytical Engine could carry out any calculation, just as Jacquard's loom could weave any pattern. All one had to do was to punch the cards with the instructions for the desired

calculation. If the Analytical Engine had been completed, it would have been a nineteenth-century computer.

24   But, alas, the Analytical Engine was not completed. The government had already sunk thousands of pounds into the Difference Engine and received nothing in return. It had no intention of repeating its mistake. Nor did Babbage's eccentricities and abrasive personality help his cause any.

25   The government may have been right. Even if it had financed the new invention, it might well have gotten nothing in return. For, as usual, the idea was far ahead of what the existing mechanical technology could build.

26   This was particularly true since Babbage's design was grandiose. For instance, he planned for his machine to do calculations with fifty-digit accuracy. This is far greater than the accuracy found in most modern computers and far more than is needed for most calculations.

27   Also, Babbage kept changing his plans in the middle of his projects so that all the work had to be started anew. Although Babbage had founded operations research, he had trouble planning the development of his own inventions.

28   Babbage's contemporaries would have considered him more successful had he stuck to his original plan and constructed the Difference Engine. But then he would only have earned a footnote in history. It is for the Analytical Engine he never completed that we honor him as "father of the computer."

29   **Lady Lovelace**   Even though the Analytical Engine was never completed, a demonstration program for it was written. The author of that program has the honor of being the world's first computer programmer. *Her* name was Augusta Ada Byron, later Countess of Lovelace, the only legitimate daughter of the poet, Lord Byron.

30   Ada was a liberated woman at a time when this was hardly fashionable. Not only did she have the usual accomplishments in language and music, she was also an excellent mathematician. The latter was most unusual for a young lady in the nineteenth century. (She was also fond of horse racing, which was even more unusual.)

31   Ada's mathematical abilities became apparent when she was only fifteen. She studied mathematics with one of the most well-known mathematicians of her time, Augustus de Morgan. At about the time she was studying under de Morgan, she became interested in Babbage's Analytical Engine.

32   In 1842, Lady Lovelace discovered a paper on the Analytical Engine that had been written in French by an Italian engineer. She resolved to translate the paper into English. At Babbage's suggestion, she added her own notes, which turned out to be twice as long as the paper itself. Much of what we know today about the Analytical Engine comes from Lady Lovelace's notes.

33   To demonstrate how the Analytical Engine would work, Lady Lovelace

included in her notes a program for calculating a certain series of numbers that is of interest to mathematicians. This was the world's first computer program.

34   "We may say more aptly," Lady Lovelace wrote, "that the Analytical Engine *weaves algebraical patterns* just as the Jacquard-loom weaves flowers and leaves." Most aptly said indeed.

BABBAGE'S DREAM COME TRUE

35 *The Harvard Mark I*   A hundred years passed before a machine like the one Babbage conceived was actually built. This occurred in 1944, when Howard Aiken of Harvard University completed the Harvard Mark I Automatic Sequence Controlled Calculator.

36   Aiken was not familiar with the Analytical Engine when he designed the Mark I. Later, after people had pointed out Babbage's work to him, he was amazed to learn how many of his ideas Babbage had anticipated.

37   The Mark I is the closest thing to the Analytical Engine that has ever been built or ever will be. It was controlled by a punched paper tape, which played the same role as Babbage's punched cards. Like the Analytical Engine, it was basically mechanical. However, it was driven by electricity instead of steam.

Photo: IBM Archives

Herman Hollerith, who pioneered the use of punched cards for data processing in the late nineteenth century. His Tabulating Machine Company was one of the organizations that would be brought together to form IBM.

Photo: Iowa State University

John V. Atanasoff's Electronic Digital Computer, developed at Iowa State University during the 1930's.

Electricity also served to transmit information from one part of the machine to another, replacing the complex mechanical linkages that Babbage had proposed. Using electricity (which had only been a laboratory curiosity in Babbage's time) made the difference between success and failure.

38   But, along with several other electromechanical computers built at about the same time, the Mark I was scarcely finished before it was obsolete. The electromechanical machines simply were not fast enough. Their speed was seriously limited by the time required for mechanical parts to move from one position to another. For instance, the Mark I took six seconds for a multiplication and twelve for a division; this was only five or six times faster than what a human with an old desk calculator could do.

39 **ENIAC**   What was needed was a machine whose computing, control, and memory elements were completely electrical. Then the speed of operation would be limited not by the speed of mechanical moving parts but by the much greater speed of moving electrons.

40   In the late 1930s, John V. Atanasoff of Iowa State College demonstrated the elements of an electronic computer. Though his work did not become widely known, it did influence the thinking of John W. Mauchly, one of the designers of ENIAC.

41   ENIAC—Electronic Numerical Integrator and Computer—was the machine that rendered the electromechanical computers obsolete. ENIAC used vacuum tubes for computing and memory. For control, it used an electrical plugboard, like a telephone switchboard. The connections on the plugboard specified the sequence of operations ENIAC would carry out.

42   ENIAC was 500 times as fast as the best electromechanical computer. A

problem that took one minute to solve on ENIAC would require eight to ten *hours* on an electromechanical machine. After ENIAC, all computers would be electronic.

43   ENIAC was the first of many computers with acronyms for names. The same tradition gave us EDVAC, UNIVAC, JOHNIAC, ILLIAC, and even MANIAC.

44 ***EDVAC***   The Electronic Discrete Variable Computer—EDVAC—was constructed at about the same time as ENIAC. But EDVAC, influenced by the ideas of the brilliant Hungarian-American mathematician John von Neumann, was by far the more advanced of the two machines. Two innovations that first appeared in EDVAC have been incorporated in almost every computer since.

45   First, EDVAC used *binary notation* to represent numbers inside the machine. Binary notation is a system for writing numbers that uses only two digits (0 and 1), instead of the ten digits (0–9) used in the conventional decimal notation. Binary notation is now recognized as the simplest way of representing numbers in an electronic machine.

46   Second, EDVAC's program was stored in the machine's memory, just like the data. Previous computers had stored the program externally on punched tape or plugboards. Since the programs were stored the same way the data was, one program could manipulate another program as if it were data. We will see that such program-manipulating programs play a crucial role in modern computer systems.

47   A stored-program computer—one whose program is stored in memory in the same form as its data—is usually called a *von Neumann machine* in honor of the originator of the stored-program concept.

THE COMPUTER GENERATIONS

48 From the 1940s to the present, the technology used to build computers has gone through several revolutions. People sometimes speak of different *generations* of computers, with each generation using a different technology.

49 ***The First Generation***   First-generation computers prevailed in the 1940s and for much of the 1950s. They used vacuum tubes for calculation, control, and sometimes for memory as well. First-generation machines used several other ingenious devices for memory. In one, for instance, information was stored as sound waves circulating in a column of mercury. Since all these first-generation memories are now obsolete, no further mention will be made of them.

50   Vacuum tubes are bulky, unreliable, energy consuming, and generate large amounts of heat. As long as computers were tied down to vacuum tube technology, they could only be bulky, cumbersome, and expensive.

Photo: Courtesy Sperry Corporation.

J. Presper Eckert and newsman Walter Cronkite discuss the use of the UNIVAC vacuum tube computer in the 1952 presidential election.

51   **The Second Generation**   In the late 1950s, the transistor became available to replace the vacuum tube. A transistor, which is only slightly larger than a kernel of corn, generates little heat and enjoys long life.

52   At about the same time, the magnetic-core memory was introduced. This consisted of a latticework of wires on which were strung tiny, doughnut-shaped beads called *cores*. Electric currents flowing in the wires stored information by magnetizing the cores. Information could be stored in core memory or retrieved from it in about a millionth of a second.

53   Core memory dominated the high-speed memory scene for much of the second and third generations. To programmers during this period, *core* and *high-speed memory* were synonymous.

54   **The Third Generation**   The early 1960s saw the introduction of *integrated circuits*, which incorporated hundreds of transistors on a single silicon chip. The chip itself was small enough to fit on the end of your finger; after being mounted in a protective package, it still would fit in the palm of your hand. With integrated circuits, computers could be made even smaller, less expensive, and more reliable.

55   Integrated circuits made possible *minicomputers*, tabletop computers small enough and inexpensive enough to find a place in the classroom and the scientific laboratory.

56   In the late 1960s, integrated circuits began to be used for high-speed memory, providing some competition for magnetic-core memory. The trend toward integrated-circuit memory has continued until today, when it has largely replaced magnetic-core memory.

57   The most recent jump in computer technology came with the introduction of *large-scale integrated circuits*, often referred to simply as *chips*. Whereas the older integrated circuits contained hundred of transistors, the new ones contain thousands or tens of thousands.

58   It is the large-scale integrated circuits that make possible the *microprocessors* and *microcomputers*. They also make possible compact, inexpensive, high-speed, high-capacity integrated-circuit memory.

59   No one has yet proclaimed a fourth generation of computers. But the recent developments just mentioned have resulted in a *microprocessor revolution*, which began in the middle 1970s and for which there is no end in sight.

FOR FURTHER READING

GLEISER, MOLLY. "Lady Lovelace and the Difference Engine." *Computer Decisions*, May 1975, pp. 38–41.

GOLDSTEIN, HERMAN H. *The Computer from Pascal to von Neumann*. Princeton: Princeton University Press, 1972.

HEATH, F. G. "Origins of the Binary Code." *Scientific American*, Aug. 1972, pp. 76–83.

LIBES, SOL. "The First Ten Years of Amateur Computing." *Byte*, July 1978, pp. 64–71.

MORRISON, PHILLIP, and MORRISON, EMILY. *Charles Babbage and His Calculating Engines*. New York: Dover Publications, 1961.

REID-GREEN, KEITH S. "A Short History of Computing." *Byte*, July 1978, pp. 84–94.

REVIEW QUESTIONS

1. How might technology have contributed to the evolution of mankind?
2. What was the most widely used method of calculation in ancient times?
3. From where do we get the words *abacus* and *calculate*?
4. Name two mathematicians and philosophers who constructed pioneering mechanical calculators.

5. Why were the early mechanical calculators unreliable?

6. What distinguishes the Jacquard loom from the abacus and the mechanical calculators?

7. What determines the pattern woven by a Jacquard loom?

8. In what century was the automatic computer invented?

9. What facets of Charles Babbage's character might have made it more difficult for him to get his inventions taken seriously?

10. What inspired Charles Babbage to start work on the Difference Engine?

11. Contrast the Difference Engine and the Analytical Engine.

12. Where did Babbage get the idea for using punched cards to control the Analytical Engine?

13. Who wrote a program for the Analytical Engine and so became the world's first computer programmer?

14. What was the main shortcoming of the Mark I and the other electro-mechanical computers?

15. What was the distinguishing feature of ENIAC?

16. What were the two distinguishing features of EDVAC?

17. What is a *von Neumann machine*?

18. Describe the technological features characteristic of each computer generation.

19. What type of computer memory was once so widely used that its name became almost synonymous with "high-speed memory"?

20. What technological developments made (a) minicomputers and (b) microcomputers possible?

READING PROBLEMS

There are two groups of words that give problems to students of English as a second language: *references* and *connectives*. In order to better prepare you for the in-depth reading you must do at the university, we will practice identifying these words in order to understand their use in the reading material of this book.

References   References are words or phrases that are used as substitutes for words or phrases used either before or (less often) after the reference in the reading material. They are used to avoid unnecessary repetition of words or phrases. For example, in the following sentence taken from the reading in this unit, the reference "these tools" is used to prevent the repetition of "the tools we have invented."

> **Example 1:** Most of the tools we have invented have aided our bodies rather than our minds. These tools help us lift and move and cut and shape.

In the second example the reference "it" is used to avoid the repetition of "information" and the reference "this" refers to the phrase "classify and modify information."

> **Example 2:** Our interest lies with machines that classify and modify information rather than merely transmitting it or preserving it. The machines that do this are the computers and the calculators, the mind tools referred to in the title of the book.

Exercise 3: References

Read the following sentences from "The Development of Computers." The references are underlined. On the lines under the sentences, write the word or phrase to which each reference refers.

> **Example:** The Latin word for *pebble* is *calculus*, from which we get the words *abacus* and *calculate*.
>
> which   *calculus*

1. We tend to think of technology as a human invention. But the reverse is closer to the truth.

   the reverse _____

2. The abacus is the counting frame that was the most widely used device for doing arithmetic in ancient times and whose use persisted into modern times in the Orient.

   whose _____

3. When was the automatic computer invented? In the 1930s or the 1940s? If you think that, you are only off by a hundred years.

   that _____

4. Babbage took issue with Tennyson's poem "Vision of Sin," which contains this couplet:

Every minute dies a man,
Every minute one is born.

one _____

5. And since people who published new tables often copied from existing <u>ones</u>, the same errors cropped up in table after table.

ones _____

6. Ada was a liberated woman at a time when <u>this</u> was hardly fashionable. Not only did she have the usual accomplishments in language and music, she was also an excellent mathematician. <u>The latter</u> was most unusual for a young lady in the nineteenth century. (She was also fond of horse racing, which was <u>even more</u> unusual.)

this_____

The latter_____

even more _____

7. A hundred years passed before a machine like the one Babbage conceived was actually built. <u>This</u> occurred in 1944, when Howard Aiken of Harvard University completed the Harvard Mark I Automatic Sequence Controlled Calculator.

This _____

8. First-generation machines used several other ingenious devices for memory. In <u>one</u>, for instance, information was stored as sound waves circulating in a column of mercury.

one_____

Connectives   Connectives are words that are used to link (connect) ideas together in some kind of relationship. Connectives can be used to signal a *cause–expected result* relationship in which the result follows logically from the cause. Notice the position of the connective in the following examples.

Example 1: We were <u>unable to make</u> the trip to Chicago <u>because</u> our car <u>broke down</u>.

        expected result   **connective**   **cause**

Other connectives used in the same position for the same purpose are *since* and *as*.

            cause   **connective**   **expected result**

Example 2: Our <u>car broke down</u>, <u>so</u> we were <u>unable to make</u> the trip to Chicago.

Other connectives used in the same position for the same purpose are *thus, therefore,* and *hence*.

Connectives can be used to signal a *cause–unexpected result* relationship in which the result does not follow logically from the cause. In fact, the result may be completely contrary to (opposite) that which is expected from the cause. Again, notice the position of the connectives in these examples.

       connective   **cause**   **unexpected result**

Example 3: <u>Although</u> our <u>car broke down</u>, we were <u>able to make</u> the trip to Chicago.

Other connectives used in the same position for the same purpose are *even though, despite the fact that, though,* and *in spite of the fact that*.

       cause   **connective**   **unexpected result**

Example 4: Our <u>car broke down</u>; <u>however</u>, we were <u>able to make</u> the trip to Chicago.

Other connectives used in the same position for the same purpose are *but, still,* and *nevertheless*.

Connectives can also signal a *conditional* sentence, in which one part of the sentence tells you the condition (situation) that must occur before the action described in the rest of the sentence takes place.

       connective

Example 5: <u>If</u> the weather is beautiful tomorrow, we will go on a picnic.

Other connectives used in the same position for the same purpose are *suppose, in case,* and *as long as*.

<u>In addition</u> to the uses already mentioned, connectives can be used to signal the addition of an idea. (Notice the use of *in addition* in this sentence, for example.) Connectives of *addition* are very useful in helping you locate the main ideas of a reading passage, because an author may use them to introduce arguments, reasons, or other supporting ideas. Connectives of addition include *also, furthermore, moreover,* and *not only . . . but also.*

    <u>Also</u>, connectives can be used to *contrast* ideas (show how they are different) in a sentence.

                                                                connective

Example 6: Some people prefer to live in a climate that is always warm, <u>while</u> others would much rather live where there is a change of seasons and plenty of cold weather.

Other connectives used in the same position for the same purpose are *whereas, although,* and *however*.

Finally, connectives can be used to signal *purpose*. Notice the difference in sentence structure between example 7 and example 8.

connector

Example 7:   We went to the movie early <u>so that</u> we could get a good seat.

connective

Example 8:   We went to the movie early <u>in order to</u> get a good seat.

Study the examples of each kind of connective <u>so that</u> you will recognize them as you read.

Exercise 4: Connectives

Find the connective(s) in the following sentences taken from "The Development of Computers." Write the connective(s) and indicate the kind of connective it is (they are) on the lines under the sentences. The kinds of connectives are: *cause/expected result, cause/unexpected result, conditional, addition, contrast,* **and** *purpose.*

> Example: We tend to think of technology as a human invention. But the reverse is closer to the truth.
>
> Connective: *but*
>
> Kind of connective: *contrast*

1. These devices transmit information or preserve it, but they do not modify it in any way.

   Connective: _____

   Kind of connective: _____

2. If the information is modified, this is considered a defect rather than a virtue, as when a defective radio distorts the music we're trying to hear.

   Connective: _____

   Kind of connective: _____

3. The calculators Pascal and Leibniz built were unreliable, since the mechanical technology of the time was not capable of manufacturing the parts with sufficient precision.

   Connective: _____

   Kind of connective: _____

4. Yet, despite his eccentricities, Babbage was a genius.

Connective: _____

Kind of connective: _____

5. Babbage set out to build a machine that not only would calculate the entries in the tables but would print them automatically as well.

Connective: _____

Kind of connective: _____

6. He called this machine the *Difference Engine*, since it worked by solving what mathematicians call "difference equations."

Connective: _____

Kind of connective: _____

7. He called the machine the *Difference Engine*, since it worked by solving what mathematicians call "difference equations." Nevertheless, the name is misleading, since the machine constructed tables by means of repeated additions, not subtractions.

Connective: _____

Kind of connective: _____

8. Even if the government had financed the new invention, it might well have gotten nothing in return.

Connective: _____

Kind of connective: _____

9. Although Babbage had founded operations research, he had trouble planning the development of his own inventions.

Connective: _____

Kind of connective: _____

10. As long as computers were tied down to vacuum tube technology, they could only be bulky, cumbersome, and expensive.

Connective: _____

Kind of connective: _____

11. Whereas the older integrated circuits contained hundreds of transistors, the new ones contain thousands or tens of thousands.

    Connective: _____

    Kind of connective: _____

12. It is the large-scale integrated circuits that make possible the microprocessors and microcomputers. They also make possible compact, inexpensive, high-speed, high-capacity integrated-circuit memory.

    Connective: _____

    Kind of connective: _____

GUESSING WORD MEANINGS

Guessing Word Meanings from Context   Because you can never know all of the English words you will encounter in your textbooks, it is very important that you be able to make good guesses about the meanings of words. Examining the context of the word (the words and phrases that come before and after it) is one way to make a logical guess about what the word means. You can also get clues to the meanings of words from punctuation. Look at the sentences that surround the word *eccentric* in the following paragraph:

> Example 1:   The inventor of that nineteenth-century computer was a figure far more common in fiction than in real life—an eccentric mathematician. Most mathematicians live personal lives not too much different from anyone else's. They just happen to do mathematics instead of driving trucks or running stores or filling teeth. But Charles Babbage was the exception.

The paragraph tells us that Charles Babbage was an *eccentric* mathematician. It tells us that most mathematicians live personal lives not too much different from those of others. And, it tells us that Charles Babbage was an exception to this. If he was an exception, then he must have led a personal life that was different from other people's. *Eccentric,* then, must mean "different." Even the phrase "a figure far more common in fiction than in real life" gives us the idea that he is unusual.

You can also guess the meanings of words by using the context to substitute a word that you know will go in the same position as the word you are having difficulty with. Look at the following sentence.

> Example 2:   ENIAC—Electronic Numerical Integrator and Computer—was the machine that rendered the electromechanical computer obsolete.

If you were to remove the word *rendered*, what word might fit in its place?

_____

The words *made* or *caused to be* fit well here. We can then guess that *rendered* has a meaning similar to "cause" or "make."

Exercise 5: Guessing Word Meanings from Context

Try to guess the meanings of the underlined words in the following sentences from "The Development of Computers." Begin by underlining the words and phrases that give you the clues necessary for you to make a good guess. Then write your definition of the word. Do not look these words up in your dictionary.

1. The widespread use of machines for information processing is a modern development. But simple examples of information-processing machines can be traced back to ancient times. The following are some of the more important <u>forerunners</u> of the computer.

2. Jacquard looms came into widespread use in the early nineteenth century, and their <u>descendants</u> are still used today. The Jacquard loom is the ancestor not only of modern automated machine tools but of the player piano as well.

3. Babbage was a <u>prolific</u> inventor, whose inventions include the ophthalmoscope for examining the retina of the eye, the skeleton key, the locomotive "cow catcher," and the speedometer.

4. Babbage's design was <u>grandiose</u>. For instance, he planned for his machine to do calculations with fifty-digit accuracy. This is far greater than the accuracy found in most modern computers and far more than is needed for most calculations.

5. ENIAC—Electronic Numerical Integrator and Computer—was the machine that rendered the electromechanical computers obsolete. ENIAC was the first of many computers with <u>acronyms</u> for names.

Guessing Word Meanings by Word Analysis   If the context of a word does not give you enough clues to guess its meaning, you may be able to determine the meaning by word analysis. This means breaking the word into its parts and using the meaning of each part to give you the clues you need to determine the meaning of the whole word.

English words are usually made up of three parts: a *prefix*, a *stem*, and a *suffix*. The stem (root) of a word provides the basic meaning of the word. For example, the stem of *contradict* is the word part *dict*, which means "to speak." There are many words that contain this stem and all of them have something to do with speaking (for example, *dictation*, *dictator*, and *dictaphone*).

The prefix of a word is placed before the stem and adds more meaning to the stem. The prefix *contra*, for example, means "against," and therefore the word *contradict* means "to speak against." This prefix can also be found in many words, adding the meaning "against" to whatever stem(s) the word contains (*contraband*, *controversy*). There are often several different forms of a word part (*contra-*, *contro-*), but they are still the same word part with the same meaning.

The suffix of a word comes at the end, and its purpose is to indicate the part of speech (noun, verb, adjective, adverb). We can take the same stem— *dict*, for example—and make it into a verb by changing it slightly and adding the suffix *-ate* (as in *dictate*). The suffix *-or* will change the word into a noun that represents a person (*dictator*—a person who dictates). Adding the suffix *-ation* also makes the word a noun, but it is now "the act of" dictating (*dictation*) rather than the person who is dictating.

Exercise 6: Guessing Word Meanings by Word Analysis

Prefixes	**Meanings**
pre- (prim-)	first, before
bi-	two, twice
trans-	across

Stems	**Meanings**
-corp-	body
-miss- (-mit-)	send
-man-	hand
-sequ- (-secut-)	follow

Use the meanings of the preceding stems and prefixes to analyze the following words and guess their meanings.

1. *primary*　The <u>primary</u> cause of a situation is (the most important cause, the least important cause, one of many causes)

　　　　　　_____ .

2. *bimanual*　*Bi* means "two" and *man* means "hand"; therefore <u>bimanual</u> must mean _____ .

3. *biweekly*　The word <u>biweekly</u> has two very different meanings. One is "occurring once every two weeks." What do you think the other meaning is? _____ .

4. *transmit*

　　　　　　To <u>transmit</u> a signal is to _____ .

5. *manufacture*　The stem *-fact-* means to "make" or "do." How has the meaning of <u>manufacture</u> changed in modern times?

　　　　　　_____

WORD–PART CHART

Write the meanings of each word part, and add more examples of words that contain these word parts.

Prefix	Meaning	Examples
pre- (prim-)	_____	previous, prevail
		_____
bi-	_____	binary, _____ ,
		_____
trans-	_____	translate, _____ ,
		_____

Stem	Meaning	Examples
-corp-	_____	incorporate, _____, _____
-miss-, (mit-)	_____	transmit, _____, _____
-man-	_____	manual, _____, _____
-sequ- (-secut-)	_____	sequence, _____, _____

SECOND READING

Read the chapter "The Development of Computers" from *The Mind Tool* again, this time carefully. As you read, try to find the main idea in each paragraph (or group of paragraphs) and underline it. Remember that the topic sentence of a paragraph (the sentence that contains the main idea) is often the first or last sentence of the paragraph, or a combination of the two. Sometimes several paragraphs together will share one main idea, or the main idea will be implied rather than stated in a sentence. Your aim should be to look for all of the important ideas and mark them, so that you can find them easily later.

POST–READING

REACTION QUESTIONS

1. What information in this chapter did you know before you read the chapter?
2. What information in the chapter was the most surprising to you?
3. What information in this chapter will be the most useful to you in your chosen field of work?

Exercise 7: Comprehension Check

Look back at the reading to answer the following questions. Circle the letter in front of the correct answer or answers.

1. According to the introduction of this chapter, the chapter concerns

    a. the tools of communication.

    b. machines that transmit or preserve information.

    c. machines that classify and modify information.

2. Information processing is

    a. a modern development.

    b. traceable to the far past.

    c. used only to do arithmetic.

3. The Jacquard loom was different from most other forerunners of the computer in that it

    a. was an information processor.

    b. was designed to do arithmetic.

    c. was not designed for hard figures.

    d. was not automatic.

4. Circle the letters in front of the statements about Charles Babbage that are true.

    a. He held a position that was once held by Isaac Newton.

    b. He was an American.

    c. He invented an instrument for examining the retina of the eye.

    d. He was an eccentric genius.

5. The mathematical tables of the nineteenth century contained many mistakes because of *all* of the following *except:*

    a. Some of the tables had not been calculated correctly.

    b. The calculations were made by steam.

    c. The printers made errors.

    d. Those who published new tables copied from the old ones.

6. The Difference Engine was not really a good name for Babbage's machine because

    a. the machine constructed tables by means of repeated subtractions.

    b. it worked by solving what mathematicians call "difference equations."

    c. the machine constructed tables by adding rather than subtracting.

    d. Babbage got a government grant to build the machine.

7. The Analytical Engine differed from the Difference Engine in that it

    a. could compute tables only by addition.

    b. was not a punched-card-controlled calculator.

    c. could carry out almost any calculation.

    d. was not completed.

8. The author of the chapter believes that

    a. mechanical technology is usually behind ideas for inventions.

    b. mechanical technology is usually ahead of ideas for how to use it.

    c. Babbage's computer was not modern in concept.

    d. the mechanical technology of the 1830s was prepared to realize Babbage's concept.

9. Circle all of the following statements about Lady Lovelace that are true:

    a. She was the world's first computer programmer.

    b. She translated a paper about the Analytical Engine from Italian into English.

    c. Her additions to the paper made up two-thirds of the translated paper.

    d. She is responsible for most of the information we have today about the Analytical Engine.

10. The Harvard Mark I

    a. was designed from Babbage's plan.

    b. was similar to the machine that Babbage conceived.

    c. was driven by steam.

    d. used complex mechanical linkages to transmit information within the machine.

11. The Harvard Mark I was obsolete just after it was finished because

    a. it could calculate only five or six times as fast as an old desk calculator.

    b. its computing, control, and memory elements were completely electric.

    c. the electromechanical machines were faster than the completely electrical machines.

12. EDVAC was more advanced than ENIAC even though they were constructed about the same time, because

    a. EDVAC used binary notation to represent numbers inside the machine, and its program was stored in the machine's memory, like the data.

    b. its program was stored externally on punched tape or plugboards.

    c. it used decimal notation to represent numbers.

    d. its innovations have been incorporated in almost every computer since.

13. First-generation computers used _____ for memory.

    a. vacuum tubes and transistors

    b. vacuum tubes and silicon chips

    c. a magnetic core and a column of mercury

    d. vacuum tubes and a column of mercury

14. According to this chapter, the kind of memory most often used currently is

    a. magnetic-core memory.

    b. vacuum tubes.

    c. integrated-circuit memory.

    d. mercury columns.

Exercise 8: Reading Analysis

Look back in the reading (pp. 9-20) to answer the following questions. Circle the letter in front of the correct answer.

1. The introduction of this chapter consists of

    a. the first five paragraphs.

b. the first three paragraphs.

c. the first paragraph.

d. the first two paragraphs.

2. "The Abacus," "Mechanical Calculators," and "The Jacquard Loom" are subtitles that indicate

   a. inventions that followed the computer.

   b. inventions that were forerunners of the computer.

   c. inventions that were subsequent to the computer.

   d. inventions that were consequences of the computer.

3. The purpose of paragraphs 12 and 13 is to

   a. add a main idea to the section on the Analytical Engine.

   b. give examples of the main idea expressed in the preceding paragraph.

   c. present arguments against the main idea of paragraph 11.

   d. make a general statement about the example given in paragraph 11.

4. The words "Yet" and "despite" in paragraph 14 indicate that the information that follows is

   a. an unexpected result of the information given in the preceding paragraphs.

   b. an expected result of the information given in the preceding paragraphs.

   c. an example of the main idea mentioned in the preceding paragraph.

   d. a conditional situation.

5. The word "since" in paragraph 16

   a. indicates a "time" clause.

   b. is used to show a cause-result relationship.

   c. is used to add an idea to the argument.

   d. indicates a contrast with the information in the previous paragraph.

6. "Nevertheless" (paragraph 19) has the same meaning as

   a. in addition.

   b. as a result.

    c. however.

    d. because.

7. Paragraph 22 tells the reader *all* of the following *except:*

    a. Babbage abandoned the Difference Engine partially because he had a better idea.

    b. Babbage wanted to build a punched-card-controlled calculator.

    c. Babbage was inspired by Jacquard's punched-card-controlled loom.

    d. His proposed automatic calculator was called the Difference Engine.

8. The word "For" in paragraph 25 has the same meaning as it does in which of the following sentences?

    a. I will go to the store <u>for</u> you if you want me to.

    b. We have known him <u>for</u> several years.

    c. We wore our raincoats today, <u>for</u> we knew that it was going to rain.

    d. <u>For</u> the last time, will you please tell me your telephone number?

9. The word "Also" that begins paragraph 27

    a. indicates the addition of another idea.

    b. indicates a contrast of ideas.

    c. indicates a result.

    d. indicates an expected results.

10. The words "Even though" that begin paragraph 29 indicate that

    a. it is strange that a demonstration program for it was written.

    b. it is logical that a demonstration for it was written.

    c. an example of this idea is being given.

    d. there is no result of this idea.

Exercise 9: Small-Group Discussion Tasks

Form a group with two or three classmates and prepare answers to each of the following essay questions. Use the chapter you have just read for the facts and examples you need. The underlined word in each sentence is the *essay-exam clue word* that tells you what to do with the facts and examples. To <u>trace</u> means to follow the progress or the history of the subject; to <u>relate</u>

means to show the connections between the things mentioned, telling how one causes another, or is like another; to compare means to show the similarities; to contrast means to show the differences. Your group answer may be given orally or in writing (whichever your instructor decides), but it must be clear and complete.

1. Trace the history of the computer from 1940s to the present.
2. Relate the abacus, mechanical calculators, and the Jacquard loom to the computer as we know it today.
3. Compare and contrast the three generations of computers mentioned in this chapter.
4. Contrast the Difference Engine with the Analytical Engine.

SOME SUGGESTED TOPICS FOR FURTHER READING

the Jacquard loom
Blaise Pascal
Wilhelm von Leibniz
Charles Babbage
IBM

binary notation
John von Neuman
core memory
ENIAC

2

More Reading Computer Science

Computer Graphics Display System, 1980's

VOCABULARY PREPARATION

The basic words for this unit are those used to speak or write about crime and those that inevitably appear when the subject of computers is discussed. Many of them can be used to talk about other subjects as well, and all of them have related words that are useful to know as part of your general academic vocabulary.

Basic Vocabulary

offender	access	authorize
apprehend	arrest	software
monitor	conviction	prosecute
suspicious	acquit	restriction
fugitive	detect	data

SKIMMING

Skimming, as mentioned in Unit 1, will give you a general impression of what you are about to read and will introduce important vocabulary used by the author. Read again the steps you should follow before reading a textbook chapter:

STEP 1: Read the main title of the chapter and all of the headings (titles for the sections of the chapter). Notice how these titles relate to one another.

STEP 2: Examine pictures, charts, and other illustrations in the chapter to get information about the chapter's contents.

STEP 3: Find the names of the people mentioned in the chapter and try to determine who they are. To do this follow these steps:

    a. Look for clues in the passage that will tell you something about the people.

    b. Look in the footnotes at the end of the chapter (or at the bottom of the page) if there is a raised footnote number at the end of the sentence containing the name.

    c. If there is no clue or footnote, look in a good English-to-English dictionary or an encyclopedia.

    d. Ask a classmate or your instructor.

STEP 4: Look at all italicized words and phrases (words and phrases in special print). Try to determine the author's reason for italicizing them.

STEP 5: Look at the review questions and bibliography at the end of the chapter (if it has them) to get more information about the chapter.

STEP 6: Rapidly read the first and last paragraph of the chapter and the first sentence of each paragraph to get an overall idea of its contents.

STEP 7: Write a few sentences explaining what you think this chapter is all about.

Exercise 1: Skimming Practice

The chapter that you are going to read in this unit is taken from the same text as that of the first unit, *The Mind Tool: Computers and Their Impact on Society* by Neil Graham. This chapter comes from a unit that includes chapters on the many uses of computers: computers in art and music, computers in medicine, and so forth.

Begin your reading of "Computers and Crime" by using the seven skimming steps to skim the chapter. As you complete each step, answer the questions that follow. (The chapter begins on page 42).

STEP 1: Read the main title of the chapter and all of the headings. Notice how they relate to one another.

    a. What are some of the ways that the police use computers in their jobs?

    b. What are the two kinds of criminal justice records?

    c. What are the areas in which computer criminals have been the most successful?

    d. What are the subtitles that describe the paragraphs that discuss computer security?

STEP 2: Examine pictures, charts, and other illustrations in the chapter to get information about the chapter's contents.

    a. How were computers used in the mid-1970s in Sugar Creek, Texas?

    b. For what purpose is the computer being used in the picture on page 45?

    c. What is the function of a security matrix?

STEP 3: Find the names of people, organizations, and so on in the chapter and try to determine who or what they are. An example of an organization name in this chapter is the FBI.

    a. What does NCIC stand for (represent)?

b. What is the purpose of the National Driver Register Service?

c. What does FBI stand for, and what is the purpose of this organization?

d. What is the Stanford Research Institute?

e. What is the National Bureau of Standards?

STEP 4: Look at all of the italicized words and phrases. Be aware of the author's reasons for italicizing them. The author uses italics in this chapter to point out important words defined in the chapter and, in one case, a phrase that is used in an unusual way.

a. *Life sentence* usually means a punishment that consists of keeping a person in prison for the remainder of his or her life. What does *life sentence* mean in paragraph 28?

b. Quickly find the definitions for :
1. encrypted _____
2. decrypted _____
3. public-key cryptosystems _____

STEP 5: Look at the review questions and bibliography at the end of the chapter to get more information about the chapter.

a. Look at the section entitled "For Further Reading" (page 53), and answer the following questions:
1. Who is the author of the book *Computer Crime?*
2. Where and when was the book called *The Secret Files They Keep on You* published?
3. What issue of which magazine published the article called "A Method for Obtaining Digital Signatures and Public-Key Cryptosystems"?

b. The review questions on page 54 are part of the chapter taken from *The Mind Tool: Computers and Their Impact on Society.* Read those questions carefully to get more information about the chapter you will read:
1. Do all people agree that computers *should* be used in law enforcement?
2. How many kinds of computer crime are discussed in this chapter?
3. Are people who commit computer crimes usually punished?
4. Are the computer systems discussed in this chapter secure?

STEP 6: Rapidly read the first and last paragraph of the chapter and the first sentence of each paragraph to get an overall idea of the chapter's contents.

STEP 7: In a sentence or two, explain what you think this chapter is about. (You may answer orally or quickly write the answer that you would give orally.)

FIRST READING

Quickly read the chapter "Computers and Crime" from *The Mind Tool* (pp. 42–54) in order to answer the following questions. You will read the chapter more thoroughly later, but for now, just read for the answers.

1. How do the police use computers to do their work more efficiently?
2. What are the arguments for distributing arrest records?
3. What are the arguments against distributing arrest records?
4. What are the arguments for distributing conviction records?
5. What are the arguments against distributing conviction records?
6. In what situations are computers most commonly used to commit crimes?
7. Why are computer criminals often not punished for their crimes?
8. What are the methods that can be used to identify people who are authorized to use a computer system? How does each work?

Computers and Crime

Neil Graham

1   No one who reads the newspapers can doubt the seriousness of crime in this country. Not a day goes by without numerous robberies, rapes, and murders being reported. In many cities, it's extremely dangerous to walk the streets at night.

2   Crime is a complex problem with many causes. Poverty, unemployment, conditions in the cities, and increasing disregard for authority all play their roles and no single remedy is going to solve the problem overnight.

3   But perhaps at least one of the causes can be dealt with—the inefficiency of the criminal justice system. For instance, the police usually are able to solve only a fraction of the crimes committed. And when offenders are apprehended, there is usually a long delay in trial and sentencing. During the delay, the offenders may be out on bail committing more crimes.

4   Much police work concerns information—information about stolen property, fugitives from justice, the methods of operation of known criminals. The computer can make an important contribution to processing this information effectively and efficiently.

5   Unfortunately, there is almost no other area in which computers inspire such fear. The reason is obvious: the police can initiate proceedings that can take a person's liberty away. And, sometimes with good reason, not everyone is convinced that those proceedings will be carried out fairly. Even worse, the police keep records that can haunt us the rest of our lives. Even those people who have the most to fear from crime may fear even more anything that increases the effectiveness of the police.

6   (The fact that large segments of the population do distrust the police is one more reason there will be no easy solutions to the problem of crime.)

7   In one way, the computer can be considered a mixed blessing for law enforcement. To be sure, it helps the police solve crimes and apprehend criminals. But it also opens up a whole new world of ways to commit crimes. As far back as 1974, authorities estimated that over $200 million were being lost each year through computer-related crime. That figure certainly has not diminished in the intervening years.

COMPUTERS AND THE POLICE

8   ***Patrol-Car Dispatching***   When you call the police, the police dispatcher has to locate the car nearest you that is free to respond. This means the dispatcher has to keep track of the status and location of every police car—not an easy task for a large department.

9   Another problem, which arises when cars are assigned to regular patrols, is that the patrols may be *too* regular. If criminals find out that police cars will pass a particular location at regular intervals, they simply plan their crimes for times when no patrol is expected. Therefore, patrol cars should pass by any particular location *at random times;* the fact that a car just passed should be no guarantee that another one is not just around the corner. Yet simply ordering the officers to patrol at random would lead to chaos.

10   A computer dispatching system can solve both these problems. The computer has no trouble keeping track of the status and location of each car. With this information, it can determine instantly which car should respond to an incoming call. And with the aid of a pseudorandom number generator, the computer can assign routine patrols so that criminals can't predict just when a police car will pass through a particular area.

11   (Before computers, police sometimes used roulette wheels and similar devices to make random assignments.)

12   Computers also can relieve police officers from constantly having to report their status. The police car would contain a special automatic radio transmitter and receiver. The officer would set a dial on this unit indicating the current status of the car—patrolling, directing traffic, chasing a speeder, answering a call, out to lunch, and so on. When necessary, the computer at headquarters could poll the car for its status. The voice radio channels would not be clogged with cars constantly reporting what they were doing. A computer in the car automatically could determine the location of the car, perhaps using the LORAN method. The location of the car also would be sent automatically to the headquarters computer.

13 *Stolen Property Files*   Often a police officer's hardest problem is recognizing stolen property as being stolen. A computerized file that lets the police quickly check descriptions and serial numbers of possible stolen items can help them recover stolen property as well as catch thieves and fences.

14   These files often are most useful and most needed for stolen cars. An officer can report the tag number of a suspicious vehicle or of one stopped for a routine traffic violation. The reply will come back while the suspected car is still in sight or in custody. Since stolen cars often are used as getaway cars in other crimes, spotting one may prevent or solve some other crime.

15 *Fugitives from Justice*   The old "Wanted Dead or Alive" posters have given way to electronic systems that let officers identify a fugitive from justice in seconds.

16   One system of this kind is the FBI's National Crime Information Center (NCIC) in Washington, D.C. NCIC maintains computerized files on both fugitives and stolen property. State police information systems throughout the nation access NCIC directly. City and county systems work through the state systems.

17   NCIC can be accessed either through a terminal or a local computer. In either case, the information requested comes back in about ten seconds. When a local computer is used, it must be limited to law enforcement and justice work. This restriction helps prevent unauthorized access to NCIC files.

18   When a police officer stops a suspicious person or automobile, he radios the information from the car registration or the person's driver's license to the police dispatcher. The dispatcher checks the information out with NCIC. Within a minute or two, the officer will know if the person is wanted or if the car or its license plate has been reported stolen.

19 *National Driver Register Service*   A person whose driver's license has been revoked may attempt to obtain a new one in another state. To curtail this, the National Driver Register Service keeps information on persons whose licenses have been denied, revoked, or suspended. Before granting a license, a state can query this computerized system to see whether or not the applicant has had his license revoked in another state. All states use this service.

CRIMINAL JUSTICE RECORDS

20 *Arrest Records*   When a person is arrested in the United States, an arrest record is forwarded to the FBI, where it becomes a part of the person's FBI file. Even if the charges are later dropped or the person is acquitted, the arrest record still will be forwarded to employers who request an FBI check.

21   (A court ruling now requires that the disposition of the case be supplied with all records sent to employers. But law enforcement officials still can get arrest records where the disposition is unknown.)

22   People who favor the distribution of arrest records argue that just because an arrest did not lead to a conviction doesn't mean it was without foundation. Members of organized crime may go unconvicted because witnesses were intimidated or murdered. Sex criminals may escape justice because the victims don't wish to subject themselves to the ordeal of a trial. And the cases against many criminals have been dismissed because the police made some technical error during arrest or questioning.

23   The people who oppose the distribution of arrest records argue that people sometimes are arrested "on suspicion" or "for investigation," particularly if they have prior police records. People who participate in political demonstrations may be arrested, sometimes with justification, sometimes without. A person's

chance of being arrested may be influenced by the person's race, sex, or social or economic status.

24   It has been estimated that one out of every two males will be arrested at some time in his life. For black males, the chances are even greater.

25   At least one court has maintained that using arrest records to deny employment constitutes racial discrimination. Residents of black ghettos are much more likely to be picked up "for questioning" or "on suspicion" than people who live in affluent, white suburbs.

26   It is a basic assumption of American justice that a person is innocent until proven guilty. It is difficult to see how the use of arrest records to deny employment and other benefits can be consistent with this assumption.

27   ***Conviction Records***   Conviction records are harder to argue against than arrest records. After all, a court has determined that a person did indeed commit a crime and has required the person to pay a penalty. Surely, the proponents of conviction records argue, employers have a right to keep convicted criminals out of their businesses.

28   And yet, when a person is convicted of a crime, society exacts a fixed penalty—so many years in jail or so many dollars for a fine. Conviction records can turn every sentence into a *life sentence* by denying the former convict employment in many areas for the rest of his life. Indeed, he may be excluded from the very job he was trained for while in prison. Unable to get work, he is all too likely to return to crime.

29   Some argue that a person's conviction record should be destroyed after a certain number of years. (Seven is a popular number.) But others argue that destroying the record after seven years is too late. After all, when a convict is first released from prison, he needs employment to further his rehabilitation.

30   So far, we haven't mentioned computers in this section. In fact, all the problems mentioned existed before anyone ever dreamed of using computers for arrest and conviction records. Now that computers are being used for some of these records, much controversy has surfaced. But the real problems lie not with the use of computers but with the records themselves.

31   This situation is typical when someone proposes storing certain types of records in a computer. People react to the proposal with alarm and concern, but usually this concern is misplaced. It should be focused not on whether the files should be stored in a computer but on whether they should exist at all. Any files that should not be allowed to exist inside a computer should not be allowed to exist outside one either.

USING COMPUTERS TO COMMIT CRIMES

32 *A New Kind of Crime*   More and more, the operations of our businesses, governments, and financial institutions are controlled by information that exists only inside computer memories. Anyone clever enough to modify this information for his own purposes can reap substantial rewards. Even worse, a number of people who have done this and been caught at it have managed to get away without punishment.

33   These facts have not been lost on criminals or would-be criminals. A recent Stanford Research Institute study of computer abuse was based on 160 case histories, which probably are just the proverbial tip of the iceberg. After all, we only know about the unsuccessful crimes. How many successful ones have gone undetected is anybody's guess.

34   Here are a few areas in which computer criminals have found the pickings all too easy.

35   *Banking*   All but the smallest banks now keep their accounts on computer files. Someone who knows how to change the numbers in the files can transfer funds at will. For instance, one programmer was caught having the computer transfer funds from other people's accounts to his wife's checking account. Often, traditionally trained auditors don't know enough about the workings of computers to catch what is taking place right under their noses.

36   *Business*   A company that uses computers extensively offers many opportunities to both dishonest employees and clever outsiders. For instance, a thief can have the computer ship the company's products to addresses of his own choosing. Or he can have it issue checks to him or his confederates for imaginary supplies or services. People have been caught doing both.

37   *Credit Cards*   There is a trend toward using cards similar to credit cards to gain access to funds through cash-dispensing terminals. Yet, in the past, organized crime has used stolen or counterfeit credit cards to finance its operations. Banks that offer after-hours or remote banking through cash-dispensing terminals may find themselves unwillingly subsidizing organized crime.

38   *Theft of Information*   Much personal information about individuals is now stored in computer files. An unauthorized person with access to this information could use it for blackmail. Also, confidential information about a company's products or operations can be stolen and sold to unscrupulous competitors. (One attempt at the latter came to light when the competitor turned out to be scrupulous and turned in the people who were trying to sell him stolen information.)

39   *Software Theft*   The software for a computer system is often more expensive than the hardware. Yet this expensive software is all too easy to copy. Crooked computer experts have devised a variety of tricks for getting these expensive programs printed out, punched on cards, recorded on tape, or otherwise delivered into their hands. This crime has even been perpetrated from remote terminals that access the computer over the telephone.

40   *Theft of Time-Sharing Services*   When the public is given access to a system, some members of the public often discover how to use the system in unauthorized ways. For example, there are the "phone freaks" who avoid long-distance telephone charges by sending over their phones control signals that are identical to those used by the telephone company.

41   Since time-sharing systems often are accessible to anyone who dials the right telephone number, they are subject to the same kinds of manipulation.

Of course, most systems use account numbers and passwords to restrict access to authorized users. But unauthorized persons have proved to be adept at obtaining this information and using it for their own benefit. For instance, when a police computer system was demonstrated to a school class, a precocious student noted the access codes being used; later, all the student's teachers turned up on a list of wanted criminals.

42 ***Perfect Crimes***   It's easy for computer crimes to go undetected if no one checks up on what the computer is doing. But even if the crime is detected, the criminal may walk away not only unpunished but with a glowing recommendation from his former employers.

43   Of course, we have no statistics on crimes that go undetected. But it's unsettling to note how many of the crimes we do know about were detected by accident, not by systematic audits or other security procedures. The computer criminals who have been caught may have been the victims of uncommonly bad luck.

44   For example, a certain keypunch operator complained of having to stay overtime to punch extra cards. Investigation revealed that the extra cards she was being asked to punch were for fraudulent transactions. In another case, disgruntled employees of the *thief* tipped off the company that was being robbed. An undercover narcotics agent stumbled on still another case. An employee was selling the company's merchandise on the side and using the computer to get it shipped to the buyers. While negotiating for LSD, the narcotics agent was offered a good deal on a stereo!

45   Unlike other embezzlers, who must leave the country, commit suicide, or go to jail, computer criminals sometimes brazen it out, demanding not only that they not be prosecuted but that they be given good recommendations and perhaps other benefits, such as severance pay. All too often, their demands have been met.

46   Why? Because company executives are afraid of the bad publicity that would result if the public found out that their computer had been misused. They cringe at the thought of a criminal boasting in open court of how he juggled the most confidential records right under the noses of the company's executives, accountants, and security staff. And so another computer criminal departs with just the recommendations he needs to continue his exploits elsewhere.

COMPUTER SECURITY

47 ***Emphasis on Access and Throughput***   For the last decade or so, computer programmers have concentrated on making it easy for people to use computer

systems. Unfortunately, in some situations the systems are all too easy to use; they don't impose nearly enough restrictions to safeguard confidential information or to prevent unauthorized persons from changing the information in a file.

48   It's as if a bank concentrated all its efforts on handing out money as fast is it could and did very little to see that the persons who requested the money were entitled to it. Of course, a real bank works just the opposite way, checking very carefully before handing out any money. Computer systems that handle sensitive personal and financial data should be designed with the same philosophy in mind.

49   ***Positive Identification of Users***   A computer system needs a sure way of identifying the people who are authorized to use it. The identification procedure has to be quick, simple, and convenient. It should be so thorough that there is little chance of the computer being fooled by a clever imposter. At the same time, the computer must not reject legitimate users. Unfortunately, no identification system currently in use meets all these requirements.

50   At present, signatures are widely used to identify credit-card holders, but it takes an expert to detect a good forgery. Sometimes even a human expert is fooled, and there is no reason to believe that a computer could do any better.

51   A variation is to have the computer analyze a person's hand movements as he signs his name instead of analyzing the signature itself. Advocates of this method claim that different persons' hand movements are sufficiently distinct to identify them. And while a forger might learn to duplicate another person's signature, he probably would not move his hand exactly the way the person whose signature he was forging did.

52   Photographs are also sometimes used for identification. But, people find it inconvenient to stop by a bank or credit-card company and be photographed. Companies might lose business if they made the pictures an absolute requirement. Also, photographs are less useful these days, when people frequently change their appearance by changing the way they wear their hair. Finally, computer programs for analyzing photographs are still highly experimental.

53   Cash-dispensing systems often use two identification numbers: one is recorded on a magnetic stripe on the identification card, and the other is given to the card holder. When the user inserts his card into the cash-dispensing terminal, he keys in the identification number he has been given. The computer checks to see that the number recorded on the card and the one keyed in by the user both refer to the same person. Someone who stole the card would not know what number had to be keyed in in order to use it. This method currently is the one most widely used for identifying computer users.

54   For a long time, fingerprints have provided a method of positive identification. But they suffer from two problems, one technical and one psychological.

The technical problem is that there is no simple system for comparing finger-prints electronically. Also, most methods of taking fingerprints are messy. The psychological problem is that fingerprints are strongly associated in the public mind with police procedures. Because most people associate being finger-printed with being arrested, they almost surely would resist being fingerprinted for routine identification

55   Voiceprints may be more promising. With these, the user has only to speak a few words into a microphone for the computer to analyze his voice. There are no psychological problems here. And technically it's easier to take and analyze voiceprints than fingerprints. Also, for remote computer users, the identifying words could be transmitted over the telephone.

56   However, voiceprints still require more research. It has yet to be proved that the computer cannot be fooled by mimics. Also, technical difficulties arise when the voice is subjected to the noise and distortion of a telephone line.

57   Even lipprints have been suggested. But it's doubtful that kissing computers will ever catch on.

58   To date, the most reliable method of positive identification is the card with the magnetic stripe. If the technical problems can be worked out, however, voiceprints may prove to be even better.

59 *Data Encryptation*   When sensitive data is transmitted to and from remote terminals, it must be *encrypted* (translated into a secret code) at one end and *decrypted* (translated back into plain text) at the other. Files also can be protected by encrypting the data before storing it and decrypting it after it has been retrieved.

60   Since it is impractical to keep secret the algorithms that are used to encrypt and decrypt data, these algorithms are designed so that their operation depends on a certain data item called the key. It is the key that is kept secret. Even if you know all the details of the encrypting and decrypting algorithms, you cannot decrypt any messages unless you know the key that was used when they were encrypted.

61   For instance, the National Bureau of Standards has adopted an algorithm for encrypting and decrypting the data processed by federal agencies. The details of the algorithm have been published in the *Federal Register*. Plans are under way to incorporate the algorithm in special purpose microprocessors, which anyone can purchase and install in his computer.

62   So the algorithm is available to anyone who bothers to look it up or buy one of the special purpose microprocessors. But the operation of the algorithm is governed by a sixty-four-bit key. Since there are about 10,000,000,000,000,000,000,000 possible sixty-four-bit keys, no one is likely to discover the correct one by chance. And, without the correct key, knowing the algorithm is useless.

63   A recent important development involves what are called *public-key cryptosystems.*

64   In a public-key cryptosystem, each person using the system has two keys, a public key and a private key. Each person's public key is published in a directory for all to see; each person's private key is kept secret. Messages encrypted with a person's public key can be decrypted with that person's (but no one else's) private key. Messages encrypted with a person's private key can be decrypted with that person's (but no one else's) public key.

65   If I wanted to send you a secret message, I would look up your public key in the directory and use it to encrypt my message. When you received the message, you would decrypt it using your private key.

66   Now, suppose I wanted to send you a *signed* message—that is, one that you could verify came from me. I would encrypt the message, using my private key, and send it to you along with an unencrypted note telling you whom it came from. You would decrypt the message using my public key. The fact that my public key works to decrypt the message proves that the message was encrypted with my private key; obviously, the message had to come from me.

67   To send a *signed, secret* message, the two techniques just described would be used in combination. That is, I would first encrypt the message using my private key, then encrypt it again using your public key. The first encryption signs the message; the second is for secrecy. You would decrypt the message twice. The first time you would use your private key, and, the second time, you would use my public key.

Protection through Software   The software of a computer system, particularly the operating system, can be designed to prevent unauthorized access to the files stored on the system.

68   The protection scheme uses a special table called a *security matrix* (see figure p. 53). Each row of the security matrix corresponds to a data item stored in the system. Each entry in the table lies at the intersection of a particular row and a particular column. The entry tells what kind of access the person corresponding to the row in which the entry lies has to the data item corresponding to the column in which the entry lies.

69   Usually, there are several kinds of access that can be specified. For instance, a person may be able to read a data item but not change it. Or he may be able to both read and modify it. If the data is a program, a person may be able to have the computer execute the program without being able either to read or modify it. Thus, people can be allowed to use programs without being able to change them or find out how they work.

70   Needless to say, access to the security matrix itself must be restricted to one authorized person.

71   Also, the software has to be reliable. Even the software issued by reputable

	Data-A	Data-B	Data-C
User-A	Read Modify Execute	Modify	Read
User-B	Read	Modify Execute	Modify
User-C	Read Modify	Read Execute	Read

Figure 1 *The security matrix specifies the rights that each individual has to each data item. For instance, User-A can read, modify, or execute Data-A, but can only modify Data-B and can only read Data-C.*

vendors may be full of bugs. One or more bugs may make it possible for a person to circumvent the security system. The security provisions of more than one computer system have been evaded by high school and college students.

72 *Restricting the Console Operator* Most computer systems are extremely vulnerable to the console operator. That's because the operator can use the switches on the computer's control panel to insert programs of his own devising, to read in unauthorized programs, or to examine and modify confidential information, including the security matrix. In the face of these capabilities, any software security system is helpless. Computer systems for handling sensitive information must be designed so that the console operator, like other users, works through the software security system and cannot override it. One solution is to incorporate the security system in firmware instead of software, so that unauthorized changes to it cannot be made easily.

FOR FURTHER READING

KNIGHT, GERALD. *Computer Crime*. New York: Walker and Co., 1973.

MEUSHAW, ROBERT V. "The Standard Data Encryption Algorithm." *Byte*, March 1979, pp. 66–74, and April 1979, pp. 110–126.

NEIER, ARYEH. *Dossier: The Secret Files They Keep on You*. New York: Stein and Day, 1975.

PARKER, DONN B. "Computer Security: Some Easy Things To Do." *Computer Decisions*, Jan. 1974, pp. 17–18.

RIVEST, R. L,; SHAMIR, A.; and ALDEMAN, L. "A Method for Obtaining Digital Signatures and Public-Key Cryptosystems." *Communications of the ACM,* Feb. 1978, pp. 120–126.

REVIEW QUESTIONS

1. Give some reasons why there are strong feelings both for and against the use of computers in law enforcement.
2. How can computers aid patrol-car dispatching?
3. What is the advantage of having patrol cars pass through any given area at random times?
4. How can computers relieve officers of the necessity of frequently reporting the status and locations of their cars?
5. Give an example of how a stolen-property file might be used.
6. What is NCIC? How is it used?
7. What is the National Driver Register Service? How is it used?
8. Give the pros and cons of making arrest records available to (1) law enforcement officials and (2) employers.
9. Repeat the arguments of question 8 for conviction records.
10. Describe six kinds of computer crime.
11. Why are computer crimes often difficult to detect?
12. Why are those who commit computer crimes sometimes able to escape punishment even if the crime is discovered?
13. What change in philosophy is necessary to design secure computer systems?
14. Describe some proposals for positively identifying computer users.
15. What is a *key*? How is it used?
16. Describe the two keys that each person using a public-key cryptosystem would possess.
17. Describe how to use a public-key cryptosystem to send a secret but unsigned message.
18. Describe how you would send a signed, secret message using a public-key cryptosystem.
19. What is a *security matrix*?
20. Describe three kinds of access that a person may have to a data item or program stored in a computer system.

VOCABULARY

Exercise 2: Basic Vocabulary Chart

Complete this chart using your English-to-English dictionary. Put the chart on a separate piece of paper so that you will have room to write all of the appropriate definitions and related words.

Word	Part of Speech	Meaning (as used in indicated paragraph)	Related Words	Synonyms
offender (3)	noun			
apprehend (7)	verb			
fugitive (16)	noun			
access (16)	verb			
suspicious (18)	adjective			
arrest (20)	noun			
acquit (20)	verb			
conviction (22)	noun			
detect (33)	verb			
software (39)	noun			
authorize (40)	verb			
prosecute (45)	verb			
restriction (47)	noun			
data (59)	noun			

READING PROBLEMS

Exercise 3: References

Read the following sentences from "Computers and Crime." The references are underlined. On the lines under the sentences, write the word or phrase to which the reference refers.

> **Example 1:** Unfortunately, there is almost no other area in which computers inspire such fear. The reason is obvious: the police can initiate proceedings that can take a person's liberty away.

the reason: the reason that computers cause fear in this area

Example 2: Sometimes with good reason, not everyone is convinced that <u>those proceedings</u> will be carried out fairly. <u>Even worse</u>, the police keep records that can haunt us the rest of our lives.

those proceedings: proceedings that can take a person's liberty away
even worse (than what?):   than that those proceedings will not be carried out fairly

1. As far back as 1974, authorities estimated that over $200 million were being lost each year through computer-related crime. <u>That figure</u> certainly has not diminished in the intervening years.

   that figure _____

2. NCIC can be accessed either through a terminal or a local computer. <u>In either case</u>, the information requested comes back in about ten seconds.

   In either case _____

3. It has been estimated that one out of every two males will be arrested at some time in his life. For black males, <u>the chances</u> are <u>even greater</u>.

   the chances (of what?)_____

   even greater (than what?) _____

4. It is a basic assumption of American justice that a person is innocent until proven guilty. It is difficult to see how the use of arrest records to deny employment and other benefits can be consistent with <u>this assumption</u>.

   this assumption _____

5. A thief can have the computer ship the company's products to addresses of his own choosing. Or he can have it issue checks to him or his confederates for imaginary supplies or services. People have been caught doing <u>both</u>.

   both _____

6. Much personal information about individuals is now stored in computer files. An unauthorized person with access to <u>this information</u> could use <u>it</u> for blackmail. Also, confidential information about a company's products or operations can be stolen and sold to unscrupulous

competitors. (One attempt at <u>the latter</u> came to light when the competitor turned out to be scrupulous and turned in the people who were trying to sell him stolen information.)

this information_____

it_____

the latter _____

7. It's as if a bank concentrated all its efforts on handing out money as fast as <u>it</u> could and did very little to see that the persons who requested the money were entitled to <u>it</u>. Of course, a real bank works just <u>the opposite way</u>, checking very carefully before handing out any money.

it_____

it_____

the opposite way (from what?)_____

Exercise 4: Connectives

Read the following sentences from "Computers and Crime." The connectives have been underlined. On the lines below the sentences, identify the kind of connective that is underlined and write the connective you choose as the best substitute (replacement) for the underlined connective. Do not consider punctuation. The kinds of connectives are *cause/expected result, cause/unexpected result, addition, conditional, purpose,* **or** *contrast.*

Example: <u>If</u> criminals find out that police cars will pass a particular location at regular intervals, they simply plan their crimes for times when no patrol is expected. <u>Therefore</u>, patrol cars should pass by any particular location at random times; the fact that a car just passed should be no guarantee that another one is not just around the corner.

If (**Because, Suppose**) **Kind of connective:** *conditional*

Substitute: *Suppose*

Therefore (**So, However**) **Kind:** *cause–expected result*

Substitute: So

1. <u>Since</u> stolen cars often are used as getaway cars in other crimes, spotting one may prevent or solve some other crime.

   Since (**Because, Although**) Kind: _____

   Substitute: _____

2. <u>Even if</u> the charges are later dropped or the person is acquitted, the arrest record still will be forwarded to employers who request an FBI check.

   Even if (**Even when, Even so**) Kind: _____

   Substitute: _____

3. The cases against many criminals have been dismissed <u>because</u> the police made some technical error during arrest or questioning.

   because (**since, while**) Kind: _____

   Substitute: _____

4. The software for a computer system is often more expensive than the hardware. <u>Yet</u> this expensive software is all too easy to copy.

   Yet (**So, Still**) Kind: _____

   Substitute: _____

5. Most systems use account numbers and passwords to restrict access to authorized users. <u>But</u> unauthorized persons have proved to be adept at obtaining this information and using it for their own benefit.

   But (**And, However**) Kind: _____

   Substitute: _____

6. <u>While</u> a forger might have to learn to duplicate another person's signature, he probably would not move his hand exactly the way the person whose signature he was forging did.

   While (**Since, Although**) Kind: _____

   Substitute: _____

7. You cannot decrypt any messages <u>unless</u> you know the key that was used when they were encrypted.

unless (**if you don't, even if**) **Kind:** _____

Substitute: _____

8. <u>Suppose</u> I wanted to send you a signed message—that is, one that you could verify came from me. I would encrypt the message, using my private key, and send it to you along with an unencrypted note telling you whom it came from.

Suppose (**Furthermore, If**) **Kind:** _____

Substitute: _____

9. If the data is a program, a person may be able to have the computer execute the program without being able to either read or modify it. <u>Thus</u>, people can be allowed to use programs without being able to change them or find out how they work.

Thus (**However, Therefore**) **Kind:** _____

Substitute: _____

Words on board

Exercise 5: Guessing Word Meanings from Context

Try to guess the meanings of the underlined words in the following sentences from "Computers and Crime." Begin by underlining the words and phrases that give you the clues you need to make a good guess, then write your definition of the word on the line under the sentence. Do not look these words up in the dictionary until *after* you have guessed their meanings.

1. Poverty, unemployment, conditions in the cities, and increasing disregard for authority all play their roles and no single <u>remedy</u> is going to solve the problem overnight.

   _____

2. For instance, the police usually are able to solve only a fraction of the crimes committed. And when <u>offenders</u> are apprehended, there

is usually a long delay in trial and sentencing. During the delay, the offenders may be out on bail committing more crimes.

---

3. In one way, the computer can be considered a <u>mixed blessing</u> for law enforcement. To be sure, it helps the police solve crimes and apprehend criminals. But it also opens up a whole new world of ways to commit crimes.

---

4. Another problem, which arises when cars are assigned to regular patrols, is that the patrols may be too regular. If criminals find out that police cars will pass a particular location at regular intervals, they simply plan their crimes for times when no patrol is expected. Therefore, patrol cars should pass by any particular location at <u>random</u> times; the fact that a car just passed should be no guarantee that another one is not just around the corner.

---

5. The officer would set a dial on this unit indicating the current <u>status</u> of the car—patrolling, directing traffic, chasing a speeder, answering a call, out to lunch, and so on.

---

6. Before granting a license, a state can <u>query</u> this computerized system to see whether or not the applicant has had his license revoked in another state.

---

7. A recent Stanford Research Institute study of computer abuse was based on 160 case histories, which probably are just the proverbial <u>tip of the iceberg</u>. After all, we only know about the unsuccessful crimes. How many successful ones have gone undetected is anybody's guess.

---

8. One programmer was caught having the computer <u>transfer</u> funds from other people's accounts to his wife's checking account.

---

9. A thief can have the computer ship the company's products to addresses of his own choosing. Or he can have it <u>issue</u> checks to him or his confederates for imaginary supplies or services.

Exercise 6: Guessing Word Meanings by Word Analysis

Prefixes	Meanings
mis-	bad, wrong, not
re-	again, back
ex-	out, from
dis-	away, not, fail to
inter-	between, among
pro-	for, before
sub- (suc-, suf-, sug-, sup-, sus-)	under, below, lower, lesser

Stem	Meaning
-voc- (-vok-)	call

Use the meanings of the preceding stems and prefixes to analyze the following words and guess their meanings.

1. *exclude*   If *include* means "to place *in* a general category, group,

   etc.," what does <u>exclude</u> mean?_____

2. *revoke*   *Re* means "back" or "again" and *-vok-* means "call." What, then, does it mean when a person has his or her license <u>revoked</u>?

   _____

3. *distrust*   If *trust* means to "place confidence in something," then

   <u>distrust</u> means_____

WORD–PART CHART

Write the meanings of each word part, and add more examples of words that contain these word parts.

Prefix	Meaning	Examples
mis-	_____	misuse, _____, _____
re-	_____	revoke, retrieve, _____
ex-	_____	exclude, _____, _____
dis-	_____	disregard, distrust, _____
inter-	_____	interval, intervene, _____
pro-	_____	proponent, _____, _____
sub- (suc-, suf-, sug-, sup-, sus-)	_____	subsidize, _____, _____

Stem	Meaning	Examples
-voc- (-vok-)		revoke, _____, _____

SECOND READING

Read the chapter "Computers and Crime" from *The Mind Tool* again, this time carefully (pp. 42–54). As you read, try to find the main idea in each paragraph (or group of paragraphs) and underline it. Remember that the topic sentence of a paragraph (the sentence that contains the main idea) is often the first or last sentence of the paragraph, or a combination of the two. Or, it may be that several paragraphs will share one main idea, or the main idea will be implied rather than stated in a sentence. Just remember to mark all of the important ideas, so that you can find them easily when you need them to answer questions or prepare for essay exams.

POST–READING

REACTION QUESTIONS

1. Which of the ways that police use computers were familiar to you?
2. Explain why you think it is good or bad for the police to use this technology.
3. What examples of computer crime have you read about or learned about that were not mentioned in this chapter.

RECOGNIZING DEFINITIONS

The definition of a word can vary from one situation to another. The same object, for example, can have different names in different parts of the country. *Bag, sack,* and *tote* are all words for the same object, but they are used in different regions of the United States. Some words have one meaning when they are used to discuss a certain subject and a different meaning when they are used to discuss another subject. The word *minor,* for instance, means one thing when it is used to talk about law, and another when it is used to refer to music. Some abstract (not concrete) words are defined again and again over time by different people. Words such as *love, patriotism,* and *culture,* for example, seem to have almost as many definitions as there are people who use the words.

It is very important to recognize definitions as they appear in your reading assignments, because they are often the most important ideas in a chapter. This is especially true in introductory courses, where you are still learning the basic vocabulary of each subject. You will need to know technical terms and common words that have special meanings in your field of study.

Some definitions are very easy to recognize. A writer will sometimes put the definition of an important word in parentheses next to the word.

Example 1: "When sensitive data is transmitted to and from remote terminals, it must be <u>encrypted</u> (translated into a secret code) at one end and <u>decrypted</u> (translated back into plain text) at the other.

Sometimes an author will use words such as *that is, or,* or *in other words* to point out the definition of an important word.

Example 2: Now, suppose I wanted to send you a <u>signed message</u>—*that is,* one that you could verify came from me.

Sometimes an author uses words such as *called, named,* or *is* to point out the word used to name what is being defined.

Example 3: Since it is impractical to keep secret the algorithms that are used to encrypt and decrypt data, these algorithms are designed so that their operation depends on a certain data item *called* the <u>key</u>.

Example 4: The protection scheme uses a special table *called* a <u>security matrix</u>.

Often, after the thing being defined is named, it will be defined more completely in the paragraph or paragraphs that follow. This extended definition gives the reader a better idea of the word's meaning.

Example 5: A recent important development involves what are *called* <u>public-key cryptosystems</u>.

　　In a public-key cryptosystem, each person using the system has two keys, a public key and a private key. Each person's public key is published in a directory for all to see; each person's private key is kept secret. Messages encrypted with a person's public key can be decrypted with that person's (but no one else's) private key. Messages encrypted with a person's private key can be decrypted with that person's (but no one else's) public key.

　　If I wanted to send you a secret message, I would look up your public key in the directory and use it to encrypt my message. When you received the message, you would decrypt it using your private key.

In example #5, the thing being defined (public-key cryptosystem) has been named in the first paragraph, explained further in the second paragraph, then illustrated with an example in third paragraph. All together, this is an *extended definition* of the term *public-key cryptosystem*.

We will work with other kinds of definitions as you progress through this book. Some are more difficult to recognize than the examples given here As you read the various kinds of textbook material in this book, look for definitions. Practice looking for the words that point out the definition, and be aware of the source of each definition. In other words, determine if this is the author's definition, or if the author is quoting someone else, perhaps with the intent of revising the other person's definition.

Exercise 7: Definitions

Define the following words, using the information given in the reading. You must reword the information in order to begin the definition as indicated. Do not use your dictionary this time to define the words.

1. encrypt (paragraph 59)

   To encrypt means to _____.

2. decrypt (paragraph 59)

To decrypt means to _____ .

3. key (paragraph 60)

A key is _____ .

4. public-key cryptosystem (paragraph 64)

A public-key cryptosystem is a system that _____

_____ .

5. signed message (paragraph 66)

A signed message is a message that _____ .

6. security matrix (paragraph 68)

A security matrix is _____ .

Exercise 8: Comprehension Check

**Look back at the reading on pp. 42–54 to answer the following questions.
Circle the letter in front of the correct answer or answers.**

1. All of the following are causes of crime mentioned in this chapter,
   except

   a. poverty.

   b. the inefficiency of the criminal justice system.

   c. increasing disregard for authority.

   d. the disintegration of the family.

2. The computer is both a good and a bad thing for law enforcement
   because

   a. it helps the police solve crimes and increases the effectiveness
   of the police.

   b. it helps the police solve crimes but also presents new ways to
   commit crimes.

   c. it can't really help the police solve crimes.

   d. the computer is often unreliable.

3. The computer dispatching system is better than old dispatching systems because (Circle the letters of <u>all</u> correct answers.)

   a. the dispatcher has to keep track of the status and location of every police car.

   b. patrol cars should pass by any particular location at random times.

   c. it can determine right away which car should respond to a call.

   d. the old system could assign patrols so that criminals couldn't predict car locations.

4. NCIC is

   a. an electronic system that lets officers identify a fugitive from justice quickly.

   b. a "Wanted Dead or Alive" poster.

   c. a state police information system.

   d. a county police information system.

5. The National Driver Register Service keeps information on persons whose licenses have been denied, revoked, or suspended so that

   a. all states can use this service.

   b. drivers who have had their license taken away for some reason in one state cannot get a new one in a different state.

   c. drivers who have had their licenses suspended in one state can get a new license in a different state.

6. All of the following things happen when a person is arrested in the United States except

   a. an arrest record is sent to the FBI.

   b. the FBI files the arrest record.

   c. the FBI sends arrest records to employers who request them.

   d. the disposition of the case is always with the arrest record.

7. The best argument against distributing conviction records is that

   a. a court has determined that a person did indeed commit a crime.

   b. the court has required a person to pay a penalty for a crime.

   c. conviction records can prevent ex-convicts from getting jobs.

   d. conviction records are harder to argue against than arrest records.

8. Computer criminals have had little difficulty in committing the following crimes. (Circle the letters of <u>all</u> correct answers.)

   a. theft of computer software and the issuing of checks for imaginary supplies and services

   b. theft of information and using time-shared services in authorized ways

   c. shipping goods to the wrong addresses and avoiding long-distance phone charges

   d. using counterfeit credit cards to buy goods in a store and stealing computer software

9. All of the following are reasons why computer criminals are often not punished, except:

   a. No one checks up on what the computer is doing.

   b. Many of the crimes we know about were detected by accident.

   c. Companies don't punish some criminals because they don't want bad publicity.

   d. Companies sometimes give the criminals severance pay and other benefits.

10. The author of this chapter feels that

    a. computer systems have too many restrictions to keep unauthorized persons from using them.

    b. some computer systems are too easy to use.

    c. computer systems that handle sensitive personal and financial data should be designed like a bank that hands out money as fast as it can.

    d. computer systems should be made easier for the general public to use.

11. The most widely used method for identifying computer users, according to this chapter, is

    a. photographs.

    b. signatures.

    c. two identification numbers, with one on a magnetic strip.

    d. fingerprints.

12. All but one of the following are kinds of access that can be specified in a security matrix:

   a. read

   b. encrypt

   c. modify

   d. execute

Exercise 9: Reading Analysis

Look back at the reading (pp. 42–54) to answer the following questions. Circle the letter in front of the correct answer.

1. The introduction for this chapter is made up of

   a. the first seven paragraphs.

   b. the first four paragraphs.

   c. the first paragraph only.

   d. the first three paragraphs.

2. In the second sentence of paragraph 8, "This" refers to

   a. calling the police.

   b. locating the nearest free car.

   c. keeping track of the status of every police car.

   d. keeping track of the location of every police car.

3. The main idea of paragraph 10 is found in

   a. the first sentence.

   b. the second sentence.

   c. the third sentence.

   d. the last sentence.

4. The word "also" in the first sentence of paragraph 12 indicates

   a. another problem that computers can solve.

   b. an example of the main idea found in paragraph 11.

   c. a result of the main idea found in paragraph 11.

   d. an unexpected result.

5. The word "Since" that begins the last sentence of paragraph 14 introduces

    a. the result of a cause–expected result relationship.

    b. the cause of a cause–expected result relationship.

    c. a time phrase.

    d. an additional idea.

6. The purpose of paragraph 24 is

    a. to give arguments against the ideas in paragraph 23.

    b. to explain the cause of the main point of paragraph 23.

    c. to give an example of the main idea of paragraph 23.

    d. to explain why some people favor the distribution of arrest records.

7. The arguments for the distribution of arrest records

    a. are all found in paragraph 22.

    b. are found in paragraphs 22 and 25.

    c. are found in paragraphs 23 and 24.

    d. are found in paragraphs 25 and 26.

8. The "and yet" at the beginning of paragraph 28 signals

    a. an example of the main idea in paragraph 27.

    b. a contrast, or an argument for the other side.

    c. the addition of another idea.

    d. the result of the main idea of paragraph 27.

Exercise 10: Small-Group Discussion Tasks

Form a group with two or three classmates and prepare answers to each of the following essay questions. Use the chapter you have just read for the facts and examples you need. The underlined word in each sentence is the *essay-exam clue word* that tells you what to do with the facts and examples. To list means to produce a numbered list of words, sentences, and so on; to discuss means to describe by giving the details and stating the pros (favorable opinions or reasons) and cons (unfavorable opinions or reasons) of something; and to explain means to give the causes and reasons for something. **Your group answer may be given orally or in writing (whichever your instructor decides), but it must be clear and complete.**

1. List the areas in which computer criminals have had an easy time committing crimes, and explain why this is so in each case.
2. Discuss the practice of distributing arrest records.
3. Discuss the practice of distributing conviction records.
4. Discuss the various kinds of identification systems that are now being used. Decide as a group which system is best.
5. Discuss the use of computers in law enforcement.

SOME SUGGESTED TOPICS FOR FURTHER READING

National Driver Register Service

FBI

computer crime

cryptosystems

computers and police work

3

Reading Environmental Science

Photo: National Parks Service

Old Faithful, Yellowstone Park

Basic Vocabulary

energy	concentrated	random
consume	dispersed	disorder
conservation	degraded	recycle
pollution	convert	deplete
wastes	transform	
potential	spontaneously	

Exercise 1: Skimming Practice

The chapter you are going to read in this unit is taken from a textbook called *Living in the Environment* by G. Tyler Miller. "Some Matter and Energy Laws" is the third chapter of the book, which is the text for an introductory environmental-science course at the university level.

Read and follow each of the seven skimming steps, answering the questions after each one as you go. (The chapter begins on page 76.)

STEP 1: Read the main title of the chapter and all of the headings. Notice how they relate to one another.

 a. What are the matter and energy laws that are discussed in this chapter?

 _____

 b. After the author explains what the matter and energy laws are, what topic are they used to discuss?

 _____

STEP 2: Examine pictures, charts, and other illustrations in the chapter to get information about the chapter's content.

 a. What are the two types of energy? Give examples of each.

 _____

 _____

b. What is the second energy law?

_____

c. What are the conditions that must exist in order for a "throwaway" society to be sustainable?

_____

d. What is required to have an "earthmanship" society?

_____

STEP 3: Find the names of people mentioned in the chapter and try to determine who they are.

    a. Who is A. F. Conventry?

_____

    b. Who is Arthur S. Eddington?

_____

STEP 4: Notice the sentences and phrases that are in italics in this chapter. Which of the following does the author seem to be doing by italicizing these words?

    a. defining important vocabulary words

    b. giving examples of the main points that have been made

    c. making sure that the reader does not miss the main point

STEP 5: Look at the section entitled "Further Readings."

    a. What is the major difference between this section and the "Further Reading" sections in Units 1 and 2 of this book?

_____

    b. Would the book *Environment, Power and Society* be appropriate for a student just beginning to study the use of human energy?

_____

    c. What is the relationship between the book *Energetics,*

Kinetics and Life: An Ecological Approach and the chapter from this book that you are currently studying?

_____

d. Which of the books listed in this section is the oldest?

_____

STEP 6: Rapidly read the first and last paragraph of the chapter and the first sentence of each paragraph to get an overall idea of the contents of this chapter.

STEP 7: Write a few sentences explaining what you think this chapter is all about.

_____

_____

FIRST READING

Quickly read the chapter "Some Matter and Energy Laws" from *Living in the Environment* (pp. 76–90) in order to answer the following questions.

1. Why is it correct to say that matter is never really consumed?
2. What does the author mean when he says, "We are faced with the problem of trade-offs"?
3. What are some examples of energy transformations?
4. What determines the amount of kinetic energy that a sample of matter has?
5. What happens to the energy that is lost by a system or collection of matter?
6. What is *net energy*?
7. What is the basic difference between concentrated heat energy and dispersed heat energy?
8. What does the author mean by an *earthmanship society*?
9. How does the author define the "throwaway" society in which we now live?
10. Why does the author reject the idea that we must become a *matter recycling society*?

11. Why doesn't the author see solar energy as the answer to our need for an infinite supply of energy?

12. What does the author mean when he says, "The more we try to order, or 'conquer' the earth, the greater stress we put on the environment"?

Some Matter and Energy Laws

E. Tyler Miller

We have for a long time been breaking the little laws, and the big laws are beginning to catch up with us.

A. F. Coventry

---

1   Look at beautiful flower, drink some water, eat some food, or pick up this book. The two things that connect these activities and other aspects of life on earth are matter and energy. **Matter,** or anything that has mass and occupies space, is of course the stuff you and all other things are made of. **Energy** is a more elusive concept. Formally it is defined as the ability or capacity to do work by pushing or pulling some form of matter. Energy is what you and all living things use to move matter around and to change it from one form to another. Energy is used to grow your food, to keep you alive, to move you from one place to another, and to warm and cool the buildings in which you work and live. The uses and transformations of matter and energy are governed by certain scientific laws, which unlike legal laws cannot be broken. In this chapter we begin our study of ecological concepts with a look at one fundamental law of matter and two equally important laws of energy. These laws will be used again and again throughout this book to help you understand many environmental problems and to aid you in evaluating solutions to these problems.

Reprinted by permission from *Living in the Environment*, 2nd ed., by E. Tyler Miller (Belmont, California: Wadsworth, Inc., 1979) pp. 32-40.

LAW OF CONSERVATION OF MATTER: EVERYTHING MUST GO SOMEWHERE

2 We always talk about consuming or using up matter resources, but actually we don't consume any matter. We only borrow some of the earth's resources for a while—taking them from the earth, carrying them to another part of the globe, processing them, using them, and then discarding, reusing, or recycling them. In the process of using matter, we may change it to another form, such as burning complex gasoline molecules and breaking them down into simpler molecules of water and carbon dioxide. But in every case we neither create nor destroy any measurable amount of matter. This results from the **law of conservation of matter:** In any ordinary physical or chemical change, matter is neither created nor destroyed but merely changed from one form to another.

3 This law tells us that we can never really throw any matter away. In other words, there is no such thing as either a consumer or a "throwaway" society. *Everything we think we have thrown away is still here with us in some form or another.* Everything must go somewhere and all we can do is to recycle some of the matter we think we have thrown away.

4 We can collect dust and soot from the smokestacks of industrial plants, but these solid wastes must then go somewhere. Cleaning up smoke is a misleading practice, because the invisible gaseous and very tiny particle pollutants left are often more damaging than the large solid particles that are removed. We can collect garbage and remove solid wastes from sewage, but they must either be burned (air pollution), dumped into rivers, lakes, and oceans (water pollution), or deposited on the land (soil pollution and water pollution if they wash away).

5 We can reduce air pollution from the internal combustion engines in cars by using electric cars. But since electric car batteries must be recharged every day, we will have to build more electric power plants. If these are coal-fired plants, their smokestacks will add additional and even more dangerous air pollutants to the air; more land will be scarred from strip mining, and more water will be polluted from the acids that tend to leak out of coal mines. We could use nuclear power plants to produce the extra electricity needed. But then we risk greater heat or thermal pollution of rivers and other bodies of water used to cool such plants; further, we also risk releasing dangerous radioactive substances into the environment through plant or shipping accidents, highjacking of nuclear fuel to make atomic weapons, and leakage from permanent burial sites for radioactive wastes.

6 Although we can certainly make the environment cleaner, talk of "cleaning up the environment" and "pollution free" cars, products, or industries is a scientific absurdity. The law of conservation of matter tells us that we will always be faced with pollution of some sort. Thus, we are also faced with the

problem of *trade-offs*. In turn, these frequently involve subjective and controversial scientific, political, economic, and ethical judgments about what is a
dangerous pollutant level, to what degree a pollutant must be controlled, and
what amount of money we are willing to pay to reduce a pollutant to a harmless
level. Now let's look at energy and the two energy laws that tell us more about
what we can and cannot do on this planet.

FIRST LAW OF ENERGY: YOU CAN'T GET SOMETHING FOR NOTHING

7   *Types of Energy*   You encounter energy in many forms: mechanical, chemical,
electrical, nuclear, heat, and radiant (or light) energy. Doing work involves
changing energy from one form to another. In lifting this book, the chemical
energy stored in chemicals obtained from your digested food is converted into
the mechanical energy that is used to move your arm and the book upwards
and some heat energy that is given off by your body.

8   In an automobile engine the chemical energy stored in gasoline is converted
into mechanical energy used to propel the car plus heat energy. A battery
converts chemical energy into electrical energy plus heat energy. In an electric
power plant, chemical energy from fossil fuels (coal, oil, or natural gas) or
nuclear energy from nuclear fuels is converted into mechanical energy that is
used to spin a turbine plus heat energy. The turbine then converts the mechanical energy into electrical energy and more heat. When this electrical energy
passes through the filament wires in an ordinary light bulb, it is converted into
light and still more heat. In all of the energy transformations discussed in this
section, we see that some energy always ends up as heat energy that flows into
the surrounding environment.

9   Scientists have found that all forms of energy can be classified either as
potential energy or kinetic energy, as shown in Figure 1. **Kinetic energy** is the
energy that matter has because of its motion. Heat energy is a measure of the
total kinetic energy of the molecules in a sample of matter. The amount of
kinetic energy that a sample of matter has depends both on its mass and its
velocity (speed). Because of its higher kinetic energy, a bullet fired at a high
velocity from a rifle will do you more damage than the same bullet thrown by
hand. Similarly, an artillery shell (with a larger mass) fired at the same velocity
as the bullet will do you considerably more harm than the bullet.

10   Stored energy that an object possesses by virtue of its position, condition,
or composition is known as **potential energy.** A rock held in your hand has
stored or potential energy that can be released and converted to kinetic energy
(in the form of mechanical energy and heat) if the rock is dropped. Coal, oil,

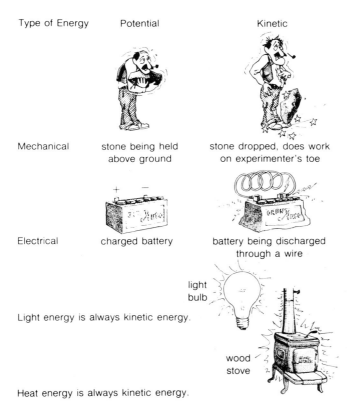

Type of Energy   Potential   Kinetic

Mechanical   stone being held   stone dropped, does work
              above ground   on experimenter's toe

Electrical   charged battery   battery being discharged
                                    through a wire

light
bulb

Light energy is always kinetic energy.

wood
stove

Heat energy is always kinetic energy.

Figure 1 *Potential and kinetic energy are the two major types of energy.*

natural gas, wood, and other fuels have a form of stored or potential energy known as chemical energy. When the fuel is burned, this chemical potential energy is converted into a mixture of heat, light, and the kinetic energy of motion of the molecules in the air and other nearby materials.

11   With this background on the types of energy, we are now prepared to look at the two scientific laws that govern what happens when energy is converted from one form to another.

12 *First Energy Law*   What energy changes occur when you drop a rock from your hand to the floor? Because of its higher position, the rock in your hand has a higher potential energy than the same rock at rest on the floor. Has energy been lost, or used up, in this process? At first glance it seems so. But according to the **law of conservation of energy,** also known as the **first law of**

thermodynamics, in any ordinary physical or chemical process, energy is neither created nor destroyed but merely changed from one form to another. The energy lost by a *system* or collection of matter under study (in this instance the rock) must equal the energy gained by the *surroundings*, or *environment* (in this instance the air).

13   Let's look at what really happens. As the rock drops, its potential energy is changed into kinetic energy (energy of motion)—both its own kinetic energy and that of the air molecules through which it passes. This causes the air molecules to move faster so that their temperature rises. This means that some of the rock's original potential energy has been transferred to the air as heat energy. The energy lost by the rock (system) is exactly equal to the energy gained by its surroundings. In studying hundreds of thousands of mechanical processes (such as the rock falling) and chemical processes (such as the burning of a fuel), scientists have found that no detectable amount of energy is created or destroyed.

14   Although most of us know this first energy law, we sometimes forget that it means in terms of energy quantity we can't get something for nothing; at best we can only break even. In the words of environmentalist Barry Commoner, "There is no such thing as a free lunch." For example, we usually hear that we have so much energy available from oil, coal, natural gas, and nuclear fuels (such as uranium). The first law of thermodynamics, however, tells us that we really have much less energy available than these estimates indicate. *It takes energy to get energy*. We must use large amounts of energy to find, remove, and process these fuels. The only energy that really counts is the *net energy* available for use after we have subtracted from the total energy made available to us the energy used to obtain it.

SECOND LAW OF ENERGY: YOU CAN'T BREAK EVEN

15 *Second Energy Law and Energy Quality*   Energy varies in its *quality* or ability to do useful work. The chemical potential energy concentrated in a lump of coal or liter of gasoline, and concentrated heat energy at a high temperature are forms of high-quality energy. Because they are concentrated, they have the ability to perform useful work in moving or changing matter. In contrast, dispersed heat energy at a low temperature is low-quality energy, with little if any ability to perform useful work. In investigating hundreds of thousands of different conversions of heat energy to useful work, scientists have found that some of the energy is always degraded to a more dispersed and less useful form, usually heat energy given off at a low temperature to the surroundings,

or environment. This is a statement of the *law of energy degradation,* also known as the **second law of thermodynamics.**

16   Let's look at an example of the second energy law. In an internal combustion automobile engine, the high-quality potential energy available in gasoline is converted into a combination of high-quality heat energy, which is converted to the mechanical work used to propel the car, and low-quality heat energy. Only about 20 percent of the energy available in the gasoline is converted to useful mechanical energy, with the remaining 80 percent released into the environment as degraded heat energy. In addition, about half of the mechanical energy produced is also degraded to low-quality heat energy through friction, so that 90 percent of the energy in gasoline is wasted and not used to move the car. Most of this loss is an energy quality tax automatically extracted as a result of the second law. Frequently the design of an engine or other heat-energy conversion device wastes more energy than that required by the second law. But the second law always ensures that there will be a certain waste or loss of energy quality.

17   Another example of the degradation of energy involves the conversion of solar energy to chemical energy in food. Photosynthesis in plants converts radiant energy (light) from the sun into high-quality chemical energy (stored in the plant in the form of sugar molecules) plus low-quality heat energy. If you eat plants, such as spinach, the high-quality chemical energy is transformed within your body to high-quality mechanical energy, used to move your muscles and to perform other life processes, plus low-quality heat energy. As shown in Figure 2, in each of these energy conversions, some of the initial high-quality

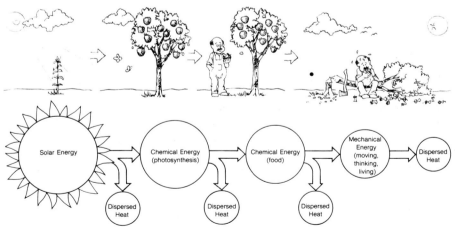

Figure 2 *The second energy law. In all energy changes some energy is degraded to low-quality heat energy that is dispersed in the environment.*

energy is degraded into low-equality heat energy that flows into the environment.

18   The first energy law governs the *quantity* of energy available from an energy conversion process, whereas the second energy law governs the *quality* of energy available. In terms of the quantity of energy available from a heat-to-work conversion, we can get out no more energy than we put in. But according to the second law, the quality of the energy available from a heat-to-work conversion will always be lower than the initial energy quality. Not only can we not get something for nothing (the first law), we can't even break even in terms of energy quality (the second law). As Robert Morse put it, "The second law means that it is easier to get into trouble than to get out of it."

19   The second energy law also tells us that high-grade energy can never be used over again. *We can recycle matter but we can never recycle energy.* Fuels and foods can be used only once to perform useful work. Once a piece of coal or a tank of gasoline is burned, its high-quality potential energy is lost forever. Similarly, the high-quality heat energy from the steam in an underground geothermal well is gone forever once it is dispersed and degraded to low-quality heat energy in the environment. This means that the net useful, or high-quality, energy available from coal, oil, natural gas, nuclear fuel, geothermal, or any concentrated energy source is even less than that predicted by the first energy law.

net high-quality energy = total high-quality
energy available

− high-quality energy needed to find,
get, and process the energy
(first law)

− energy quality lost in finding,
getting, and processing the energy
(second law)

From this we see that both the first and second energy laws must be used to evaluate our energy options.

20 *Second Energy Law and Increasing Disorder*   The second energy law can be stated in a number of ways. Another way of looking at this law is to realize that energy tends to flow or change spontaneously from a compact and ordered form to a dispersed and random, or disordered, form. Heat always flows spontaneously from hot to cold. You learned this the first time that you touched a hot stove. A cold sample of matter has its heat energy dispersed in the random, disorderly motion of its molecules. This is why heat energy at a low temperature can do little if any useful work.

21   Let's look at other spontaneous changes in the world around us. A vase

Figure 3 *The spontaneous tendency toward increasing disorder of a system and its surroundings.*

falls to the floor and shatters into a more disordered state. A dye crystal dropped into water spontaneously dissolves, and the fact that color spreads is evidence that its molecules spontaneously tend toward a more dispersed and disordered state throughout the solution. A woman dies and the highly ordered array of molecules in her body decays to many smaller molecules that are dispersed randomly throughout the environment. Your desk and room seem spontaneously to become more disordered after a few weeks of benign neglect (Figure 3). Smoke from a smokestack and exhaust from an automobile disperse spontaneously to a more random or disordered state in the atmosphere. Pollutants dumped into a river or lake tend to spread spontaneously throughout the water. Indeed, until we discovered that the atmosphere and water systems could be overloaded, we assumed that such spontaneous dilution solved the problem of pollution.

22   These observations all suggest that a *system* of matter spontaneously tends toward increasing randomness, or disorder. But is this hypothesis valid? You may have already thought of some examples that contradict this hypothesis. As its temperature decreases to 0°C, liquid water spontaneously increases its order and freezes into ice. What about living organisms with their highly ordered systems of molecules and cells? You are a walking, talking contradiction to the idea that systems tend spontaneously toward disorder. We must look further.

23   Most of the examples cited concern an apparent increase in disorder in matter. Since we are looking for an energy law, perhaps we should focus on energy. Any change in matter requires either an input of energy or a release of energy. When water freezes and goes to a more ordered state, heat energy

is given off to the surroundings. In changing from liquid water to solid ice, the order in the system increases. But the heat given off during this change increases the disorder in the surroundings. Measurements reveal that this increase in disorder in the surroundings is greater than the order created in the system.

24   The way out of our dilemma then is not to look at changes in disorder or order in the system only, but to look at such changes in both the system *and its environment.* Look at your own body. To form and preserve its highly ordered arrangement of molecules and its organized network of chemical reactions, you must continually obtain energy and raw materials from your surroundings. This means that disorder is created in the environment—primarily in the form of low-quality heat energy. Just think of all the disorder in the form of heat that is added to the environment to keep you alive. Planting, growing, processing, and cooking foods all require energy inputs that add heat to the environment. The breakdown of the chemicals in food in your body gives off more heat to the environment. Indeed, your body continuously gives off heat equal to that from a 100-watt light bulb—which explains why a closed room full of people gets hot. Measurements show that the disorder, in the form of low-quality heat energy, that is added to the environment to keep you alive is much greater than the order maintained in your body. This does not even count the enormous amounts of disorder added to the environment when concentrated deposits of minerals and fuels are extracted from the earth and burned or dispersed to heat the buildings you use, to move you around in vehicles, and to make the clothes, shelter, and other things that you use.

25   In considering the system and surroundings as a whole, scientists find that there is *always* a net increase in disorder with any spontaneous chemical or physical change. For any spontaneous change, either (1) the disorder in both the system and the environment increases, (2) the increase in disorder in the system is greater than the increase in order created in the environment, or (3) the increase in disorder in the environment is greater than the order created in the system. Experimental measurements have demonstrated this over and over again. Thus, we must modify our original hypothesis to include the surroundings or environment. *Any system and its surroundings as a whole spontaneously tend toward increasing randomness or disorder,* or in other words, if you think things are mixed up now, just wait. This is another way of stating the second energy law, or **second law of thermodynamics.**

26.   Scientists frequently use the term **entropy** as a measure of relative randomness or disorder. A random, or disorderly, system has a high entropy, and an orderly system has a low entropy. Using the entropy concept, we can state the second energy law as follows: Any system and its surroundings as a whole spontaneously tend toward increasing entropy.

27   No one has ever found a violation of this law. In most apparent violations,

the observer fails to include the greater disorder (entropy) increase in the surroundings when there is an increase in order in the system.

MATTER AND ENERGY LAWS
AND THE ENVIRONMENTAL CRISIS

28 As we shall see throughout this book, the law of conservation of matter and the first and second laws of energy (see summary box) give us keys for understanding the environmental crisis and for dealing with it. These laws tell us why any society living on a finite planet like earth must eventually become an *earthmanship society* based on recycling and reusing matter and reducing the rate at which matter and energy are used. Energy flows to the earth from the sun and then goes back into space, but for all practical purposes little matter enters or leaves the earth. We have all of the supply of matter that we will ever have. Romantic and technological dreams that we can get new supplies of matter from space and other planets fail to consider that these efforts, even if the supplies were available on inhospitable planets, might require more of the earth's resources than we could bring back. Since we won't get any large amounts of new matter from beyond the earth, and since the law of conservation of matter tells us that no breakthrough in technology will create any new matter, we must learn to live with the matter we now have.

29   Our present one-way or "throwaway" society is based on using more and more of the earth's resources at a faster and faster rate (Figure 4). To sustain such growth rates requires an essentially infinite and affordable supply of mineral and energy resources. Technology can help us stretch these supplies and perhaps find substitutes, but sooner or later we must face up to the finiteness of the earth's supplies as discussed in Enrichment Study 3. The present environmental crisis and rising prices of key resources are warnings that these limits to growth may be closer than we like to think.

30   Some say we must become a *matter recycling society* so that growth can continue without depleting matter resources. As high-grade and economically affordable matter resource supplies dwindle, we must, of course, recycle more and more matter. But there is a catch to such a recycling society. In using resources such as iron, we dig up concentrated deposits of iron ore (because they are the cheapest). Then we disperse this concentrated iron over much of the globe as we fashion it into useful products, discard it, or change it into other chemical substances. To recycle such widely dispersed iron, we must collect it, transport it to central recycling centers, and melt and purify it so that it can be used again. This is where the two energy laws come in. *Recycling matter always requires energy.* However, if a resource is not too widely scat-

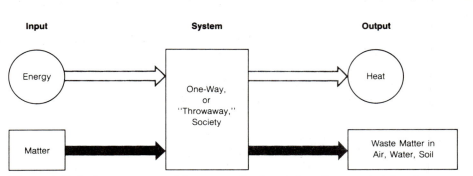

Figure 4 *Today's one-way, or "throwaway," society is based on maximizing the rates of energy flow and matter flow in an attempt to convert the world's mineral and energy resources to trash, pollution, and waste heat as fast as possible. It is sustainable only with essentially infinite supplies of mineral and energy resources and an infinite ability of the environment to absorb the resulting heat and matter wastes.*

tered, recycling often requires less energy than that needed to find, get, and process virgin ores. In any event, a recycling society based on ever increasing growth must have an essentially inexhaustible and affordable supply of energy. And energy, unlike matter, can never be recycled. Although experts disagree on how much usable energy we have, it is clear that supplies of fossil fuels and nuclear fuels are finite. Indeed, affordable supplies of oil, natural gas, and nuclear fuel may last no longer than several decades.

31   "Ah," you say, "but don't we have an essentially infinite supply of solar energy flowing into the earth?" The laws of energy help us to evaluate this option. Sunlight reaching the earth is dispersed energy. In order to use it to heat water to high temperatures, to melt metals, or to produce electricity, this dispersed energy must be collected and concentrated. This requires energy—lots of it. This means that we must have an almost infinite supply of some other energy source, such as nuclear or fossil fuels. We are apparently in a vicious circle.

32   For the moment, however, let's assume that nuclear fusion energy (still only a faint technological dream) or some other energy breakthrough comes to our rescue. Even with such a technological miracle, the *second energy law tells us why continued growth on a finite planet is not possible. As we use more and more energy to transform matter into products and then recycle these products, the disorder in the environment will automatically increase.* We will have to disrupt more and more of the earth's surface and add more and more low-quality heat energy and matter pollutants (many of which are small gaseous molecules created by breaking down larger, more ordered systems of matter) to the environment. Low-quality heat energy flows back into space, but if we create it at a faster rate than that at which it can flow back, the earth's atmos-

phere could heat up and create unknown and possibly disastrous ecological and climatic changes. Thus, paradoxically, the more we try to order, or "conquer," the earth, the greater the stress we put on the environment. From a physical standpoint, the environmental crisis is a disorder, or entropy, crisis, and the second energy law tells us why. Failure to accept the fact that no technological breakthrough can repeal the second energy law can only result in more and more damage to the quality of life on this planet.

33   Why do many think we can ignore or repeal the second energy law? Part of the problem is ignorance. Most people have never heard of the second law, let alone understood its significance. In addition, this law has a cumulative rather than individual effect. You accept the law of gravity because it limits you and everyone else on a personal level. However, though your individual activities automatically increase the disorder in the environment, this individual impact seems small and insignificant. But the cumulative impact of the disorder-producing activities of billions of individuals trying to convert all of the world's resources to trash and garbage as fast as possible can have a devastating impact on the life-support system that sustains us all. *The second energy law tells us that we are all interconnected whether we like it or not.*

34   This may seem like a rather gloomy situation, but it need not be. The second energy law, along with the first energy law and the law of conservation of matter, tell us what we *cannot* do. But even more important and hopeful, these laws tell us what we *can* do. They show us that the way out is to shift to an *earthmanship society* (Figure 5), which is based on a deliberately reduced

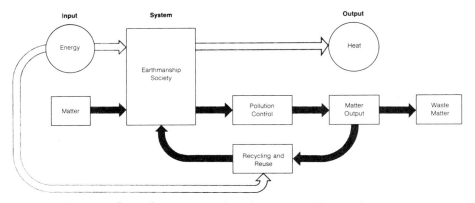

Figure 5 *An earthmanship society is based on energy flow and matter recycling. It requires reusing and recycling finite mineral resources, conserving energy (since it can't be recycled), increased pollution control, and deliberately lowering the rate at which we use matter and energy resources so that the environment is not overloaded and resources are not depleted.*

rate of use of matter and energy so that the entropy or disorder limits of the environment are not exceeded and resources are not depleted. This requires matter recycling, but more important it requires reuse of matter (which takes less energy than recycling), making products that last, increased pollution control, and emphasizing conservation of matter and energy (which cannot be recycled). Only by conserving and not wasting matter and energy supplies can we conserve and preserve life and life quality. This is the key to earthmanship.

35   To make the exciting and necessary transition to an earthmanship society, we must stop thinking of earth as a spaceship that we can pilot—and resupply—at will. Far from "seizing the tiller of the world," as Teilhard de Chardin would have us do, we must stop trying to steer completely. Somehow we must tune our senses and hearts to nature, though we will never completely understand its marvelous complexity. We must learn anew that we belong to the earth and not the earth to us. As part of nature, we will always attempt to shape it to some extent for our own benefit, but we must do so with ecological wisdom, care, and restraint.

MATTER AND ENERGY LAWS

Law of conservation of matter: In any ordinary physical or chemical change, matter is neither created nor destroyed but only transformed from one form to another.

or

We can never really throw matter away.

or

Everything must go somewhere.

First law of energy or thermodynamics (law of conservation of energy): In any ordinary physical or chemical change, energy is neither created nor destroyed but merely changed from one form to another.

or

You can't get something for nothing in terms of energy quantity, you can only break even.

or

There is no such thing as a free lunch.

Second law of energy or thermodynamics (law of energy degradation): In all conversions of heat energy to work, some of the energy is always degraded to a more dispersed and less useful form, usually heat energy given off at a low temperature to the surroundings, or environment.

or

You can't break even in terms of energy quality.

or

Energy can never be recycled.

or

Any system and its surroundings (environment) as a whole spontaneously tend toward increasing randomness, disorder, or entropy.

or

If you think things are mixed up now, just wait.

The law that entropy increases—the second law of thermodynamics—holds, I think, the supreme position among laws of nature. . . . If your theory is found to be against the second law of thermodynamics, I can give you no hope; there is nothing to do but collapse in deepest humiliation.

Arthur S. Eddington

FURTHER READINGS

ANGRIST, S. W., and L. G. HEPLER. 1967. *Order and Chaos*. New York: Basic Books. Excellent nontechnical introduction to thermodynamics emphasizing its fascinating historical development.

BENT, HENRY A. 1971. "Haste Makes Waste: Pollution and Entropy." *Chemistry*, vol. 44, 6–15. Excellent and very readable account of the relationship between entropy (disorder) and the environmental crisis.

BOULDING, KENNETH E. 1964. *The Meaning of the 20th Century*. New York: Harper & Row. Penetrating discussion of our planetary situation by one of our foremost thinkers. See especially Chapters 4, 6, and 7 on the war, population, and entropy (disorder) traps.

COOK, EARL. 1976. *Man, Energy, Society*. San Francisco: Freeman. Superb discussion of energy and energy options.

COTTRELL, F. 1955. *Energy and Society*. New York: McGraw-Hill. Survey of our development of energy sources.

MILLER, G. TYLER, JR. 1971. *Energetics, Kinetics and Life: An Ecological Approach.* Belmont, Calif.: Wadsworth. My own attempt to show the beauty and wide application of thermodynamics to life. Amplifies and expands the material in this chapter at a slightly higher level.

ODUM, HOWARD T. 1971. *Environment, Power and Society.* New York: Wiley-Interscience. Important and fascinating higher-level discussion of human energy use.

ODUM, HOWARD T., and ELISABETH C. ODUM. 1976. *Energy Basis for Man and Nature.* New York: McGraw-Hill. Outstanding discussion of energy principles and energy options at a somewhat higher level.

PRIEST, JOSEPH. 1973. *Problems of Our Physical Environment: Energy, Transportation, Pollution.* Reading, Mass.: Addison-Wesley. Slightly more technical but highly readable treatment of energy principles.

STEINHART, CAROL E., and JOHN S. STEINHART. 1974. *Energy: Source, Use, and Role in Human Affairs.* North Scituate, Mass.: Duxbury Press. Excellent treatment of energy principles and options.

THIRRING, HANS. 1958. *Energy for Man.* New York: Harper & Row. Informative overview of our use of energy.

Exercise 2: Basic Vocabulary Chart

Use your English-to-English dictionary to complete this chart. Put the chart on a separate piece of paper so that you will have room to write all the appropriate definitions and related words.

Word	Part of Speech	Meaning (as used in chapter)	Related Words	Synonyms
energy (1)	noun			
consume (2)	verb			
conservation (2)	noun			
pollution (4)	noun			
wastes (4)	noun			
potential (10)	adjective			
concentrated (15)	adjective			
dispersed (15)	adjective			
degraded (15)	adjective			
convert (16)	verb			

Word	Part of Speech	Meaning (as used in chapter)	Related Words	Synonyms
transform (17)	verb			
spontaneously (20)	adverb			
random (20)	adjective			
disorder (22)	noun			
recycle (30)	verb			
deplete (30)	verb			

Exercise 3: Word Substitution with Basic Vocabulary

This exercise contains some of the basic vocabulary of the chapter. Check your understanding of these words by choosing one of the following words to replace the underlined word in each sentence. Write the word on the line in parentheses next to the underlined word.

consuming   dispersed   depleting

transformations   random

potential   hypothesis

1. In all of the energy changes (_____) discussed in this section, we see that some energy always ends up as heat energy that flows into the surrounding environment.

2. These observations all suggest that a system of matter spontaneously tends toward increasing randomness, or disorder. But is this proposition (_____) valid?

3. We always talk about using up (_____) matter resources, but we actually just change them to another form.

4. Heat energy that is sent off in various directions (_____) at a low temperature is low-quality energy.

5. Some say we must become a matter-recycling society so that growth can continue without exhausting (_____) matter resources.

6. Coal, oil, natural gas, wood, and other fuels have a form of stored (_____) energy known as chemical energy.

7. Another way of looking at this law is to realize that energy tends to flow or change spontaneously from a compact and ordered form to

a dispersed and haphazard (_____) form.

READING PROBLEMS

Exercise 4: References

Read the following sentences from "Some Matter and Energy Laws." The references are underlined. On the lines under the sentences, write the word or phrase to which the reference refers.

> Example: Matter, or anything that has mass and occupies space, is of course the stuff you and all other things are made of. Energy is a <u>more elusive concept</u>.
>
> more elusive concept   <u>more elusive than the concept of matter</u>

1. The amount of kinetic energy that a sample of matter has depends both on its mass and its velocity (speed). Because of its higher kinetic energy, a bullet fired at a high velocity from a rifle will do more damage than the same bullet thrown by hand. <u>Similarly</u>, an artillery shell (with a larger mass) fired at the same velocity as the bullet will do considerably more harm than the bullet.

Similarly (What two things are being compared, and how are they similar?)

_____

_____

2. What energy changes occur when you drop a rock from your hand to the floor? Because of its higher position, the rock in your hand has a higher potential energy than the same rock at rest on the floor. Has energy been lost, or used up, in <u>this process</u>? At first glance it seems <u>so</u>.

this process _____

so _____

3. As the rock drops, <u>its</u> potential energy is changed into kinetic energy (energy of motion)—both <u>its</u> own kinetic energy and <u>that</u> of the air molecules through which <u>it</u> passes. <u>This</u> causes the air molecules to move faster so that <u>their</u> temperature rises. <u>This</u> means that some of the rock's original potential energy has been transferred to the air as heat energy.

its _____

its _____

that _____

it _____

This _____

their _____

This _____

4. In investigating hundreds of thousands of different conversions of heat energy to useful work, scientists have found that some of the energy is always degraded to a more dispersed and less useful form, usually heat energy given off at a low temperature to the surroundings, or environment. <u>This</u> is a statement of the law of energy degradation, also known as the second law of thermodynamics.

This _____

5. Fuels and foods can be used only once to perform useful work. Once a piece of coal or a tank of gasoline is burned, its high-quality potential energy is lost forever. <u>Similarly</u>, the high-quality heat energy from the steam in an underground geothermal well is gone forever once it is dispersed and degraded to low-quality heat energy in the environment.

Similarly (What two things are being compared, and how are they similar?)

_____

_____

Exercise 5: Connectives

Read the following sentences from "Some Matter and Energy Laws." The connectives have been removed from the sentences. Decide what kind of relationship is indicated in each sentence, then choose the connective that correctly expresses this relationship. Disregard any punctuation requirements when choosing your answer. The kinds of relationships are:

cause—expected result

cause—unexpected result

conditional

purpose

addition

contrast

(See pages 22–24 to review these relationships.)

Example: _____ we can certainly make the environment cleaner, talk of "cleaning up the environment" and "pollution free" cars, products, or industries is a scientific absurdity. (**Although, Because, Also**)

Kind of Relationship: unexpected result _____

Connective: Although _____

1. Cleaning up smoke is a misleading practice, _____ the invisible gases and very tiny particle pollutants left are often more damaging than the large solid particles that are removed. (**in order to, because, and**)

Kind of Relationship: _____

Connective: _____

2. We could use nuclear power plants to produce the extra electricity needed. _____ then we risk greater heat or thermal pollution of rivers and other bodies of water used to cool such plants. (**Because, So that, But**)

Kind of Relationship: _____

Connective: _____

3. _____ its higher position, the rock in your hand has a higher potential energy than the same rock at rest on the floor. (**Therefore, Because of, In addition**)

   Kind of Relationship: _____

   Connective: _____

4. _____ most of us know this first energy law, we sometimes forget that it means in terms of energy quantity we can't get something for nothing. (**Although, Because, Thus**)

   Kind of Relationship: _____

   Connective: _____

5. The chemical potential energy concentrated in a lump of coal or liter of gasoline, and concentrated heat energy at a high temperature are forms of high-quality energy. (a) _____ they are concentrated, they have the ability to perform useful work in moving or changing matter. (b) _____ dispersed heat energy at a low temperature is low-quality energy, with little if any ability to perform useful work.

   (a. **Because, However, So that**)   (b. **In contrast, Also**)

   (a) _____   (b) _____

   _____   _____

6. Only about 20 percent of the energy available in the gasoline is converted to useful mechanical energy, with the remaining 80 percent released into the environment as degraded heat energy.

   _____, about half of the mechanical energy produced is also degraded to low-quality heat energy through friction, so that 90 percent of the energy in gasoline is wasted and not used to move the car. (**Therefore, Because, In addition**)

   Kind of Relationship: _____

   Connective: _____

7. Energy flows to the earth from the sun and then goes back into space,

   _____ for all practical purposes little matter enters or leaves the earth. (**but, so, because**)

   Kind of Relationship: _____

   Connective: _____

8. (a) _____ we won't get any larger amounts of new matter from beyond the earth, and (b) _____ the law of conservation of matter tells us that no breakthrough in technology will create any new matter, we must learn to live with the matter we have now.

   (a. **If, While, Since**)   (b. **although, since, while**)

   (a) _____   (b) _____

   _____   _____

9. _____ experts disagree on how much usable energy we have, it is clear that supplies of fossil fuels and nuclear fuels are finite. (**In order that, While, Because**)

   Kind of Relationship: _____

   Connective: _____

10. _____ make the exciting and necessary transition to an earthmanship society, we must stop thinking of earth as a spaceship that we can pilot—and resupply—at will. (**Because, In order to, Furthermore**)

    Kind of Relationship: _____

    Connective: _____

Exercise 6: Guessing Word Meanings from Context

Try to guess the meaning of the underlined words in the following sentences from "Some Matter and Energy Laws." Begin by underlining the words

and phrases that give you the clues you need to make a good guess, then write your definition of the word on the line under the sentence. Do not look these words up in your dictionary.

Example: <u>Matter</u>, or anything that has mass and occupies space, is of course the stuff you and all other things are made of.

Matter is anything that has mass and occupies space.

1. The uses and transformations of matter and energy <u>are governed by</u> certain scientific laws, which unlike legal laws cannot be broken.

2. Coal, oil, natural gas, wood, and other fuels have a form of stored or <u>potential</u> energy known as chemical energy.

3. We always talk about <u>consuming</u> or using up matter resources, but actually we don't consume any matter.

4. Concentrated heat energy at a high temperature is a form of high-quality energy. Because it is concentrated, it has the ability to perform useful work in moving or changing matter. In contrast, <u>dispersed</u> heat energy at a low temperature is low-quality energy, with little if any ability to perform useful work.

5. In investigating hundreds of thousands of different conversions of heat energy in useful work, scientists have found that some of the energy is always <u>degraded</u> to a more dispersed and less useful form.

6. Pollutants dumped into a river or lake tend to spread spontaneously throughout the water. Indeed, until we discovered that the atmosphere and water systems could be overloaded, we assumed that such spontaneous <u>dilution</u> solved the problem of pollution.

7. These observations all suggest that a system of matter spontaneously

tends toward increasing randomness, or disorder. But is this hypoth-esis valid? You may have already thought of some examples that contradict this hypothesis.

hypothesis _____

valid _____

Exercise 7: Guessing Word Meanings by Word Analysis

Prefixes	**Meanings**
re-	back, again
con- (co-, col-, com-)	with, together
trans-	across
in- (ir-, im-, il-)	not
dis-	away, not, fail to

Stems	**Meanings**
cycl-	circle, wheel
-vers (-vert-)	turn
-fin-	end

Use the meanings of the preceding stems and prefixes to analyze the follow-ing words and guess their meanings.

1. *convert*   If you are converted to a new religion, does it mean that you believe in this religion or that you do not believe in it?

   _____

2. *disorder*   When your room is in a state of disorder, is it clean and organized or messy?

   _____

3. *finite*   Is space finite, or infinite?

   _____

4. *recycle*   When you <u>recycle</u> something, do you throw it away, or use it again?

_____

5. *irresponsible*   Can you trust someone who is <u>irresponsible</u> to do an important job for you?

_____

WORD-PART CHART

Write the meanings of each word part and add more examples of words that contain these word parts.

Prefix	Meaning	Examples
re-	_____	recycle, _____, _____
con- (co-, col-, com-)	_____	convert, _____, _____
trans-	_____	transform, _____, _____
in- (ir-, im-, il-)	_____	infinite, _____, _____
dis-	_____	disorder, _____, _____

Stems	Meaning	Examples
-cycle-	_____	recycle, _____, _____
-vers- (-vert-)	_____	convert, _____, _____
-fin-	_____	finite, _____, _____

SECOND READING

Read the chapter "Some Matter and Energy Laws" from *Living in the Environment* (pp. 76–90) again, this time carefully. As you read, underline the main idea in each paragraph (or paragraphs). This time, when you finish reading each section of the chapter, go back and reread the sentences that you have underlined. Try to write a brief summary of each section of the chapter, incorporating all the main ideas you picked out.

POST-READING

RECOGNIZING DEFINITIONS

You were told in Unit 2 that writers can point out a definition to the reader by using clue words or phrases. Because definitions are so important in textbook reading, you should be able to locate the words being defined and, using the definition clues, find the words and phrases that define the word. Here are some examples that show you how to do this.

> **Example 1:** Matter, or anything that has mass and occupies space, is of course the stuff you and all other things are made of.

In Example 1, the word that is being defined is *matter*. The clue that points out the definition is the word "or" and the commas that separate this definition from the main part of the sentence. The phrase that can be used to define the word is "anything that has mass and occupies space."

> **Example 2:** Energy is a more elusive concept. Formally it is defined as the ability or capacity to do work by pushing or pulling some form of matter. Energy is what you and all living things use to move matter around and to change it from one form to another. Energy is used to grow your food, to keep you alive, to move you from one place to another, and to warm and cool the buildings in which you work and live.

Example 2 contains a more extended definition than that in example 1. Three definition clues are used in this definition of energy: "is defined as," "is," and "is used to." Key words and phrases that define *energy* are:

> a. "the ability or capacity to do work by pushing or pulling some form of matter";
> b. what you and all living things use to move matter around and to change it from one form to another."

The definition clue "is used to" introduces more specific examples of what the author means when he says, "to move matter around and to change it from one form to another."

Exercise 8: Recognizing Definitions

Find the following words in the paragraphs indicated by the number before each word. Write the definition clue used in the reading on the line next to the words, then define the words on the lines under them.

    Example: (9) kinetic energy (definition clue) <u>is</u>

               (**Definition**) <u>Kinetic energy is the energy that matter has because of its motion.</u>

1. (9) velocity (**definition clue**) _____

   (**Definition**) Velocity is _____

   _____ .

2. (10) potential energy (**definition clue**) _____

   (**Definition**) Potential energy is _____

   _____ .

3. (10) chemical energy (**definition clue**) _____

   (**Definition**) Chemical energy is _____

   _____ .

4. (15) energy quality (**definition clue**) _____

   (**Definition**) Energy quality is _____

   _____ .

5. (26) entropy (**definition clue**) _____

   (**Definition**) Entropy is _____

   _____ .

UNDERSTANDING PARAPHRASING

Paraphrasing is the act or process of restating or rewording a text, paragraph, or sentence. As a university student, you will need to understand paraphrasing in order to succeed in your academic work. To thoroughly understand and use the information you read in your textbooks, you should be able to recognize when an author has restated (reworded) an idea, saying it in another way. You also need to be able to recognize restatements in order to succeed on multiple-choice exams (exams that require you to choose the correct answer from among several choices). Finally, you must be able to paraphrase, or put into your own words, information that you read so that you can write essay exams, summaries, and research papers.

There are several ways that a writer can restate an idea.

1. The writer can use synonyms (words that have the same meaning) of words used in the original statement.

Example: This car consumes a lot of gas.

Paraphrase: This car uses up a lot of gas.

2. The writer can change the emphasis of the sentence by using a different subject (the person or thing that is performing the action of the sentence). For example, the writer can change the verb from active to passive. This change will make the original subject of the sentence less important than the original object (the person or thing that is receiving the action of the sentence).

Example: In every case we neither create nor destroy any measurable amount of matter.

Paraphrase: In every case, no measurable amount of matter is either created or destroyed.

3. The writer can use a different connective to show the relationship of ideas in the sentence or paragraph. This change often includes a change in the word order and structure of the sentence, not just the substitution of one word for another.

Example: Since electric car batteries must be recharged every day, we will have to build more electric power plants.

Paraphrase: Electric car batteries must be recharged every day; therefore, we will have to build more electric power plants.

4. The writer may use relative clauses to combine sentences that were originally separate.

Example: We begin our study of ecological concepts with a look at one fundamental law of matter and two equally important laws of energy. These laws will be used again and again throughout this book to help you understand many environmental problems.

Paraphrase: We begin our study of ecological concepts with a look at one fundamental law of matter and two equally important laws of energy, all three of which will be used again and again throughout this book to help you understand many environmental problems.

Here is an illustration of the various ways that a writer can restate an idea.

Original Sentence: To sustain such growth rates requires an essentially infinite and affordable supply of mineral and energy resources.

This sentence can be rewritten by any of the first three methods mentioned, or a combination of two or three of them.

Example 1: Our society needs an essentially infinite and affordable supply of mineral and energy resources in order to sustain these growth rates.

What has been changed to make the second sentence from the first?

Example 2: In order to continue growing at the same rate, our society needs a virtually unending and economically satisfactory supply of mineral and energy resources.

How is Example 2 different from the original sentence?

The first step in learning to paraphrase is to recognize paraphrases that are made by other writers. You will practice recognizing paraphrases throughout the rest of this book to increase your understanding of the material you read and to help you with multiple-choice exams.

You will notice as you do paraphrase exercises throughout the book that there are many ways to restate an idea. Try to find paraphrases in the readings and try to paraphrase as you answer the questions that follow each reading.

EXERCISE 9: *Recognizing Paraphrases*

Circle the letter of the answer that best paraphrases the original sentence.

1. Matter, or anything that has mass and occupies space, is of course the stuff that you and all other things are made of.

   a. Matter takes up space.

    b. Matter is what you and everything else consist of.

    c. Matter, which has mass and takes up space, is what everything is made of.

    d. Everything is made up of matter, which is mass and space.

2. The uses and transformations of matter and energy are governed by certain scientific laws, which, unlike legal laws, cannot be broken.

    a. Certain scientific laws govern the uses and transformation of matter and energy, and these laws cannot be broken, as legal laws can.

    b. The scientific laws that govern the uses and transformation of matter and energy can be broken, as legal laws can.

    c. Scientific laws that govern the uses and transformation of matter and energy cannot be broken, just as legal laws cannot be broken.

    d. The scientific laws that govern the uses and transformation of matter and energy are breakable.

3. We always talk about consuming or using up matter resources, but actually we don't consume any matter.

    a. We actually don't consume any matter because we always talk about consuming or using up matter resources.

    b. Although we always talk about consuming or using up matter resources, actually we don't consume any matter.

    c. We always talk about consuming or using up matter resources; moreover, we actually don't consume any matter.

    d. We always talk about consuming or using up matter resources so that we don't consume any matter.

4. We can reduce air pollution from the internal combustion engines in cars by using electric cars. But since electric car batteries must be recharged every day, we will have to build more electric power plants.

    a. The use of electric cars can reduce air pollution from the internal combustion car engines; however, we will need to build more electric power plants to recharge their batteries every day.

    b. Air pollution can be reduced by the use of electric cars, but it will be necessary to build more electric power plants and to recharge the electric car batteries every day.

    c. The use of elecltric cars will result from building more power plants.

    d. Air pollution from internal combustion engines can be reduced by building more electric power plants.

5. Because of its higher position, the rock in your hand has a higher potential energy than the same rock at rest on the floor.

   a. The rock in your hand has a higher potential energy than the same rock at rest on the floor since it has a higher position.

   b. Although the rock in your hand has a higher position, it has a higher potential energy than the same rock at rest on the floor.

   c. The rock in your hand has a higher potential energy than the same rock at rest on the floor, and it has a higher position.

   d. The rock in your hand has a higher position so that it has a higher potential energy than the same rock at rest on the floor.

6. Once a piece of coal or a tank of gasoline is burned, its high-quality heat energy is lost forever.

   a. The high-quality heat energy in a piece of coal or a tank of gas is temporarily lost when it is burned.

   b. Burning a piece of coal or a tank of gas causes its high-quality heat energy to get lost.

   c. The high-quality heat energy of a piece of coal or a tank of gas can never be recovered once the coal or gas is burned.

   d. When we burn a piece of coal or a tank of gas, we must replace its high-quality energy by treating it.

7. These observations all suggest that a system of matter spontaneously tends toward increasing randomness, or disorder.

   a. These observations indicate that a system of matter spontaneously tends to become more random and disordered.

   b. According to these observations, all matter spontaneously moves toward decreasing randomness and disorders.

   c. The observations we have made prove that a system of matter spontaneously tends toward increasing randomness or disorder.

8. Some say that we must become a matter recycling society so that growth can continue without depleting matter resources.

   a. Some people say that we must become a matter recycling society because growth can continue without depleting matter resources.

   b. Some say that we need to become a matter recycling society; furthermore, growth can continue without depleting matter resources.

   c. Some say we have to become a matter recycling society in order for growth to continue without depleting resources.

    d. Some say that growth must continue without depleting matter resources although we must become a matter recycling society.

Exercise 10: Comprehension Questions

Look back at the reading (pp. 76–90) to find the answers to the following questions. Circle the letter in front of the correct answer or answers.

1. The following statements about the laws of energy and matter are true:

    a. They can be broken.

    b. They cannot be broken.

    c. They govern the activities of human beings.

    d. There is no punishment for breaking them.

2. It is inaccurate to say that we "consume" resources because

    a. the resource matter is neither created nor destroyed; it is changed.

    b. the resource matter is not changed from one form to another.

    c. the resource matter cannot be recycled if it is discarded.

    d. matter can be thrown away only under certain conditions.

3. It is misleading to say that we can clean up smoke because

    a. the solid particles cannot really be removed from the smoke.

    b. smoke cannot be prevented in any way.

    c. the most dangerous pollutants in smoke are invisible or very tiny.

    d. industries are not willing to spend the money to clean up their smoke.

4. All of the following will result from the use of electric cars except:

    a. We will have to build more electric power plants.

    b. Coal-fired plants may be used, which will cause pollution problems.

    c. Nuclear power plants may be used, which will cause more pollution problems.

    d. All problems of pollution related to the use of cars will be solved.

5. This chapter informs the reader that

   a. it is possible to get rid of all pollution.

   b. it is impossible to make the environment cleaner.

   c. we must determine what levels of pollution are acceptable.

   d. no level of pollution should be accepted by the public.

6. All of the following are kinds of energy except:

   a. radiant

   b. chemical

   c. coal

   d. heat

7. The energy transformations in paragraph 8 have the following result in common:

   a. Chemical energy is converted to electrical energy.

   b. Heat energy flows into the surrounding environment.

   c. Mechanical energy is converted to electrical energy.

   d. Chemical energy is converted to mechanical energy.

8. The amount of kinetic energy matter has depends on

   a. its mass.

   b. its velocity.

   c. both its mass and its velocity.

   d. neither its mass nor its velocity.

9. The following is an example of potential energy:

   a. unburned coal or wood

   b. burning oil

   c. a dropped rock

   d. electricity passing through a wire

10. The energy lost by a system or collection of matter

   a. is greater than the energy gained by the environment.

   b. is less than the energy gained by the environment.

   c. is equal to the energy gained by the environment.

11. The chemical potential energy in a lump of coal is high-quality energy because

   a. it is dispersed heat energy.

   b. it is degraded to a less useful form.

   c. it is concentrated.

   d. it is heat energy given off to the environment at a low temperature.

12. Paragraph 16 says that

   a. only 20 percent of the energy in gasoline is actually used to move the car.

   b. friction degrades about half of the mechanical energy produced in an internal combustion engine.

   c. the internal combustion engine wastes energy just because the design of the engine is not good.

   d. it is not necessary to waste or lose energy quality if the energy is properly designed.

13. The second energy law indicates that

   a. we can recycle energy but we can never recycle matter.

   b. high-grade energy is rarely degraded after use.

   c. high-grade energy can't be replaced.

   d. foods and fuels can be used more than once to perform useful work.

14. Energy tends to flow from

   a. a compact, random form to a disordered form.

   b. a compact ordered form to a disordered form.

   c. a dispersed, random form to a disordered form.

   d. a dispersed, random form to a compact, ordered form.

15. If they consider the system and surroundings as a whole, scientists find that

   a. there is invariably a net increase in disorder when there is spontaneous chemical or physical change.

   b. a spontaneous chemical or physical change always causes the disorder in both the system and the environment to increase.

   c. a spontaneous chemical or physical change always causes an increase in the disorder of the system.

d. a spontaneous chemical or physical change invariably causes more of an increase in the disorder of the environment than in the disorder of the system.

EXERCISE 11: Anticipating Essay Questions

In the first two units of this book you were asked to organize answers to several essay questions as part of a small group. Typically, every reading assignment given to you in university-level courses contains material for several essay questions, and it is likely that you will be asked to answer these essay questions as part of your professor's evaluation of your understanding of the material. You can prepare for essay exams if you learn to look for possible questions as you read the textbook, and prepare answers for them ahead of the exam. You will usually have to write the answer itself in class, but you can plan how you will write it outside of class. This is an excellent way to organize and remember the information you will need in order to do well on the exam.

Subtitles are very useful in determining the author's method of organization and the important topics of the chapter. Often, making these subtitles into questions will provide you with possible essay-exam questions. Here are the topics of "Some Matter and Energy Laws":

1. Law of Conservation of Matter: Everything Must Go Somewhere.
2. First Law of Energy: You Can't Get Something for Nothing.
3. Second Law of Energy: You Can't Break Even.
4. Matter and Energy Laws and the Environmental Crisis.

Read and think about the five essay questions that follow. The underlined word in each sentence is the *essay-exam clue word* that tells you what to do with the information in the chapter. To underline **explain means to make clear by giving the details; to** compare **means to show the similarities and differences; to** evaluate **means to give your opinion or some expert's opinion of the truth or importance of the concept; to** illustrate **means to make something clear by giving concrete examples, comparisons, or analogies; and to** relate **means to show the connections between things, telling how one causes the other or is like the other.**

1. Explain the law of conservation of matter.
2. Compare the first law of energy with the second law of energy.
3. Evaluate the law of conservation of matter.

4. <u>Explain</u> and <u>illustrate</u> the first and second laws of energy.
5. <u>Relate</u> the environmental crisis to the matter and energy laws in this chapter.

Which of these five questions do you think a professor might ask? Why are the other questions not likely to be asked?

_____

_____

Answer the essay questions that you chose. Make sure that your answers are both clear and complete.

SOME SUGGESTED TOPICS FOR FURTHER READING

pollution (water, air, soil)

conservation

recycling

energy laws

laws of matter

kinetics

ecology

4

More Reading Environmental Science

Hindu Pilgrims, Rajastan, India

Basic Vocabulary

voluntary	eliminate	immigration
abortion	predominant	controversial
compel	extend	fetus
ethical	commune	coercive
legal	sterilize	diverse

Exercise 1: Skimming Practice

The chapter you are going to read is also from *Living in the Environment* by G. Tyler Miller. This reading is from a series of enrichment articles included in the book to give students supplemental reading related to the main chapters of the book. As mentioned in Unit 3, Living in the Environment is a textbook used to teach introductory environmental science at the university level.

Do each step, one at a time, answering the questions before you go on to the next step. (The chapter begins on page 115.)

STEP 1: Read the main title of the chapter and all of the headings. Notice how these relate to one another.

    a. What are the methods of population control discussed in this chapter?

    b. What are the four aspects of the abortion issue discussed in this chapter?

    c. What is one kind of involuntary population control?

STEP 2: Examine pictures, charts, and other illustrations in the chapter to get information about the chapter's contents.

    a. What is the function of the table on page 123?

STEP 3: Find the names of people, organizations, and so on (proper names) mentioned in the chapter and try to determine who or what they are.

    a. In paragraph 2 you will see the following:
       (Davis 1967, 1972a, 1978, Echols 1976, Ehrlich et al. 1977, Hauser 1973, Lappé & Collins 1977, Stokes 1977, Willing 1971)

What is the significance of the names and dates between parentheses in this chapter?

   b. Who is Cardinal Cushing?

   c. What is Medicaid?

   d. Who is Robert Coles?

   e. Who is Desmond Morris?

   f. Who is Garrett Hardin? (See "Further Readings" for a clue.)

STEP 4: Look at all of the italicized words and phrases. Be aware of the author's reasons for italicizing them. The author of this chapter italicizes terms that he is defining and words used to emphasize a point.

   a. Find the definitions for the following terms:

   1. *Clostridium welchii* _____

   2. *nuclear family* _____

   3. *extended family* _____

   4. *multiadult extended family* _____

   5. *positive incentives* _____

   6. *negative incentives* _____

   b. List the words that are italicized to emphasize a point.

STEP 5: Look at the review questions and the bibliography at the end of the chapter to get more information about the chapter.

   a. What aspect of population control is discussed in *Who Shall Live?*

   b. Which other books and/or magazine articles discuss the same aspect of population control as that discussed in *Who Shall Live?*

   c. Does the author think that *Abortion: Law, Choice and Morality* is a thorough survey of the issue?

   d. What company published *Exploring New Ethics for Survival?*

STEP 6: Rapidly read the first and last paragraphs of the chapter and the first sentence of each paragraph.

STEP 7: In a sentence or two, explain what you think this chapter is about. (You may answer orally or quickly write the answer that you would give orally.)

FIRST READING

Quickly read the chapter from *Living in the Environment*. This time you do not have questions to guide your reading. As you read, try to pick out and underline the main ideas of each section. In the margin next to the main ideas, write a note to yourself, reminding yourself what the paragraphs are about. This will allow you to quickly find answers to the questions asked at the end of the chapter and organize the information for essay exams.

Population Control Methods

E. Tyler Miller

1   There is considerable debate over whether world population growth can be controlled by (1) economic development, (2) voluntary family planning programs, (3) beyond family planning programs, (abortion, education, changing women's roles, economic incentives and disincentives, and involuntary control), or (4) some combination of these three methods. This enrichment study will examine beyond family planning methods for population control.

IS VOLUNTARY FAMILY PLANNING ENOUGH?

2   Voluntary family planning is an extremely important method for helping control world population growth, but many observers feel that it must be coupled with economic development and with methods that go beyond family planning (Davis 1967, 1972a, 1978, Echols 1976, Ehrlich et al. 1977, Hauser 1973, Lappé & Collins 1977, Stokes 1977, Willing 1971). This view is based on the beliefs that family planning programs alone will not be able to slow world population growth rapidly enough and that family planning is not really a method for population control.

3   Supporters of family planning point to a number of successes in reducing fertility rates over the past 25 years (see Cutright & Jaffe 1976, Dryfous 1976, Hull et al. . . .1977, Maudlin 1975, Nortman 1977, Nortman & Hofstatler 1978, Ravenhold & Chao 1974, Staff report 1972b, 1978h, Worrall 1977) and the fact that by 1976, 136 million women in the world were using some form of contraception (Staff report 1978j). Critics, however, point out that after over 20 years of family planning efforts throughout the world, an estimated 263 million women

Reprinted by permission from *Living in the Environment*, 2nd ed., by E. Tyler Miller (Belmont, California: Wadsworth, Inc., 1979) pp. E57–E63.

were not using any form of birth control in 1976 (Staff report 1978j, Stokes 1977). In other words, in 1976 about two out of three of the potentially fertile women in the world were not using any form of contraception to prevent unwanted pregnancies (Staff report 1978f). Critics use these data to show that family planning methods are too slow to have significant impact on world population growth. Supporters of family planning programs, however, argue that this is not the fault of family planning programs but represents the failure of governments to provide enough funds and personnel to make such efforts more effective.

4   Another criticism of family planning is that it is not designed to be a method for population control (Davis 1967, 1972a, 1978). The announced aim of family planning is to help couples have the number of children they want when they want them. Without family planning most couples have more children than they want, but with family planning they still have more children than many observers feel can be supported by available resources. The problem is that many couples want so many children that world population will continue to grow at a relatively high rate, especially in developing nations, unless economic development and beyond family planning methods are used (Davis 1967, 1973, Echols 1976, Ehrlich et al. 1977, Willing 1971).

VOLUNTARY LIBERALIZED ABORTION

5   *Freedom of Choice or Murder?*   Liberalization of abortion laws and easy availability of abortion are often suggested as important additions to voluntary methods for fertility control. Abortion, however, is a highly emotional issue that does not lend itself to compromise or cool debate. Basically, the argument is between those who regard abortion as murder and those who believe that a woman should have the right to choose whether to bear a child.[1] One side emphasizes the basic right of a pregnant woman to control her own body, while the other emphasizes the rights of the unborn child.

6   Proponents view antibortion laws as a form of "compulsory pregnancy" that denies each woman the right to control her fertility according to her own beliefs and needs (Hardin 1968a, 1969c, 1974b). The attitude is that no one should be required to have an abortion, but at the same time no one should be compelled to go through a pregnancy. Making abortion illegal imposes the religious views

---

[1]For a discussion of the ethical and other issues involved in abortion and population control, see the following: American Friends Service Committee 1970, Augenstein 1969, Barr & Abelow 1977, Callahan 1970, 1972, Connery 1977, Djerassi 1972, Dyck 1971, 1977, Hardin 1970b, 1974a, 1974b, 1977, Noonan 1970, Omran 1971, 1976, Ransil 1969, Sarvis & Rodman 1972, Shinn 1970, Veatch 1977.

of one group on another group who feels that this choice should be made by the individual.

7   Some individuals, however, have strong moral and religious beliefs that view abortion as an act of murder and thus believe that the "right to life" of an unborn child should take precedence over a pregnant woman's "right to choose" whether to terminate her pregnancy. The issue is fraught with inconclusive and controversial medical, theological, and legal debate about when life begins—at conception, at birth, or at some difficult-to-define point in between. Is the fetus only a piece of unborn living matter that is a potential human being, or is it human from the moment of conception? For some, the question "When does life begin?" makes no sense, since they consider life to be a continuous process (Hardin 1974b). Others make the distinction between an embryo and a viable fetus (one sufficiently developed to survive outside the uterus). Because of incubators and modern medical techniques, survival is now possible after 28 weeks and in rare circumstances after 24 weeks. Neither the Catholic church nor any other Christian church, however, baptizes or demands that an aborted fetus less than seven months old be given proper burial and death rites. Indeed, the Catholic church permitted early abortions under some circumstances until a papal decree in 1969 (Behrens 1977).

8   No court ruling will settle these ethical questions. Indeed, as legal restraints are removed, the ethical issues emerge even more strongly for the individual. To some religious leaders, forcing individuals to face up to these moral decisions rather than allowing them to hide behind legal reasons represents an improvement. More and more Catholics agree with Cardinal Cushing's statement that "Catholics do not need the support of civil law to be faithful to their own religious convictions."

9   *The Extent of Abortion*   In spite of strong antiabortion laws throughout human history, abortion has been and still is one of the most widely used methods of birth control in the world (Devereux 1955, Freedman 1965, Robbins 1973, United Nations 1972). The total number of legal and illegal abortions throughout the world each year is estimated at between 30 and 55 million, about half of these performed illegally (Brown & Newland 1976, Tietze & Lewit 1977, Tietze & Munstein 1975).

10   According to the lower estimate there is about one abortion for every four live births; according to the higher estimate, there is one abortion for every two live births (Tietze & Lewit 1977). Obviously laws banning abortion have been among the most ineffective laws of all time.

11   By making abortions illegal, a country encourages dangerous abortions that kill thousands every year, particularly poor women who cannot afford to travel to a region where abortion is legal. In Colombia, for example, which has one of the strictest abortion laws in the world, the largest maternity hospital in

Bogota must devote half its beds to cases of complications arising from illegal abortions (Brown & Newland 1976).

12   Perhaps half of all illegal abortions are self-induced. Wowmen swallow large and dangerous doses of chemicals such as quinine, which are sold as "home remedies." Should this method fail, they resort to a back-street abortionist or a knitting needle. Most poor women throughout the world still abort themselves with a sharpened stick. Infection is understandably a major killer. The most dangerous bacterium, *Clostridium welchii*, kills in only 12 hours unless medical treatment is provided immediately. Antibiotics decrease the risk but again must be given quickly; most are often not available in developing nations.

13   **Health and Psychological Risks**   The most common modern procedure for legal abortion—vacuum aspiration—takes about 5 minutes, and in 1978 cost about $185 in a U.S. clinic. With this method, a legal abortion done under medical supervision within the first 12 weeks of pregnancy is 4 to 6 times safer than childbirth (Rudel et al. 1972, Tietze & Lewit 1977, Zero Population Growth 1976a).

14   There has been much discussion and mixed evidence concerning the potential psychological problems associated with abortions. These problems are very real for some women, particularly those who are masochistic or acutely depressed. But legal abortion clinics in New York State have found psychological problems much rarer than expected. Apparently if legal and moral stigmas are removed, many women do not experience guilt feelings. In contrast, many problems can arise from being denied an abortion—broken careers, forced teenage marriages (which have very high divorce rates), abandoned and disturbed children and "battered babies." Compared with wanted children, unwanted children born to women denied an abortion tend to have a higher incidence of illness, slightly poorer school marks, and poorer social adjustment (Dytrych et al. 1975).

15   **Worldwide Abortion Liberalization**   One of the major social trends throughout the world during the past decade has been the legalization of abortion (Brown & Newland 1976, Omran 1976, Tietze & Lewit 1977). In 1971, 38 percent of the world's people lived in countries where abortion was legal. By 1977 this figure had increased to 66 percent, or two-thirds, of the world's people (Brown & Newland 1976, Tietze & Lewit 1977). About one-third of the world's people live in countries with nonrestrictive abortion laws, which allow pregnancies to be terminated on request during a specified stage of pregnancy (usually 10 to 24 weeks). Another third of the world's people are in nations with moderately restrictive abortion laws, where unwanted pregnancies may be terminated for specific medical, psychological, and socioeconomic reasons (Tietze & Lewit 1977). The remaining third live in countries where abortion is completely illegal

or is allowed only if there is a severe threat to a woman's life or health. The three major reasons for the worldwide liberalization of abortion are (1) the awareness of how much death and illness are caused by illegal abortion, (2) court decisions (as is the case in the United States), and (3) the growth of women's movements, especially in developed nations (Brown & Newland 1976).

16   In 1973 the Supreme Court made a historic decision, stating that during the first three months (12 weeks) of pregnancy, the decision about having an abortion must be left up to a woman and her doctor. This decision thus made unconstitutional all antiabortion laws in the United States. A state may regulate but not deny abortions in the third through sixth months of pregnancy; after this period, each state can draw up its own statutes.

17   Between 1973 and 1977 the number of legal abortions in the United States almost doubled, rising from almost 745,000 to 1.27 million (Forrest et al. 1978, Sullivan et al. 1977). Of the women who had legal abortions in 1976, about 75 percent were unmarried, 67 percent were white, and 33 percent were teen-agers, and 23 percent had their abortions paid for by Medicaid through federal and state funds (Forrest et al. 1978). In 1977, 28 percent of pregnant women in the United States chose to terminate their pregnancy by a legal abortion and an estimated 30 percent of the women who wanted legal abortions, were unable to obtain them because services were unavailable in their communities (Forrest et al. 1978). In 1977 a nationwide survey showed that 77 percent of all Americans and 73 percent of all American Catholics polled believed either that abortion should be legal under any circumstances (22 percent of all Amer-icans and 20 percent of American Catholics) or under certain circumstances (Arney & Treschler 1976, Staff report 1978l).

18   In spite of widespread approval by Americans, a small but militant minority in the Catholic church and in right-to-life groups is still applying intense orga-nized pressure against legal abortion. In 1977 the Supreme Court ruled that even though every woman has a legal right to an abortion, the government is not obliged to pay for it. Under intense pressure from antiabortion forces, Congress eliminated federal Medicaid funding for most abortions for the poor in 1977. By 1978 only 16 states continued to fund such abortions. During the past few years, eight legal abortion clinics in Minnesota, Vermont, Nebraska, Iowa, and Ohio have been hit by fire, and another eight clinics have been vandalized. Although abortion is legal and supported by most Americans, the intense ethical, religious, and political controversy over this issue has clearly not ended.

CHANGES IN EDUCATION, WOMEN'S ROLES, AND FAMILY STRUCTURE

19 *An Earthmanship Curriculum*   Education through both mass communication and formal education can play an important part in population control (Ahmed 1974, Population Reference Bureau 1970d, Simmons 1970, Worrall 1977). In the United States a comprehensive earthmanship education program should be designed for kindergarten through college that emphasizes our relationship to and responsibilities for the ecosphere (Branson 1972, Brown 1971c, U.S. Department of the Interior 1971, Vivian 1973). Special efforts should be directed at the preschool and elementary levels, where many values are introduced or at least heavily reinforced. Although there has been some improvement during the last five years, many elementary school readers and other materials in the United States are still ecological and sexist disaster areas (Ahlum & Fraley 1973, Hardin 1978, Russo 1973).

20   Instead of showing all American families with two or three children and two cars, we should introduce other models. Some families might have only Dick or only Jane, and we might introduce the couple down the street who married at the age of 30 and have a meaningful life with no children and a small car. There might be visits from Uncle George, a happy bachelor who rides a bicycle, and Aunt Sally, an unmarried woman who is a doctor, senator, executive, judge, or lawyer. We must display a diverse array of identity options to young children (Russo 1973). We must destroy the myths that couples without children can't be happy (Peck 1971, Pohlman 1969, Silka & Kiesler 1977, Silverman & Silverman 1971) and that unmarried persons, especially women, lead less fulfilling lives. Contrary to popular opinion, research studies comparing married and unmarried women indicate that personal fulfillment does not depend on marriage or parenthood (Baker 1966, Looft 1971).

21   Somehow we must be made aware that the quality, not the quantity, of parenthood is important. Some people have the ability and compassion to provide quality parenthood for more than two children, and these rare individuals should not be discouraged. But many couples should stop at two, or one, or none (Lieberman 1970, Peck & Gronzig 1978, Zero Population Growth 1976b). In all education and persuasion programs, however, the emphasis *must* be on positive reinforcement and showing other options rather than on punishment and making people feel guilty.

22 *Changes in Cultural Patterns*   To many, the birth of a child is an essential and fulfilling event. Psychiatrist Robert Coles (1964) recorded this statement about what a new child means to a poverty-stricken black mother:

> *To me having a baby inside me is the only time I'm really alive. I know I can*

make something, do something, no matter what color my skin is, and what names people call me. When the baby gets born you can see the little one grow and get larger and start doing things, and you feel there must be some hope, some chance that things will get better.

But many women are trapped into motherhood as a role that society expects of them. It does little good, however, to talk about altering motivation toward childbearing without offering women the opportunity to become educated and to express their lives in work and other meaningful social roles.[2] In most developing societies women do not have equitable access to education. Nearly two-thirds of the world's 800 million illiterates are women, and almost everywhere males are given preference in education and vocational training (McGrath 1976). In subsistence agriculture societies in developing nations women typically do 50 percent of the work associated with growing food, take care of any children, do the housekeeping, and suffer the most malnutrition because men and children are given first claim to the limited food supplies (Newland 1977).

23   The percentage of women in various occupations varies throughout the world, as shown in Table 1 (Blake 1974, Senderowitz 1978). An average of 30 percent of the world's work force in 1977 was female, ranging from 51 percent in the Soviet Union to 1.8 percent in Algeria; the figure was 40.5 percent in the United States (Senderowitz 1978). In the United States most working women have clerical and service jobs and earn an average of 41 percent less than male workers (Senderowitz 1978). Although women make up 85 percent of the elementary school teachers and 51 percent of the high school teachers, they make up only 11 percent of full university professors, 5 percent of school superintendents, and 1 percent of college presidents (Senderowitz 1978).

24   One of the most significant events of this century is the drive to recognize and guarantee women's rights in the United States. This movement is important primarily in its recognition of human dignity and freedom, but it is also a crucial element in any successful effort to control U.S. population. Providing women with equal work opportunities causes a marked change in the family structure and can lead to later marriage and smaller families (as it has in the U.S.S.R. and China) (Blake 1974).

25   We must support and encourge efforts to eliminate male domination, which is an outdated frontier role. This will not be easy, but cultural patterns can change, and equality for women is a much-needed earthmanship rule. It can

---

[2]For more details on women's roles and rights, see the following: Ahlum & Fralley 1973, Blake 1974, Boston Women's Health Center 1976, Boulding 1976a, Ceres 1975, Chafe 1972, Cordell & McHale 1975, De Beauvoir 1949, Dixon 1975a, 1975b, Editorial Research Reports 1977, Firestone 1970, Friedan 1963, Gornick & Moran 1972, McGrath 1976, Newland 1977, Organization for Economic Co-operation and Development 1975b, Peck 1971, Population Reference Bureau 1975d, Rossi 1973, Safilios-Rothschild 1974, Silverman & Silverman 1971, Tangni 1976.

Percentage of Women in Selected Occupations throughout the World in 1977

Occupation	Soviet Union	United States	Sweden	Japan	India	Chile
Physicians	70	13	18	10	7	8
Lawyers	35	9	8	2	1	10
Members of national legislature	35	3	21	3	5	7
Managerial positions	32	20	11	5	2	9
Union members	60	21	33	28	12	—
Agricultural workers	44	16	26	50	20	3

Source: Senderowitz 1978

be achieved through laws, education, and increasing the sensitivity of males to the conscious and unconscious ways in which women's rights are denied.

26   Family structure patterns may also be changing, especially in some developed nations. Through much of human cultural evolution, the predominant family pattern has been the *extended family*, consisting of the mother, father, grandfather, grandmother, children, grandchildren, and other relatives living together or at least nearby. During the past 50 years, the extended family in the United States has largely been replaced by the *nuclear family*, composed of the mother, father, and their children. Some observers feel that the nuclear family may be replaced by a *multiadult extended family*, consisting of networks of intimate friends who may or may not live together (Ramey 1976).

27   The possible cultural need for an extended family, coupled with the lack of age diversity in the nuclear family, may account in part for the thousands of experimental communes that have sprung up in the United States and western Europe in recent years. There is great variety among the estimated 3,000 communes formed in the United States since 1965. They range from rural to urban and religious to economic, and they share everything from income to beds and board (Conover 1973, Fairfield 1972, Kanter 1972, Roberts 1971, Zableck 1971).

28   Most communes are volatile, short-lived, and beset with problems. Desmond Morris (1969) observed that most rural communes don't last because people brought up in an urban society have in effect lost their "social virginity." At first, fugitives from a highly stimulating urban society find a return to simplicity satisfying. Eventually, however, disillusionment and boredom may set in. At this point the group either collapses from internal stress or stirs itself into economic or other activities that place it back into the rat race. One weakness of most rural and urban communal experiments is that they are structured horizontally around one age group or a common set of problems or interests

rather than vertically, with an array of ages and interests. Often such diversity can provide more long-term social and economic stability.

29   The importance of communes must not be underestimated. Most represent attempts to break out of the small nuclear family and to return to the extended families that are more characteristic of our evolutionary past (Roberts 1971). In addition, they serve as important flesh-and-blood examples of alternatives to the urban-industrial life-style and temporary halfway houses for people suffering from cultural battle fatigue. We need to encourage these experiments, which are designed to help us establish a richer network of meaningful human relationships in a stressful urban world.

ECONOMIC INCENTIVES AND DISINCENTIVES

30 There has been considerable interest in using economic incentives and disincentives to reduce population growth (Barnett 1969, Berman 1970, Enke 1966, Kangas 1970, Lipe 1971, Marriot 1968, Pohlman 1971a, 1971b, Ridker & Museat 1973, Spengler 1966, 1969). There are two approaches: positive (or economic-reward) incentives and negative (or economic-penalty) approaches. *Positive incentives* include direct cash payments, savings certificates, free contraceptives, free abortion and sterilization, free health plans, free old-age pensions, and free education for individuals and couples who delay marriage or child-bearing, limit their number of children, or agree to use contraceptives or to be sterilized.

31   *Disincentives* or, *negative incentives*, include elimination of income tax deductions for some or all children; elimination of welfare, health, maternity, housing, or educational benefits after more than the allotted number of children; and taxes on marriage, children, and child-related goods and services. All incentive approaches are based on the reasonable assumption that economic rewards and penalties provide effective motivation.

32   Positive incentives have the advantage of redistributing wealth to the poor, since they would have greater need and are more inclined to accept such rewards. Thus, incentives may be particularly useful in developing countries, where most people are poor. In such countries a combination of small, immediate cash rewards plus an old-age security plan might simultaneously reduce population and raise economic well-being. It must be remembered that in these countries one of the main reasons for having children is to provide parents with security in their old age, which might be their thirties or forties. Positive incentives are noncoercive in principle. But they may be considered coercive in practice for the poor who might have little choice but to accept them even though they strongly want to have children.

33   Economic disincentives that add taxes, eliminate child-related services, or

increase the costs of children would be unjust to both the poor and the lower middle classes and to the children who would have to bear the brunt of reduced economic income. But the children are also penalized when parents plan poorly and have more children than they can support. Positive incentives appear particularly effective in developing countries, but they might have little impact on middle and upper classes anywhere, for whom negative incentives or penalties might be more effective.

34   A diverse array of carefully planned incentive and disincentive programs must be tried on a pilot basis throughout the world over the next few decades. We need to know what types of incentives and disincentives will work (Leibenstein 1969). Because of vast cultural, economic, and political differences even within a single country, approaches will vary considerably. Kangas (1970) cautioned us to stop looking for the "one best incentive or disincentive" and develop a broader, integrated package of multiple and reinforcing social and economic incentives and disincentives at the individual, small-group, community, and national levels. Such incentives and disincentives should be part of a carefully planned program for raising the economic and social well-being of the population.

INVOLUNTARY POPULATION CONTROL

35 *Arguments for Coercion*   To most people the use of coercive measures for population control is either unthinkable or at best a last resort. Some argue that the world population situation is already bad enough to justify instituting some forms of involuntary control (Boot 1974, Boulding 1964, Chasteen 1971, Daly 1977, Ehrlich 1968, Ehrlich & Harriman 1971, Hardin 1968b, 1970b, 1974b, 1978, Heer 1975). They argue that our life-support system is already threatened by overpopulation or will be within 50 to 70 years. They also believe that voluntary and even extended voluntary methods either will not work or will be too slow. Garrett Hardin (1968b, 1970b, 1972a, 1974b, 1977, 1978) has argued that voluntary programs won't work because individuals do not see their own actions as a threat to others—the "do-your-own-thing" myth. The impact of people who voluntarily give up their right to breed or pollute can be minimized if they constitute a dwindling proportion of the total population. It is also argued that the various coercive proposals do not *completely* deny the individual freedom to have children. Instead they limit the number of children to one or two.[3]

36 *What is Coercion?*   To draw a sharp line between voluntary and involuntary

---

[3] For discussions of the freedom issue in population control, see the following: Callahan 1972, Day 1968, Dyck 1971, Pilpel 1971.

approaches to population control is impossible. Every day we engage in actions falling somewhere between the two approaches in other areas. We stop at red lights and pay taxes. We have coercive prohibitions of crime, coercive school attendance, restrictions on the number of wives or husbands we can have at one time, and a host of others. We surrender certain freedoms to do as we please to gain other, more important ones—to drive safely, to be free from certain diseases, and to live in a community providing education, fire and police protection, streets, parks, and other services.

37   So perhaps restricting the number of children that a couple can have is a justifiable limitation of individual liberty that protects the air, water, and land resources for present and future generations. But any involuntary approach must be clearly justified and enforceable. Unenforceable legislation can be a disaster, as the United States learned during Prohibition and as India learned recently when it tried to coerce people to be sterilized. Before any involuntary approach is used, several important questions must be answered: Is the approach really necessary for security, survival, or freedom? Does it represent the least possible coercion, have the fewest harmful consequences, and minimize injustice? How will it be enforced? Are there other alternatives?

38   Nearly all successful forms of social control are developed by employing those measures that are the least onerous to the people concerned. People resent compulsion less than unfairness in the distribution of rewards and punishments. For example, how would we punish people who had too many children? Would they be sent to jail? Fined? In either case, the "sins" of the parents could be passed on to innocent children.

39 *Restricting Immigration*   One coercive approach to limiting the population of a particular country already exists: restricting immigration. For 200 years America had an open door immigration policy, but beginning with laws passed in 1921 and 1924, quotas were set, and in 1965 even stricter immigration laws were enacted (Bouvier et al. 1977, Keely 1974). In spite of this, legal immigration in the 1970s accounted for about 20 percent of the U.S. population growth each year, compared with 11 percent in the 1950s. The United States admits more immigrants than any other country in the world. In contrast, the Soviet Union, China, Japan, Hungary, Czechoslovakia, and several other countries admit almost no immigrants (Bouvier et al. 1977).

40   Whether to decrease further or even eliminate immigration into the United States is an extremely difficult and controversial question. Present immigration policies also pose several ethical dilemmas. One is the "brain drain," a policy that encourages trained and skilled persons in developing nations to immigrate to the United States (House Foreign Affairs Committee 1974). An estimated one-third of the scientists in the United States came from developing countries (UNESCO 1971, Ward 1976); of the 11,323 scientists and engineers who immi-

grated to the United States in 1972, 9,581 came from developing nations, especially India and the Philippines (House Foreign Affairs Committee 1974). Currently about 7,000 of the 14,000 new physicians each year in the United States are immigrants, mostly from India, the Philippines, and other developing nations (House Foreign Affairs Committee 1974). It is agreed that this immigration policy deprives developing countries of their most valuable resource, educated citizens, and is a reverse form of foreign aid from the poor nations to the rich nations (House Foreign Affairs Committee 1974). Should the United States eliminate all immigration or only that of trained personnel? These are agonizing questions for a country that has considered itself the "melting pot" of the world.

41   In this enrichment study we have seen that there are many possible approaches to controlling population, each with specific advantages and disadvantages. Because people and countries have exciting and necessary uniqueness and diversity, each approach must be analyzed in relation to the needs and political realities of each culture (Dyck 171, Mamdani 1973, Nash 1972, Polgar 1972). We all have a role to play: the couples who decide to have one, two, or no children; the couples who believe they can truly provide *quality* parenthood for more than two children; those who find life can be meaningful without marriage; the druggist who displays contraceptives; the newspaper executive who decides to accept ads for birth control; people who insist that each woman has a right to avoid birth by having an abortion; people who oppose abortion on moral grounds; the courageous politician who introduces liberalized abortion or sex education laws; the insurance executive who insists that abortion costs be covered in health plans; the leaders who insist that their country institute an official population stabilization policy; and all people who by acting in these and other ways are practicing earthmanship.

If policies and programs can be designed to help women achieve their goals by means other than motherhood, two very important objectives can be met at once: raising the status of women and lowering the birth rate.

Kathleen Newland

FURTHER READINGS

AMERICAN FRIENDS SERVICE COMMITTEE. 1970. *Who Shall Live?* New York: Hill and Wang. Examines ethics of human control over life and death.

AUGENSTEIN, L. 1969. *Come Let Us Play God*. New York: Harper & Row. Good discussion of ethics of population control.

BROWN, WILLIAM E. 1971. *Islands of Hope*. Washington, D.C.: National Recreation and Park Association. Excellent discussion of environmental education.

CALLAHAN, DANIEL. 1970. *Abortion: Law, Choice and Morality*. New York: Macmillan. Comprehensive survey of the abortion issue.

CALLAHAN, DANIEL. 1972. "Ethics and Population Limitation." *Science*, vol. 175, 487–494. Very good discussion of ethical issues of population control.

CONNERY, JOHN. 1977. *Abortion: The Development of the Roman Catholic Perspective*. Chicago: Loyola University Press. Excellent overview.

HARDIN, GARRETT. 1974. *Mandatory Motherhood: The True Meaning of "Right to Life."* Boston: Beacon Press. Superb discussion of abortion issue.

HARDIN, GARRETT. 1978. *Exploring New Ethics for Survival*. 2nd ed. New York: Viking. Another superb contribution by this prominent human ecologist. Explores ethics of population control policies.

KANGAS, L. W. 1970. "Integrated Incentives for Fertility Control." *Science*, vol. 169, 1278–1283. Superb analysis of incentive approach with call for a broader multifaceted approach. Important article.

KANTER, ROSABETH M. 1972. *Commitment and Community*. Cambridge, Mass.: Harvard University Press. One of the best analyses of communes and utopias.

NEWLAND, KATHLEEN. 1977. *Women and Population Growth: Choice beyond Childbearing*. Washington, D.C.: Worldwatch Institute. Superb discussion of women's roles. Highly recommended.

POHLMAN, EDWARD A. 1971. *How To Kill a Population*. Philadelphia: Westminster. Excellent presentation of the case for using incentives for population control.

POLGAR, STEPHEN, 1972. "Population History and Population Policies from an Anthropological Perspective." *Current Anthropology*, vol. 13, no. 2, 203–241. Most population control programs fail because they are not tailored to the cultural characteristics of each group.

ROBBINS, JOHN. 1973 "Unmet Needs in Family Planning: A World Survey." *Family Planning Perspectives*, vol. 5, no. 4, 232–236. Good summary of failure of family planning to make a significant impact. Summarizes findings of a 1971 world survey by the International Planned Parenthood Federation.

SARVIS, BETTY, and HYMAN RODMAN. 1972. *The Abortion Controversy*. New York: Columbia University Press. Excellent balanced discussion.

SILVERMAN, ANNA C., and ARNOLD SILVERMAN. 1971. *The Case against Having Children*. New York: McKay. Excellent discussion of alternatives to motherhood.

TERRY, MARK. 1971. *Teaching for Survival*. New York: Ballantine. Outstanding book showing how environmental concepts can be worked into any course.

TIETZE, CHRISTOPHER, and SARAH LEWIT. 1977. "Legal Abortion." *Scientific American*, vol. 236, no. 1, 21–27. Excellent discussion of the spread of legal abortion throughout the world.

ZERO POPULATION GROWTH. 1976. *The One Child Family*. Washington, D.C.: Zero Population Growth. Excellent pamphlet summarizing advantages of a one-child family.

Exercise 2: Basic Vocabulary Chart

Use your English-to-English dictionary to help you complete this chart. Put the chart on a separate sheet of paper so that you will have room to write all of the appropriate definitions and related words.

Word	Part of Speech	Meaning (as used in indicated paragraph)	Related Words	Synonyms
voluntary (1)				
abortion (5)				
compel (5)				
fetus (7)				
ethical (8)				
legal (9)				
diverse (20)				
eliminate (24)				
predominant (25)				
extend (25)				
commune (27)				
sterilize (37)				
immigration (39)				
controversial (40)				
coercive (35)				

Exercise 3: Recognizing the Correct Definition from Context

The following basic vocabulary words have more than one definition. Circle the letter of the appropriate definition for the word as it is used in the sample sentence.

1. <u>Voluntary</u> family planning is an extremely important method for help-ing control world population growth, but many observers feel that it must be coupled with economic development and with methods that go beyond family planning.

   a. supported by private funds

   b. proceeding from free choice

2. By making abortions illegal, a country encourages dangerous abor-tions that kill thousands every year, particularly poor women who cannot afford to travel to a region where <u>abortion</u> is legal.

   a. the natural premature expulsion of a fetus; miscarriage

   b. partial or complete arrest of development

   c. artificially produced expulsion of a fetus

3. The most common modern procedure for <u>legal</u> abortion—vacuum aspiration—takes about 5 minutes, and in <u>1978</u> cost about $185 in a U.S. clinic.

   a. of or concerned with law

   b. established, authorized, or permitted by law

   c. characteristic of or appropriate to those who practice law

4. Under intense pressure from antiabortion forces, Congress elimi-nated (<u>eliminate</u>) federal Medicaid funding for most abortions for the poor in <u>1977</u>.

   a. to get rid of

   b. to remove a contestant from further competition by defeating

   c. to remove a quantity from a system of algebraic equations

5. Through much of human cultural evolution, the <u>predominant</u> family pattern has been the extended family, consisting of the mother, father, grandfather, grandmother, children, grandchildren, and other relatives living together or at least nearby.

   a. superior in power

b. superior in number

c. superior in influence

6. The possible cultural need for an extended (extend) family, coupled with the lack of age diversity in the nuclear family, may account in part for the thousands of experimental communes that have sprung up in the United States and western Europe in recent years.

   a. to give or offer to give

   b. to open or stretch to full length

   c. to spread out, expand

7. Most communes are volatile, short-lived, and beset with problems.

   a. verb: to converse intimately

   b. noun: a group of people who, though not forming a single family, share a house or land

   c. noun: the smallest political division of France, Italy, Belgium, and other countries

8. Positive incentives for population control include direct cash payments, free contraceptives, free abortion and sterilization (sterilize), and free health plans.

   a. to deprive of productive or reproductive power

   b. to make barren

   c. to free from infective or pathogenic microorganisms

Exercise 4: Word Substitution with Basic Vocabulary

For each of the following sentences, choose one of the following words or phrases that has the same meaning as the underlined word or phrase. Write the answer in the blank.

unborn child	varying	allowed by law
got rid of	involuntary	moral
forced	disputable	

1. No one should be compelled to go through a pregnancy.

   _____

2. Neither the Catholic church nor any other Christian church baptizes

or demands that an aborted <u>fetus</u> less than seven months old be given proper burial and death rites.

_____

3. No court ruling can settle <u>ethical</u> issues about abortion.

_____

4. In 1971, 38 percent of the world's people lived in countries where abortion was <u>legal</u>.

_____

5. Under intense pressure from antiabortion forces, Congress <u>eliminated</u> federal Medicaid funding for most abortions for the poor in <u>1977</u>.

_____

6. We must display a <u>diverse</u> array of identity options to young children.

_____

7. To most people the use of <u>coercive</u> measures for population control is either unthinkable or at best a last resort.

_____

8. Whether to decrease further or even eliminate immigration into the United States is an extremely difficult and <u>controversial</u> question.

_____

READING PROBLEMS

Exercise 5: References

Read the following sentences from "Population Control Methods." The references are underlined. On the lines under the sentences, write the word or phrase to which the reference refers.

> **Example:**   Voluntary family planning is an extremely important method for helping control world population growth, but many observers feel that <u>it</u> must be

coupled with economic development and with methods that go beyond family planning.

it   voluntary family planning _____

1. Critics point out that after over 20 years of family planning efforts throughout the world, an estimated 263 million women were not using any form of birth control in 1976. In other words, in 1976 about two out of three of the potentially fertile women in the world were not using any form of contraception to prevent unwanted pregnancies. Critics use these data to show that family planning methods are too slow to have significant impact on world population growth.

   these data _____

2. Basically, the argument is between those who regard abortion as murder and those who believe that a woman should have the right to choose whether to bear a child. One side emphasizes the basic right of a pregnant woman to control her own body, while the other emphasizes the rights of the unborn child.

   One side (of what?) _____

   the other _____

3. The most common modern procedure for legal abortion—vacuum aspiration—takes about 5 minutes, and in 1978 cost about $185 in a U.S. clinic. With this method, a legal abortion done under medical supervision within the first 12 weeks of pregnancy is 4 to 6 times safer than childbirth.

   this method _____

4. There has been much discussion and mixed evidence concerning the potential psychological problems associated with abortions. These problems are very real for some women, particularly those who are masochistic or acutely depressed.

   These problems _____

5. In 1971, 38 percent of the world's people lived in countries where abortion was legal. By 1977 this figure had increased to 66 percent, or two-thirds, of the world's people.

   this figure _____

6. A state may regulate but not deny abortions in the third through

sixth month of pregnancy; after this period, each state can draw up its own statutes.

this period _____

7. Under intense pressure from antiabortion forces, Congress eliminated federal Medicaid funding for most abortions for the poor in 1977. By 1978 only 16 states continued to fund such abortions.

such abortions _____

8. One of the most significant events of this century is the drive to recognize and guarantee women's rights in the United States. This movement is important primarily in its recognition of human dignity and freedom, but it is also a crucial element in any successful effort to control U.S. population.

This movement _____

9. For 200 years America had an open door immigration policy, but beginning with laws passed in 1921 and 1924, quotas were set, and in 1965 even stricter immigration laws were enacted. In spite of this, legal immigration in the 1970s accounted for about 20 percent of the U.S. population growth each year, compared with 11 percent in the 1950s.

this _____

10. Present immigration policies also pose several ethical dilemmas. One is the "brain drain," a policy that encourages trained and skilled persons in developing nations to immigrate to the United States.

One _____

Exercise 6: Guessing Word Meanings from Context

Try to guess the meanings of the underlined words in the following sentences from "Population Control Methods." Begin by underlining the words and phrases that give you the clues you need to make a good guess, then write your definition of the word on the line under the sentence. Do not look these words up in your dictionary until *after* **you have guessed their meanings.**

Example: The argument is between those who regard abortion as murder and those who believe that a woman should have the right to choose whether to bear a child.

Since the sentence is about <u>abortion</u> and it talks about the <u>right to choose whether</u> to bear <u>a child</u>, *to bear* probably means the same thing as "<u>to give birth to</u>."

to give birth to
_____

1. Voluntary family planning is an extremely important method for helping control world population growth, but many observers feel that it must be <u>coupled with</u> economic development and with methods that go beyond family planning.

_____

2. Abortion is a highly emotional issue that <u>does not lend itself to</u> compromise or cool debate.

_____

3. <u>Proponents</u> of legal abortion view antiabortion laws as a form of "compulsory pregnancy" that denies each woman the right to control her fertility according to her own beliefs and needs.

_____

4. Some individuals, however, have strong moral and religious beliefs that view abortion as an act of murder and thus believe that the "right to life" of an unborn child should <u>take precedence over</u> a woman's "right to choose" whether to terminate her pregnancy.

_____

5. In spite of strong antiabortion laws throughout human history, abortion has been and still is one of the most widely used methods of birth control. The total number of legal and illegal abortions throughout the world is estimated at between 30 and 55 million, about half of these performed illegally. Laws <u>banning</u> abortion have been among the most ineffective laws of all time.

_____

6. In spite of widespread approval by Americans, a small but <u>militant</u> minority in the Catholic church and in right-to-life groups <u>is still</u> applying intense organized pressure against legal abortion.

_____

7. In most developing societies women do not have <u>equitable</u> access to education. Nearly two thirds of the world's 800 million illiterates are women, and almost everywhere males are given preference in education and vocational training.

Exercise 7: Guessing Word Meanings by Word Analysis

Prefixes	**Meanings**
contra-	against
anti-	against
un-	not, opposite, reverse
super- (supra-)	above, over, higher or greater than
pro-	for, before
il- (im-, in-, ir-)	not

Stems	**Meanings**
-bio-	life
-vis- (-vid-)	see
-cent-	hundred
-ben- (-bon-)	good

Use the meanings of the preceding stems and prefixes to analyze the following words and guess their meanings.

1. *contraception*   If <u>conception</u> is the beginning of pregnancy or the act of fertilization, then what is <u>contraception</u>?

   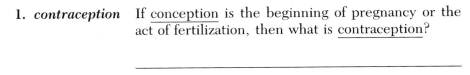

2. *antiabortion*   What is the goal of <u>antiabortion</u> laws?

3. *supervisor*   What is the job of a <u>supervisor</u>?

4. *benefactor*   The stem *-fact-* means "do"; therefore, a <u>benefactor</u> is

a person who _____.

5. *century*   How many years are there in a <u>century</u>? _____

6. *television*   The stem *-tele-* means "long-distance" or "far." What, then, is the purpose of <u>television</u>?

_____

7. *proponent*   Do <u>proponents</u> of abortion think it should be legal or illegal?

_____

8. *contradict*   The stem *-dic-* means "say" or "tell." What, then, does it mean to <u>contradict</u> someone?

_____

SECOND READING

Carefully read the chapter "Population Control Methods" from *Living in the Environment* (pp. 115–126). Revise your notes in the margin, so that they are easier to use. Use your revised notes to write a brief summary of each section of the chapter.

POST-READING

REACTION QUESTIONS

1. With which ideas in this chapter do you disagree?
2. Which statistics in the chapter were the most surprising to you?
3. Which of the methods of population control discussed in this chapter are used in your country? Are they effective there?
4. Is the control of population growth important to your country at this time?
5. Is your country using any other methods of population control than those discussed in this chapter?

Exercise 8: Short-Answer Comprehension Questions

The questions in this exercise are based on the main ideas found in this chapter. As you answer them check to see how many are answered by information that you underlined while you thoroughly read the chapter. If you underlined the important ideas in the chapter, most of them should be.

1. What are the arguments given in this chapter against the effectiveness of voluntary family planning as a method of controlling world population growth?

2. Why is it difficult to debate the issue of abortion?

3. What information is given in this chapter to prove that laws prohibiting abortion have been very ineffective?

4. What does the author say is the result of making abortions illegal?

5. What information is given to prove that allowing legal abortions causes fewer problems than does making abortions illegal?

6. How many of the world's people live in parts of the world where abortion is completely illegal?

7. What is the difference between nonrestrictive abortion laws and moderately restrictive abortion laws?

8. What are the three reasons why abortion has been liberalized worldwide?

9. What was the immediate result of the 1973 Supreme Court decision on abortion?

10. What was the Supreme Court ruling on abortion in 1977, and what result did it have?

11. What does the author mean by an *earthmanship curriculum?*

12. Although to many, having children is an essential and fulfilling event, the author thinks that many women have children for another reason. What is this reason?

13. Why does the author think that the women's rights movement is significant to the control of world population?

14. What are the three family patterns mentioned in this chapter, and how is each defined?

15. What are the reasons given in paragraph 28 to explain why most rural communes don't last long?

16. Why are communes important even though so many of them fail?

17. What are some examples of positive incentives?

18. What are some examples of negative incentives?

19. In what case are positive incentives most effective?

20. What arguments does the author give that coercion as a means of population control may be justified under certain circumstances?

21. What ethical dilemma caused by current immigration policies in the United States is discussed in this chapter?

SCANNING FOR DETAILS

It is impossible to remember all of the details of a chapter after you have read it. For this reason you need to know how to rapidly scan a chapter to find the details you need. You can determine generally where in the chapter a statistic or a name might be found by quickly reading the topic headings in the chapter and then the first sentence of each paragraph under the appropriate heading. For example, if you are looking for the number of women who used some kind of contraceptive in 1976, it is logical to look under the heading "Is Volunteer Family Planning Enough?" If you read the first sentence of each paragraph under this heading, you will find that the second paragraph begins by discussing successes in reducing fertility rates, and that the statistic you are looking for is in the second part of that sentence.

It is important to be able to scan for details, because you will often have to read quickly through a chapter to find information for your notes, to support your arguments in class discussions, or to give supporting evidence in an essay-question answer. Practice this skill by doing Exercise 9 as quickly as possible.

Exercise 9: Scanning for Details

On the first line below the question write the heading under which you think you will find the answer. Then, find the answer and write it on the second line.

1. How many women throughout the world were not using any form of birth control in 1976?

    Heading: _____

    Answer: _____

2. What does Cardinal Cushing say about abortion?

   Heading: _____

   Answer: _____

3. How many abortions take place throughout the world each year?

   Heading: _____

   Answer: _____

4. What percentage of the world's people lived in countries where abortion was legal in 1971?

   Heading: _____

   Answer: _____

5. How many legal abortions took place in the United States between 1973 and 1977?

   Heading: _____

   Answer: _____

6. What percentage of the world's work force in 1977 was female?

   Heading: _____

   Answer: _____

7. What family-structure pattern has become the most common in the United States during the last fifty years?

   Heading: _____

   Answer: _____

8. What are three examples of positive incentives used to control population growth?

   Heading: _____

   Answer: _____

9. What are three examples of negative incentives used to control population?

   Heading: _____

   Answer: _____

10. When did the United States first set quotas on the number of people who are allowed to immigrate into the country?

   Heading: _____

   Answer: _____

UNDERSTANDING PARAPHRASING

In Unit 3 you learned four ways that a writer can paraphrase a sentence: by using synonyms, by changing the emphasis of a sentence with a different subject, by substituting one connective for another, and by combining sentences with relative clauses. There are many ways to restate an idea. As you do the paraphrasing exercises in this book and as you read, be aware of the variety of ways that a writer can say the same thing with different words.

Exercise 10: Recognizing Paraphrases

Circle the letter of the answer that best paraphrases the original sentence.

1. Voluntary family planning is an extremely important method for helping control world population growth, but many observers feel that it must be coupled with economic development and with methods that go beyond family planning.

   a. Voluntary family planning is an extremely important method for helping control world population growth, so many observers feel that it must be coupled with economic development and with methods that go beyond family planning.

   b. Although voluntary family planning is an extremely important method for helping control world population, many observers feel that economic development and methods that go beyond family planning must be used at the same time.

   c. Many observers think that economic development and methods that go beyond family planning should be used instead of family planning.

2. By making abortions illegal, a country encourages dangerous abortions that kill thousands every year, particularly poor women who cannot afford to travel to a region where abortion is legal.

a. Countries that make abortion against the law encourage women to have dangerous abortions, which kill thousands every year, especially poor women who don't have money to go to a place where abortion is legal.

b. When a country makes abortion illegal, it discourages abortions, which kill thousands a year, especially poor women who can't afford to travel to places where abortions are legal.

c. Dangerous abortions, which kill thousands of poor women every year, are caused by a country's making abortion legal.

3. In 1973 the Supreme Court made a historic decision, stating that during the first 3 months (12 weeks) of pregnancy, the decision about having an abortion must be left up to a woman and her doctor.

a. During the first three months of pregnancy, a woman can illegally obtain an abortion, according to a 1973 Supreme Court decision.

b. Because of the 1973 Supreme Court decision, a woman could choose to have an abortion legally after the first three months of pregnancy.

c. The historic decision made by the Supreme Court in 1973 said that as long as it was in the first three months of pregnancy, a woman and her doctor could decide on an abortion.

4. Whether to decrease further or even eliminate immigration into the United States is an extremely difficult and controversial question.

a. It is both difficult and controversial to decrease or eliminate immigration into the United States.

b. The question of whether to further decrease or possibly discontinue immigration into the United States is controversial and difficult to answer.

c. Everyone agrees that it is difficult to decrease or eliminate immigration into the United States.

5. Nearly all successful forms of social control are developed by employing those measures that are the least onerous to the people concerned.

a. Almost all forms of social control that succeed are developed by taking action that is the least offensive to the people involved.

b. The people concerned require beneficial measures in order for a form of social control to be successful.

c. In order for a government to suceed at social control, the people concerned must be willing to eagerly accept the actions taken by that government.

Exercise 11: Beginning Paraphrasing

Paraphrase these sentences by following the directions after each.

1. We surrender certain freedoms to do as we please to gain other, more important ones.

   a. Substitute a synonym for <u>surrender</u>.

   b. Use a connective of purpose other than <u>to</u> (*in order to, so that*). Note: Remember that the connective *so that* must be followed by a clause with a subject and a verb—for example, "I went to the dentist's office so that <u>I could get my teeth cleaned</u>."

   _____

   _____

2. Positive incentives have the advantage of redistributing wealth to the poor since they would have greater need and are more inclined to accept such rewards.

   a. Use a connective of cause–expected result other than <u>since</u> (*because, as*).

   b. Rephrase "they would have greater need." (Try using *need* as a verb.)

   _____

   _____

3. Because of vast cultural, economic, and political differences even within a single country, approaches will vary considerably.

   a. Substitute a synonym for <u>considerably</u>.

   b. Use a connective of cause–expected result other than <u>because of</u>.

   _____

   _____

4. At first, fugitives from a highly stimulating urban society find a return to simplicity satisfying. Eventually, however, disillusionment and boredom may set in.

   a. Substitute synonyms for <u>satisfying</u>, <u>stimulating</u>, and <u>eventually</u>.

   b. Use a connective of cause–unexpected result other than <u>however</u> (*but, nevertheless*).

   _____

   _____

5. Instead of showing all American families with two or three children and two cars, we should introduce other models.

   a. Substitute a synonymous phrase for <u>instead of</u>.

   b. Change the verb in "we should introduce other models" from *active* to *passive*.

   _____

   _____

PASSING ESSAY EXAMS: ORGANIZING YOUR ANSWER

If you have prepared well for your essay exam, you should know the information you want to include in your answers. The next problem is to organize the material. A good essay-question answer has three basic parts: the *introduction* statement, the *body* of the answer, and the *concluding* statement.

The introductory statement tells the reader the topic of the paragraph (or more) and what you will say about this topic. The introductory statement should be short and to the point. For example, suppose the essay question is "Discuss the various kinds of systems that are currently being used to identify computer users." You learned in Unit 2 that *discuss* means "to describe by giving the details and stating the pros and cons of something." Your introductory statement should tell the reader that you are going to talk about the different kinds of identification systems and that you will explain the pros and cons of each.

   Example 1   Introductory
                 Statement: There are seven kinds of systems that are currently being used to identify computer users, and each one has its good and bad points.

If the essay question is an actual question, you might turn the question into a statement, adding the necessary information to make your introduction complete.

   Example 2   Question: How do the police use computers to make their work easier and more efficient?

Introductory

Statement: The police use computers in four ways that make their work easier and more efficient: to dispatch patrol cars, to keep stolen-property files, to locate fugitives from justice, and to provide a national driver-registration service.

After you have written the introductory statement, you should make a brief outline of the points you wish to include in the body of your answer. These points will be the support for the main idea presented in the introductory sentence. Support can consist of definitions, reasons, or details and examples. Here is a sample outline you might make to support the introductory statement in example 1.

Outline Example 1

A. Signatures
　　1. widely used
　　2. detected only by an expert
　　3. can fool computers

B. Hand movements
　　1. different from signature movements
　　2. distinct: forger might imitate signature, but not movement

C. Photographs
　　1. inconvenient
　　2. not reliable
　　　　a. people change appearance
　　　　b. computer program for analyzing still experimental

D. Identification numbers
　　1. two numbers
　　2. most widely used method

E. Fingerprints
　　1. no simple method to compare
　　2. messy
　　3. associated with police procedures—a psychological problem

F. Voiceprints
　　1. no psychological problems
　　2. technically easier to analyze
　　3. can be transmitted over the telephone

G. Lipprints

After you make the outline, check to be sure that the ideas are balanced.

Each idea with the same marker (letters, numbers) should have the same value. Suppose, for example, your outline looked like this:

Outline Example 2

Introductory
Statement: The police use computers in four ways.

A. To dispatch patrol cars

B. To keep stolen-property files

C. Stolen-property files are used by police all around the country.

D. To locate fugitives from justice

E. To provide a national driver-registration service

Outline example 2 is not a balanced outline because while A, B, D, and E are all uses of the computer in police work, C is actually a point that helps explain B. The idea in C should be marked with a *1.* and located under B to show that it supports B.

In addition to keeping the points in your outline balanced, you should also put them in order of importance. Put the most important either first or last and then arrange the other points in order in between.

When you have corrected your outline for balance and order of importance, write the transition word or phrase that you plan to use to introduce each supporting idea next to it. Transition words are important for good organization, and if you add them to your outline, you will not forget to include them in your answer.

Final Outline for Example 2

The police use computers in four ways.

First,   **A.** To dispatch patrol cars

Another,   **B.** To keep stolen-property files
                   1. Stolen property files are used by police all around the country.

Third,   **C.** To locate fugitives from justice

Finally,   **D.** To provide a national driver-registration service

As you write the essay-exam answer, carefully follow your outline. Include only definitions, reasons, and details and examples that explain the ideas you have included in your outline.

The last sentence of your answer should be a concluding statement that summarizes the main points you have made in the body of your answer. Do not add any new ideas here.

Exercise 12: Organizing an Essay-Question Answer

Choose one of the following essay questions, then follow the four steps to organize your answer.

Essay Questions

1. Discuss the arguments given in this chapter both for and against abortion.
2. Trace the development of worldwide abortion liberalization in the past decade.
3. How have changes in cultural patterns affected the control of world population growth?
4. Explain the use of economic incentives and disincentives as a means of population control.

STEP 1: Write an introductory statement to begin your answer. Be sure that it mentions the topic and tells the reader what you will say about that topic.

STEP 2: Put your main supporting points in outline form under the introductory statement. Check to see that they are balanced and in order of importance.

STEP 3: Add a transition word or phrase next to each main supporting idea.

STEP 4: Write a concluding sentence that summarizes your main points. Check to be sure that you have not added any new ideas in your concluding sentence.

This is how your final outline (including the introductory and concluding statements) should look.

The police use computers in four ways that make their work easier and more efficient.

First,	A.	to dispatch patrol cars
Another,	B.	to keep stolen-property files
Third,	C.	to locate fugitives from justice

Finally,   D. to provide a national driver-registration service

These are the four ways that the police use computers to make their work easier and more efficient.

You can now use your completed outline to write an answer to the essay question.

SOME SUGGESTED TOPICS FOR FURTHER READING

family planning

abortion

fertility control

antiabortion laws

right-to-life groups

population control

zero population growth

immigration

5

Reading Business

Crystal City, Texas, 1939

Basic Vocabulary

promotion	in the long run	slogan
enhance	hypothesis	logo
media	(sales) pitch	deceptive
motivation	ultimate	bargain
hierarchy	tact	redeem
prospects	diplomacy	endorsement
potential	volume	
drive	worthwhile	

Exercise 1: Skimming

"Promotional Aspects of Marketing" is the twelfth chapter of a book called *Introduction to Modern Business* by Vernon A. Musselman and John H. Jackson. The book is used for an introductory business course at the college level. This chapter is part of a unit called "Marketing."

Do each step, one at a time, answering the questions before you go on to the next step. (The chapter begins on page 152.)

STEP 1: Read the main title of the chapter and all of the sub-headings. Notice how these relate to one another.

    a. What is the basic definition of *promotion?*

    b. What are the various types of promotion?

    c. What are the steps in the personal-selling process?

    d. Which of the following topics about advertising does this chapter discuss?

        1. the purpose of advertising

        2. the types of advertising

        3. the definition of advertising

        4. slogans used in advertising

        5. various media used for advertising

        6. the amount of money spent on advertising

    e. What are the types of advertising discussed in this chapter?

    f. What are the media that are used to advertise?

g. What are the sales-promotion activities that are mentioned in this chapter?

STEP 2: Examine pictures, charts, and other illustrations in the chapter to get information about the chapter's contents.

a. What does Figure 1 illustrate?

b. What is the purpose of Figure 4?

c. What kind of advertising does the ad in Figure 8 represent?

d. Why do the Campbell kids look slightly different now compared with the past?

e. According to Table 1, which company had the biggest increase in the amount of money spent on advertising? Which company decreased its advertising budget the most?

f. According to Figure 10, which medium spends the most money for advertising?

STEP 3: Find the names of people, organizations, and so on (proper names) mentioned in the chapter and try to determine who or what they are.

a. What is Pike's Peak?

b. Who is Abraham H. Maslow?

c. What is AIDA?

d. What does Donald Moine do?

e. In what area of business is Frederick E. Webster an expert?

f. Who is Victor Kiam II?

g. What is the Federal Trade Commission?

h. What is the Better Business Bureau?

STEP 4: Look at all of the italicized words and phrases. Be aware of the author's reasons for italicizing them. The author of this chapter uses italics to indicate definitions and subheadings.

You've already looked for subheadings in STEP 1. Quickly find the definitions given in this chapter for the following words:

a. promotion

b. selling

c. motivation

d. advertising

e. point-of-purchase display

f. publicity

STEP 5: Look at the review questions and the bibliography at the end of the chapter to get more information about the chapter.

(Review questions and bibliography are not included in this chapter.)

STEP 6: Rapidly read the first and last paragraph of the chapter and the first sentence of each paragraph.

STEP 7: In a sentence or two, explain what you think this chapter is about. (You may answer orally or quickly write the answer that you would give orally.)

FIRST READING

Quickly read the chapter "Promotional Aspects of Marketing" from *Introduction to Modern Business*. As you read, underline the main ideas and label each paragraph or so by putting notes in the margin. When you finish the chapter, reread your notes and use them to make a set of questions about the chapter. This is a technique that many Americans use to prepare for exams. Be sure your questions are general enough that they ask about main ideas.

Promotional Aspects of Marketing

Vernon A. Musselman
John H. Jackson

If you think advertising doesn't pay—
there are 25 mountains in Colorado
higher than Pike's Peak; name one.

The American Salesman

---

1   Promotion is the third element in the marketing mix. . . .
2   A company may well have a fine product or service offering and it may be priced correctly. It may also have an adequate distribution system tailored to its target market. But it must reach that market. **Promotion** refers to efforts to reach the customers in that market and persuade them to act.
3   In this chapter, we look at four different aspects of promotion. The first two are personal selling and advertising. Then we turn to sales promotion and public relations. Together, these four factors make up the **promotion blend.**

NATURE AND TYPES OF PROMOTION

4   As a marketing term, PROMOTION is *a firm's efforts to influence customers to buy.* Promotion includes the elements of giving information and influencing customer behavior. Its purpose is to enhance the firm's image or increase the sales of the firm's products.
5   Promotion includes all selling activities. The most important of these are personal selling, advertising, sales promotion, and public relations. The way in which these activities are combined make up a company's "promotion blend."

Vernon A. Musselman, John H. Jackson, *Introduction to Modern Business*, 9th ed., © 1984, pp. 296-319. Reprinted by permission of Prentice-Hall, Inc., Englewood Cliffs, N.J.

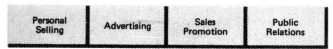

| Personal Selling | Advertising | Sales Promotion | Public Relations |

Figure 1 *The Promotion Blend*

The way the different components of the promotion blend are put together depends upon the firm's marketing objectives. Promotional strategy is designed to achieve those objectives. Promotion's role depends on the other elements in the marketing mix. For example, if a company chooses to use a high-pricing strategy, promotion assumes a major role.

6   Developing a promotional effort consists of choosing communication media and blending them into an effective program. Seldom does a company rely on a single type of promotional activity—a combination of methods is used to communicate with customers.

Promotion Is Communication

7   **Promotion is communication, since the marketer is the sender of a sales message, and the customer is the receiver.** Promotion includes all the methods used to get the message through clearly.

8   The first purpose of the message is to inform. But its real objective is a response from the potential buyer. Marketers send promotional messages through sales manuals, news releases, artwork, displays, samples, prizes, and personal sales presentations. These make up the communication channel. Personal selling uses personal contacts, the telephone, and the mail. Advertising uses mostly the mass media—newspapers, radio, and television. Sales promotion uses displays, exhibits, sampling, and so on. Public relations encompasses all of these. These activities share the common objective of getting feedback in the form of a purchase.

The Communication Flow

| The Marketer (Sender) | Promotion (Messages) | Customer (Receiver) |

Figure 2 *Promotion as Communication*

PERSONAL SELLING AS PROMOTION

9   A simplified definition of SELLING would be *"the art of personal persuasion employed to induce others to buy."* Personal selling is the oldest method of selling. This method is unique, for it involves a two-way exchange of ideas between buyer and seller. In our treatment of personal selling, we discuss:

1. The behavioral approach in selling
2. The selling process
3. Successful personal selling
4. Sales management

Behavioral Approach In Selling

10   In recent years, marketing executives have received valuable information from behavioral scientists regarding human behavior in the marketplace. The study of behavior starts with an understanding of motivation. MOTIVATION is *an inner force that moves people toward satisfying a need*. Motivation involves a three-stage cycle consisting of a need or want, a drive, and a goal. The drive may be physical, such as the need for water, food, or sleep. Or it may be psychological, such as the need for recognition or security. The drive is the stimulation to act, which is created by the need or want. The third stage, reaching the goal that satisfies the need, is the result of the drive.

11   For some years now, psychologists have recognized that human behavior is motivated by both environmental conditions and individual characteristics.

12   Abraham H. Maslow formulated a theory of motivation, which received considerable attention in marketing. He brought together the viewpoints of several schools of psychological thought. Maslow identified a hierarchy of five levels of needs, which he arranged in the order he felt people seek to satisfy them.

13   These needs are significant to marketers. The physiological needs relate to what a product does—automobiles transport people. Safety needs relate to people's security—homes provide safe and comfortable living quarters. The belongingness needs relate to products that make one personally attractive or acceptable, and so on.

The Personal–Selling Process

14   The successful personal-selling process involves five basic steps. They are the same whether the sale is conducted in one presentation or over a period of time. They cannot always be precisely timed or sharply distinguished from one another. These steps are shown in Figure 3.

5.   Closing the sale.

4.   Handling objections.

3.   Conducting the interview.

2.   Creating sales presentation.

1.   Locating prospects.

Figure 3 *Basic Steps in the Personal-Selling Process*

15 *Locating the Prospective Customer*   **Prospects** are potential customers. In some businesses, salespeople are supplied with a list of prospects. In others, potential customers must be discovered by the salesperson. Such customers can be found among one's acquaintances, through inquiries of friends and business associates, through social contacts, and through advertising.

16 *Creating a Sales Presentation*   The presentation may be informal or tightly structured. Many presentations use visual materials, charts, graphs, slides, or filmstrips. The presentation should be flexible so that it may be adapted to suit the situation.

17 *Conducting the Sales Interview*   The third step in the selling process is conducting the interview. One useful approach is the **"AIDA"** persuasion process. This process involves four stages through which the purchaser passes mentally—*attention, interest, desire,* and *action*. After gaining the prospect's attention, the presentation must develop the buyer's interest. Product samples, models, or a special price discount are effective in doing this. Moving into the desire and action stages sometimes requires more than one interview. A salesperson must know when to stop the presentation to avoid "overselling."

18 *Handling Objections*   The progress of the sales interview may hinge on the effectiveness of the salesperson's handling of objections. Seldom do interviews follow the script, for the customer raises questions. The customer may want time to think the idea over, or may not like the price. Or the item's quality may be questioned. The salesperson must learn how to answer questions and objections, and move the interview toward completion.

19 *Closing the Sale*   At some point, the customer reaches a decision to buy or not to buy. If the presentation is successful, the sale will be made. Sales are not always closed at the end of the initial presentation. If more meetings are required, a date should be established for the first follow-up interview.

20   A successful salesperson studies the prospect carefully and discovers which

Photo: Laura Latulippe

Closing the Sale. At some point the customer reaches a decision to buy or not to buy.

technique will be most effective in closing the sale. For example, the sales-person determines how the customer wishes to pay for the article, and then moves along smoothly to the right closing technique without offending the customer.

21   One sales manual of instructions says this about closing a sale:

1. When your prospect begins to pause in making the final decision, this is the time to step in and close.

2. Watch your prospect's facial expression. If the prospect indicates by a smile or a twinkle of the eye that he or she is pleased with the article, then get out your order book.

3. Listen to the prospect's voice; if there is a slight inflection or a raising or lowering tone, this is your tip to make your closing remarks.

22 *Follow-up Contacts*   Sometimes a follow-up visit is needed to close a sale. But follow-up contacts should be made in many cases even though they are not needed. The follow-up contact is an important complement to the selling proc-ess. How well is the customer satisfied with the product or service? What postsale servicing is needed? Is needed servicing being provided promptly and pleasantly? And, of course, is another sale in order?

Successful Personal Selling

23   Every salesperson wishes to be successful; the professional salesperson works consciously to become more effective. **To progress in successful selling, one must want to succeed, exercise self-discipline, and develop good selling techniques.** Purpose, planning, enthusiasm, confidence, and drive are all ingredients in selling success. Sales personnel may be directed by management, but self-motivation is most important.

24   Psychologist Donald Moine said that the best salespeople use indirect hypnosis in selling without even knowing it. By changes in their rate of speech, its volume, or its tone, certain phrases have the effect of commands. After a

---

SUCCESS IN SELLING

Success in selling employs a variety of techniques. Here are a few that are often mentioned by successful salespeople:

1. Find out what your customer's real wants and needs are. Listen as they tell you what they are interested in.

2. Know all about your product and what it can do for your customer. Product knowledge is a "must" in personal selling because it creates customer confidence, builds enthusiasm, and gives a professional touch to the situation. Stress the unique advantage of your product over others.

3. Present a positive rather than a negative approach. The sales presentation is more effective when the salesperson says, "May I help you?" than when he or she says, "You wouldn't like to see our new model, would you?" A negative approach calls for a negative answer.

4. Prepare yourself to handle objections. If the prospect says the price is too high, you might reply, "Yes, the price may be a little higher than you planned. However, in the long run you'll save money because of the superior quality of this product." In any event, don't argue with your prospect about whether a price is too high.

5. Use praise judiciously.

customer's confidence is won, the sales pitch begins. Fact is linked with suggestion, just as a hypnotist does it. For example, "You have a wife and three children, and we think you need $80,000 protection for them."

25 **Personal selling is a two-way flow of communication. It should concentrate on need satisfaction, not on the hard sell.**

Words That Sell

26 Closing a sale is an agent's ultimate goal. Both a reputation and income are determined by the sales record. Therefore, a successful sales representative pays special attention to the words he or she uses. Some words encourage a sale's closing, and others produce a negative reaction. In the comparison below, words that help to sell are matched against words that don't.

Words That Sell	Words That Don't
Agreement	Contract
Analysis	Estimate
Certify	Claim
Economic value	Low price
Inexpensive	Cheap
Investment	Cost
Negotiate	Bargain
Offer	Give
OK it, please!	Sign it!
Opportunity	Deal
Own	Buy
Quality	Expensive
Service	Sell
Specialist	Expert

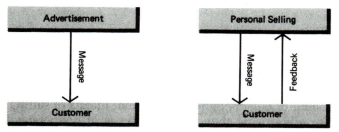

Figure 4 *Personal Selling Is Two-Way Communication*

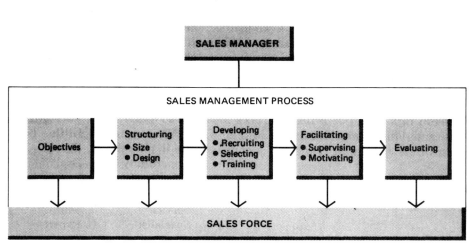

Figure 5 *The Sales-Management Process*

Sales Management

27   Frederick E. Webster, Jr., interviewed the chief executive and operating officers in thirty major corporations. He found that they believe that marketing is the most important management function in their businesses. They also see it becoming even more important in the future.[1]

28   As a major part of marketing, sales management differs very little from management in other areas of a business firm. . . .

29   The main task in sales management consists of coordinating the selling efforts of individuals. This is a very personal thing and requires administrative ability, tact, and diplomacy. Various aspects of sales management include the following:

1. Establishing sales-force objectives

2. Planning an organizational structure

3. Recruiting, selecting, and training

4. Directing the sales force—motivation, supervision, compensation

5. Evaluating and then determining promotions and rewards

30   The sales-management process is illustrated in Figure 5.

---

[1]Frederick E. Webster, Jr., "Top Management's Concerns about Marketing: Issues for the 1980's," *Journal of Marketing*, Vol. 45 (Summer 1981), 16.

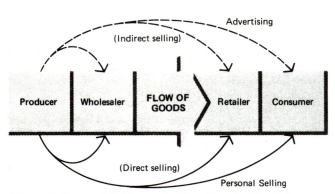

Figure 6 *Personal Selling and Advertising in Marketing*

ADVERTISING AS PROMOTION

31 Most companies use a blend of personal and nonpersonal means of selling. More money is spent for advertising than for other types of nonpersonal promotion. The parallel relationship of personal selling to advertising in promoting the flow of goods is shown in Figure 6.

32   To the homemaker, advertising may mean the grocery ad in Wednesday's local newspaper. To the sales manager, advertising is a method of communicating with the public to make the selling job easier. To the accountant, advertising is one of the costs of doing business; and to the economist, it is an integral part of today's business system.

33   All of us have been influenced to buy certain things because of some form of advertising. It is universally recognized that advertising conveys selling messages better than other techniques in certain situations.

What Is Advertising?

34   The Definitions Committee of the American Marketing Association defines ADVERTISING as *any paid form of nonpersonal presentation and promotion of ideas, goods, or services by an identified sponsor."* Two things are important in this definition: payment for the advertisement, and a sponsor who pays for it. At times it is possible to communicate without cost to the sponsor—for example, through editorial comments by newspapers or magazines about a firm or a product. This type of information is considered publicity rather than advertising. Usually public relations is more concerned with developing a favorable image with the public than with directly promoting the sale of products.

Purposes of Advertising

35   **The overall purpose of advertising is to influence the level of product sales and thereby increase the advertiser's profits.** Sometimes a firm is forced to advertise because of the actions of competitors or government. In such instances, the opportunity to increase profits may be slim. Yet failure to advertise could result in either reduced sales and less profit or legal action.

36   As a tool of marketing, advertising generally serves the following purposes (sometimes called "the three Rs of advertising"):

1. *Retain "loyal" customers:* Persuade present customers to increase their buying. An example is Eastman Kodak's appeal in its advertising that reads, "Don't forget to feed your camera this weekend."

2. *Retrieve "lost" customers:* Slow down the flow of present customers away from the preferred brand. The Florida Citrus Commission changed strategy when it started advertising, "It isn't just for breakfast any more."

3. *Recruit "new" customers:* Increase the flow of customers toward the advertised product. Replace those lost to competitors. Widen the total market. Johnson & Johnson appealed to adults to use the shampoo they had earlier pushed for babies. They featured Fran Tarkenton shampooing his hair and saying, "Everyone knows about no more tears."

Most companies think all this is very important—in fact, vital—to their sales. How important? Well, consider this: Of the 192 pages in a recent issue of *Business Week*, 128 pages were advertising. (Sixty percent of the advertisements were in color.)

Measuring the Results of Advertising

37   **For a determination of the effectiveness of advertising, its results should be evaluated. And they must be evaluated in relation to its objectives.** A practical way to measure its effectiveness is through increased sales volume.

38   Sales for a period of time following an advertising campaign can be compared with those for a prior period. A second way is to determine how well the advertising message is received. As with product-test markets, advertising-test markets are often used before a nationwide campaign is launched.

Types of Advertising

39   Advertising can be classified into certain types, depending upon its use and purpose.

40 *Product Advertising*   This type of advertising is designed to sell one or more

VICTOR K. KIAM II

Victor K. Kiam stars in his own commercials. You may have seen him on television. He has appeared using a Remington Shaver, telling you it will shave as close as a blade or he'll give you your money back

Kiam graduated from Yale with a B.S. degree in 1947 and a B.A. in 1948, and received a master's degree in Business Administration from Harvard in 1951. He was with Lever Brothers from 1951 to 1955, the International Latex Corporation from 1955 to 1968, and the Benrus Corporation from 1968 to 1977. He was chairman and CEO of Benrus from 1971 to 1977. Since 1979, he has been chairman and president of Remington Products, Inc.

Remington once ranked first in electric shavers, but its market share declined and it was losing money. Kiam bought the company in 1979. He trimmed overhead, lowered prices, and stepped up advertising. He turned the company into a profit maker. He believes that in addition to producing a quality product, you have to let people know about it.

Victor Kiam is a ranked tennis player, the holder of several U.S. patents, and an internationally recognized speaker. He is the founder of the School of Entrepreneurial Studies at the University of Bridgeport. He is a member of the World Business Council, a Fellow of the Institute of Directors in London, and a trustee of the University of Bridgeport.

Kiam is married to the former Ellen Lipscher of New York City, and they have three children. They make their home in Stamford, Connecticut.

definite and identified products or services. It usually describes and praises their features and good qualities and may even emphasize their prices. Product advertising is used to sell both consumer and industrial goods. Consumer and industrial goods have different marketing characteristics. They are sold in different trade channels, to different markets, under different pricing policies, and by different selling methods. Edward G. Harness, former

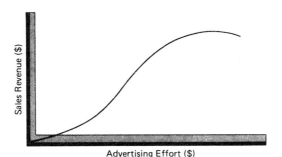

Figure 7 *The Sales Response Function*

board chairman of Procter & Gamble, had this to say about advertising as it relates to products:

> *Advertising has no life of its own. It has no unique power to persuade. It is not a separate and distinct life force in our society. It should not be praised or criticized for its own sake. It is simply a part of a total marketing process which, to be successful, must be based on a worthwhile product.*

41 ***Institutional Advertising*** This type tries to create a favorable attitude toward the company offering to sell a good. It tries to build goodwill that will generate long-run rather than immediate sales. For example, a manufacturer may run an institutional advertisement to tell the public about the firm's efforts to reduce air pollution. Large corporations can afford to spend money on institutional advertising.

42 ***National Advertising*** This type is used to sell nationally distributed brands by using a medium with nationwide circulation. It is generally associated with advertising by the manufacturer rather than by a retailer or local advertiser. Moreover, national advertising refers only to the *level of the advertiser*. It has no relation at all to geographic coverage. If such a manufacturer places an advertisement in only one city, it is still called national advertising.

CASHING IN ON A NAME

Sophia Loren receives a 5 percent commission on each vial of Sophia perfume sold. John McEnroe received $500,000 for endorsing Dunlop tennis rackets, plus a small commission on each sale above that amount.

THE PFIZER HEALTHCARE SERIES

A pain in the stomach that comes from the heart.

You feel a sense of fullness. Of pressure. A sharp pain in the chest. A heaviness. Maybe you're short of breath. Symptoms we innocently mistake for indigestion may also be symptoms of a heart condition called angina pectoris. More typically, you may have an unusual sensation in your left arm. A pain in your left shoulder or neck. Even a pain in your jaw or teeth.

The right diagnosis can be life-saving if your heart is warning that it is not getting enough blood and is short in oxygen and nutrients.

Who can diagnose angina?
You cannot. Your doctor can.
Diagnosis of angina is usually simple and straightforward. Treatment depends upon the type of angina you have.
Angina occurs:

1. When there is coronary vessel spasm.
2. When blood flow is limited by vessel wall thickening.
3. When a combination of vessel spasm and wall thickening reduces blood, oxygen and nutrients to the heart.

You can reduce the workload on your heart by reduction of weight, smoking, tension and stress, and also by recreation and rest. Moderate exercise helps, too. Medicines can increase blood flow in the vessels of your heart. And if your angina is related to high blood pressure, your doctor may prescribe medicines to help bring it down.

Obviously, you cannot be your own doctor. You need a support system. We call it...

Partners in Healthcare
You are the most important partner.
Only you can spot the warning signs and report them to your physician. And it's you who must decide to accept the guidance and counseling of your physician and pharmacist. When medicines are prescribed, only you can take them as directed.

Your doctor interprets the warning signs, orders your tests, and makes the diagnosis.
He also prescribes the best medication for you among those available—considering each drug's characteristics—and monitors your progress.

All those who discover, develop and distribute medicines complete the partnership.
Pfizer's ongoing research brings you essential medicines for a wide range of diseases. Through our development of these and many other medications, we are fulfilling our responsibility as one of your partners in healthcare.

 PHARMACEUTICALS · A PARTNER IN HEALTHCARE

Figure 8 *Example of an Advocacy Ad. (Courtesy of Pfizer Pharmaceuticals.)*

43 *Local Advertising*   Local (or retail) advertising is placed by a local merchant. It usually differs from national advertising by being more specific in terms of price, quality, and quantity. In national advertising, the purpose is to build a general demand for a product that may be sold in many stores. In local advertising, the stress is on the store where the product is sold.

44 *Corrective Advertising*   Corrective advertising takes place to correct specific false or misleading claims that might have been made in previous advertising. Classic examples of corrective advertising include the following: STP's corrective ads to clarify the claim that STP oil treatment will stop cars from burning oil; Anacin's $24 million worth of corrective advertising disclosing that Anacin is not a tension reliever; Listerine's correcting an earlier claim that it "fights colds." These and other corrective ads have been ordered by courts to rectify earlier misleading advertisements.

45 *Advocacy Advertising*   Many companies carry on advertising programs devoted to public-service themes. The Warner-Swazey Company features this type of message regularly in its advertising. The Mobil Oil Corporation ran a series of such ads during the energy crisis. Motorola and Pfizer had such series in the early 1980s. Companies use advocacy advertising when, in their opinion, the news media are not presenting both sides of an issue. Advocacy advertising is similar to the editorials that appear in business magazines and newspapers. Stephen A. Kliment defines advocacy advertising as:

> *. . . any kind of paid public communication or message from an identified source and in a conventional medium of public advertising, which presents information or a point of view bearing on a publicly recognized controversial issue.*[2]

46   Bradley Graham, in his article, "The Corporate Voice," published in *The Washington Post,* March 25, 1979, said: "Weyerhauser in its ads doesn't sell paper, it preaches conservation. Kellogg doesn't peddle cereal, it promotes nutrition. Bethlehem Steel argues the fine points of U.S. Trade policy."

ADVERTISING SLOGANS

47 Amtrak launched an ad campaign to convince leisure travelers of the uniqueness of the train experience. The ads took advantage of what nature supplied Amtrak at no extra charge for four-color: beautiful, exciting scenery right outside its own picture windows. The copy line was, "See America at see level." The results: For six months seats and/or sleeping accommodations were completely sold out on 733 of its trains. Amtrak had 17 percent of its ad budget in magazine advertising.

48   If you had your preference, would you ruther go to Druthers? Or wouldn't you rather have a Buick? And sooner or later you'll own Generals!

49   Slogans do help sell merchandise. Many American businesses use slogans

---

[2]Stephen A. Kliment, "Advocacy Advertising by U.S. Corporations: Can Money Buy Friends?" *Madison Avenue,* February 1981, p. 29.

Photo: Courtesy of The Coca Cola Company.

The familiar Coke bottle with logo in Chinese script.

to identify their products. One of the best known uses of slogans relates to Coke. The Coca-Cola Company has used slogans for years. You can recall several, but you probably don't realize how often the slogan has changed. Here is a review of some of the Coke slogans:

Some of Coca-Cola's Ad Themes Through the Years

1886	Drink Coca-Cola
1905	Coca-Cola revives and sustains
1906	The Great National Temperance Beverage
1922	Thirst knows no season
1925	Six million a day
1927	Around the corner from everywhere
1929	The pause that refreshes
1938	The best friend thirst ever had
1948	Where there's Coke there's hospitality
1949	Along the highway to anywhere
1952	What you want is a Coke
1956	Makes good things taste better
1957	Sign of good taste
1958	The cold, crisp taste of Coke
1963	Things go better with Coke

1970	It's the real thing
1971	I'd like to buy the world a Coke
1975	Look up, America
1976	Coke adds life
1979	Have a Coke and a smile
1982	Coke is It

50   Logos sell merchandise too. Companies use logos at their places of business and in their advertising. Do you have an alligator, a fox, or a hound on any of your clothing? The Izod-Lacoste alligator is one of the best-known logos. Since General Mills bought David Crystal, the alligator logo has really been popularized. It appears on dresses, shirts, jeans, jackets, sweaters, swimwear, socks, pajamas, and what have you. More than 30 million Izod alligator items are sold every year.

51   The marketing of shampoo products is a good illustration of competition through advertising. This is a billion dollar market, and one where brand loyalty is weak. A company can spend millions in launching a new product only to see market share fade in a couple of years. Gillette Company spent $45 million to launch "Silkience"; Helene Curtis spent $35 million in a promotion blitz; and Procter & Gamble spent $50 million to bring out "Pert."

Competition in Advertising

52   If a competitor advertises a product similar to yours, you return the favor. In a single issue of *Business Week* magazine, fourteen different computer companies advertised their products. Here are some examples of their attention-catching captions:

Sticklers for accuracy are sold on T.I. computers.

Texas Instruments

Making a quick decision isn't enough. You've got to make the right one. And with HP 125, you can do both.

Hewlett-Packard

E.F. Hutton simplifies life with Apples.

Apple Computer

Don't let a microcomputer that only performs solo get your goat.

Get an i Bex

53   *Business Week* itself advertised as follows:

> *Join the 800,000 plus subscribers whom* Business Week *is guiding more smoothly through 1982. With our "focused information for management" you're ready for opportunities, turning points, crises. You're perking with new ideas, techniques, solutions.*

54 Shortly thereafter, *Forbes* responded with:

> *Do you know anybody who is somebody in business who does not read* Forbes Magazine?

55   Companies not only compete for business by advertising; they also compete *in* their advertising. For example, Savin Corporation used a full-page ad in *The Wall Street Journal* to take a jab at the Xerox Corporation. The top half of the page said, in letters an inch and a half high:

> *We created a new way of copying, more revolutionary than xerography.*

56   And Xerox advertised as follows:

> *Our New Typewriter Has More Memory Than What's Their Name's.*

57   Soon after Avis advertised offering to rent "Cadillacs at the Cutlass price" and said, "Trying Harder makes Avis Second to None," Hertz used a full-page ad in *The Wall Street Journal* to say:

> *Now Avis claims to be second to none. That should read "Second to no. one."*

ADVERTISING AND THE PUBLIC

58   **Advertising alone will not persuade consumers to pay what they feel is an unreasonable price.** Yet consumers often believe that a nationally advertised brand is worth a higher price than an unadvertised brand. For example, customers are willing to pay a little more for Armour's canned ham than for an unknown brand. Their experience leads them to think that it will taste better. The consumer may determine this added value by prior use, or may accept the claims of the advertiser. However, if the advertised brand has no important differences, its price may be no higher than that of unadvertised competitors.

59   **Is advertising an economic waste?** Critics question the social value of advertising. For one thing, they claim that advertising fails to create new demands and merely results in switching brands. For such consumer goods as toothpaste, cosmetics, detergents, and gasoline—where advertising is highly competitive—the total per capita consumption has risen steadily over the years. To say that all advertising is purely competitive and therefore wasteful suggests

that competition itself is wasteful. From the advertiser's standpoint, the potential dollar sales should produce enough gross-margin dollars—the excess of sales over cost of goods sold—to pay the advertising costs. Advertising is expected to pay for itself in added sales. Evidence shows that mass advertising is essential to maintain both mass consumption and mass production.

60 **Truth in Advertising** There are, of course, dishonest advertisers. As the watchdog for the American public, the Federal Trade Commission (FTC) is constantly battling with companies about their alleged exaggerations or untruths. What do we mean by "tell the truth"? Is the advertisement expected to tell the literal truth, or merely to give a reasonably accurate impression? On this subject, the Supreme Court has made these statements:

Advertising as a whole must not create a misleading impression even though every statement separately considered is literally truthful.

Advertising must not obscure or conceal material facts.

Advertising must not be artfully contrived to distract and divert readers' attention from the true nature of the terms and conditions of an offer.

61 The FTC embarked on a strong truth-in-advertising campaign in the early 1970s. It demanded that advertisers be prepared to substantiate their claims. An FTC resolution states that advertisers are not voluntarily meeting the public's needs for more objective information about their claims. The resolution adds:

Public disclosure can enhance competition by encouraging competitors to challenge advertised claims which have no basis in fact. . . .

62 In another area of concern, the FTC is seeking to prevent deceptive price advertising. Typical practices that the commission warns advertisers to avoid are contained in its publication, "Guides against Deceptive Pricing." This publication is available to businesses in cooperation with Better Business Bureaus.

63 A recent study published by the *Harvard Business Review* gives some business executives' views regarding advertising:

1. Only one out of three believes that advertisements really give a true picture of the product.

2. Two out of five believe that the general public's faith in advertising is at an all-time low.

3. Nine out of ten feel that advertisers should be required to prove their claims.

64 Much advertising can be considered truthful. Still, there are too many unscrupulous advertisers who make misleading or half-true statements about

their products. Exaggerated claims for killing germs, curing colds, and inducing sleep have been challenged by government agencies.

65   In 1938, Congress passed the Wheeler-Lea Act, amending the Federal Trade Commission Act of 1914. The act gives the FTC power over "unfair or deceptive acts or practices." Several statutes aimed at specific industries grant the FTC authority to act on matters related to labeling and advertising.

ADVERTISING MEDIA

66   **If an advertising message is to reach its audience, some type of carrier must be chosen.** In the field of advertising, these carriers are called **MEDIA**. (A specific advertising medium is sometimes called a **vehicle**.) The success of advertising depends upon both the message and the medium selected. The media most commonly used for advertising purposes are these:

Newspapers	Outdoor advertising
Magazines	Transportation advertising
Direct mail	Point-of-purchase displays
Radio	Specialty
Television	

Kinds of Media

67   Some large companies use almost all the media listed above. But small companies, for financial reasons, may use only one or two. Many factors must be evaluated in selecting the proper media. These include the cost, extent of coverage (circulation), size of the selection from which to choose, degree of flexibility, timeliness, and nature of coverage (geography).

68 *Newspapers*   There are approximately 1,800 daily newspapers in the United States, with a combined circulation of 62 million; and there are about 700 daily newspapers with Sunday editions, with a combined circulation of over 55 million. There are 8,000 weekly newspapers.[3] In terms of spending, the newspaper is the leading medium. It accounts for 28.5 percent of the total advertising dollar. This vehicle is very effective when a business is seeking to cover a single metropolitan area. Copy can be prepared and submitted only a few hours before press time, although most newspapers specify that copy be turned in several days in advance. However, the short life of each newspaper edition and the

---

[3] *Editor and Publisher Yearbook*, 1981.

Figure 9 *The Campbell Kids are slimming down to fit a new weight-conscious image emphasizing nutrition and athletics. (Courtesy Campbell Soup Company.)*

poor reproductive quality of illustrations are two limiting factors. Studies show that the average length of time a person reads a newspaper is only twe𝚗ʹy minutes. **The newspaper advertisement is used when the appeal attempts to reach the general public, not a select group.**

69 *Television*   Television is a mass medium. It can be used either on a nationwide or on a regional basis, or it can be concentrated on the local market. As with radio, television has the advantage of immediate reception, providing timeliness to an even greater extent than newspapers. A magazine or newspaper may be in print several hours or days before it is read by the subscriber, but the TV message is received by the listener at once. Television's greatest advantage is that it combines sight, sound, motion, and demonstration. And for many viewers, it does all this in color—a unique combination for advertising. On the other hand, its message is short-lived, and production costs are high. Expend-

itures for TV advertising are the second largest. TV claims one-fourth of all advertising dollars.

70   Ninety-five percent of all American households have television sets, and 80 percent of all adults (18 years of age and older) view television daily. It is a mass medium that appeals to all age groups.

71   Most prime time is given to the national networks. Because of its broad coverage at prime time, advertising on the national network is expensive. Nabisco paid CBS and NBC $4.5 million to sponsor the Rose Parade on both networks on January 1, 1983. This was thought to be the first time that one company had 4½ hours of *exclusive* sponsorship on two networks—a total of seventy-six commercials. A 30-second commercial in prime time for the 1984 Olympics cost about $250,000. The ten companies that spent the most for network TV advertising during a recent year, in order of the amount spent, are shown in Table 1.

72   Complaints about the frequency of TV advertisements are causing the networks to consider carefully how many ads are "enough." Affiliated stations have been unhappy because the increase in the number of national network commercials reduces the number of advertising minutes they can sell locally.

73 ***Direct-Mail Advertising***   Direct-mail advertising ranks third behind newspapers and television in the amount of money spent. More than 10,000 companies currently use mail-order advertising. Direct-mail advertising averages over $10

TABLE 1   Big Advertisers on TV (in order of amount spent)

Rank	Name of Company	Increase or Decrease of Expenditure Over Previous Year
1	Procter & Gamble Co.	+15%
2	General Foods Corp.	+1
3	American Home Products	+2
4	Ford Motor Co.	+28
5	PepsiCo	+22
6	General Motors Corp.	+0.2
7	General Mills	−4
8	Bristol-Myers	−8
9	McDonald's	−5
10	Philip Morris Inc.	+20

billion. It is estimated that 85 percent of third-class mail and between 10 and 15 percent of first-class mail are direct-mail advertising.[4]

74   **The chief advantage of direct-mail advertising is that the advertiser can select precisely the audience to be reached,** which is not possible with other media. Segmentation makes it possible to have inquiry lists by product class, dollar amount, merchandise class, recentness of purchase, method of ordering, or method of payment. Direct-mail advertising is the most flexible, for it may serve a local, regional, or national market. Also, it offers an opportunity to make one's message personal. It provides great flexibility in production design and accurate timing in its scheduling. Direct-mail advertising does not require the purchase of time or space, as the other media do. The cost of direct-mail advertising is for printing, securing mailing lists, and postage.

75 *Magazines*   In contrast to newspaper ads, magazine advertising reaches a more selective group. People buy magazines intended for them as members of special groups, such as teachers, doctors, engineers, farmers—and, yes, even advertising personnel. Magazines are generally printed on high-quality paper that enhances creative designs and the use of color. Copy must be submitted weeks in advance of the publication date. People keep magazines much longer than newspapers and thumb through them again and again. Magazines provide a wide range of prospects, reaching people with many and special interests.

76   The W. R. Simmons Company reported that 90 percent of the nation's adult population (18 years of age and older) are magazine readers. The Daniel Starch research organization reported a study covering 12 million inquiries. This organization found that 54 percent of all inquiries to any single magazine ad are received within one week after its publication. Another 25 percent are received during the second week. By the end of the sixth week, 95 percent of the return is in.

77   Advertising rates are based on circulation. The cost of reaching customers can be determined in this way:

$$\frac{\text{Page rate} \times 1,000}{\text{Circulation}} = \text{Cost per thousand readers}$$

78   The twelve companies that spent the largest sums for magazine advertising in a recent year, in order of the amount spent, are listed in Table 2.

79 *Radio*   Radio as an advertising medium is considerably different from what it was before television. Some people thought that television would destroy radio advertising. To the contrary, it has increased greatly. In total, the more than

---

[4]Direct Mail Advertising Association.

TABLE 2   Top 12 Magazine Advertisers, 1981

Rank	Company	Ad Dollars in Magazines
1	Philip Morris Inc.	$102,834,866
2	Reynolds, R J Industries, Inc.	89,264,693
3	Seagram, Co. Ltd.	67,517,826
4	General Motors Corp.	65,503,848
5	BAT Industries, Ltd.	61,166,983
6	Sears Roebuck & Co.	58,911,949
7	Ford Motor Co.	55,078,100
8	General Foods Corp.	37,165,667
9	Loews Corp.	36,486,469
10	Time Inc.	36,455,029
11	Procter & Gamble Co.	35,737,289
12	American Tel. & Tel. Co.	35,167,071

SOURCE: *Magazine Publishers Association.*

4,000 AM stations and more than 2,000 FM stations reach 80 percent of the population on any given day. Whereas there may be only one or two daily newspapers in a specific market, there are several radio stations. Radio messages are designed for special audiences, such as homemakers, farmers, and youth groups.

80   **Spot advertising on the radio gives individual market selection.** The advertiser can therefore tailor the message to the market coverage selected. Spot advertising enables a business firm to present its message at the most favorable time in an individual market. It provides the greatest flexibility in time, wording, station, and market.

Expenditures for Advertising

81   The total spent for advertising exceeds $54.8 billion annually. When taken as a whole, the amount of money that American corporations spend for advertising equals the amount they pay to their stockholders in dividends. A study completed by the Association of National Advertisers shows that for most companies dealing in consumer goods, advertising is among the three largest

IN A RECESSION, CUT ADVERTISING FIRST?

When sales and profits drop during a recession, management looks for ways to cut expenses. One of the most tempting areas is advertising costs. But is it one of the wisest? Here is what happened during the five most recent recessions:

According to the American Business Press, companies that maintained or increased advertising expenditures posted greater sales and profits than companies that cut theirs.

What happened during the 1974–75 recession is of particular interest. Companies that did not cut their ad budgets in either year had higher sales and income during those two years than companies that cut in either or both years.

expenditures. For retailers, advertising ranks as the number-two expenditure, exceeded only by salaries.

82   The percentages spent by the various media are shown in Figure 10.

SALES PROMOTION

83 Sales promotion is basically a motivational activity. It is neither personal selling nor advertising, yet it has some of the characteristics of both. Advertising relies

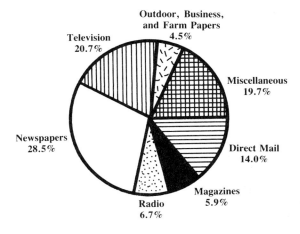

Figure 10
Advertising Expenditures by Medium, 1980. (Graph based on data published in Advertising Age, January 5, 1981.)

FREEZE FREEZES FLORIDA FRUIT ADS

Florida had a severe freeze in citrus land in the winter of 1982. It damaged 84 percent of the state's citrus crop. The Florida Citrus Commission placed a 10-day embargo on the shipment of fresh fruit. It also cut $1 million from its $20 million advertising budget for the year.

on outside media to broadcast messages about companies and their products. **The basic means used in sales promotion are internally created and distributed.**

84   Sales promotions are special functions and should be tied to personal selling or advertising. More money is spent on sales promotion than on advertising. It is estimated that in 1982, almost 60 percent of the promotional dollar went for sales promotion.

85   Sales promotion is aimed largely at three groups: company sales personnel, middlemen, and consumers. Devices aimed at company people and intermediaries are sales manuals, training films, exhibits, catalogs, and demonstrations. The major types of sales-promotion activities that are directed toward consumers are point-of-purchase displays, sampling, coupons, premiums, and contests.

Point–of–Purchase Displays

86   The POINT–OF–PURCHASE DISPLAY is *a device by which a product is displayed to stimulate an immediate purchase*. It consists of displays inside stores, close to the place where the goods are stacked. These displays are intended to stimulate impulse buying—decisions made on the spot without prior planning to buy. Supermarkets make space available for representatives to set up a display and perhaps cook sausage, hot dogs, and the like.

Product Sampling

87   Distributing a small sample of a product is a good way to promote it. Sampling puts into practice the axiom that "a good product promotes itself." To be most effective, sampling programs should be coordinated with advertising efforts. The samples should be distributed soon after the product is advertised. Samples are distributed largely by mail and through house-to-house delivery.

Photo: Laura Latulippe

*Consumers appreciate
the bargains they get
with coupons.*

Couponing

88   Cashing in a coupon is a quick and easy way to get a bargain. Quite often the consumer knows little more than that about the coupon process. But couponing has become a $1.3 billion business operation.[5]

89   The cents-off coupon goes directly to the consumer. This ensures that the ultimate user receives the saving. The rest of the process is carried out in one of several ways. Perhaps the manufacturer gives the wholesaler a discount on the purchase. The agreement might be that the wholesaler would pass the saving along to the retailer. The retailer would then lower the price and give the saving to the consumer.

90   In a recent year, 90 billion coupons were issued, but customers redeemed only a little over 4 billion. A. C. Nielsen estimates that 76 percent of all U.S. households used coupons. Nielsen's research arm reported that newspapers print and distribute the bulk of these.

---

[5]According to estimates, this consists of $604 million in production, distribution, and handling costs, and $740 million in redemption costs.

91   Cash refunds are sometimes used in lieu of the cents-off coupon. The cash refund or rebate specifics are usually printed right on the package; thus they do not cost much to distribute.

Premiums

92   A premium is offered the consumer as a reason for buying a specific good. If the purchase is made, the premium is received as a gift. Toys and other gimmicks are returned to buyers in exchange for box tops, universal product codes, or bottle caps. Premiums are seldom related to the product being sold. The premium leads the buyer into thinking that he or she is receiving "something for nothing."

93   Some premiums cost the manufacturer very little. In addition to the box top, the consumer must send in a certain amount of money. This sum comes close to paying the producer's net cost of the premium. The seller must pay, of course, the promotion and handling costs. The buyer still saves money, since the item usually costs less than its price in local stores.

94   For several years, Texaco offered a toy fire engine and gasoline truck as a premium at a price well under $5. More than a million of these premiums were distributed annually. And it has been estimated that Texaco gained more than 100,000 new customers each year the company used this premium. Premiums such as recipe booklets, packets of flower seeds, or plastic toys cost less than the average cents-off coupon.

95   Trading stamps represent a different form of premium. Their use is a long-term promotional effort. Trading stamps may be strong for a few years and then wane in popularity. But some retailers prefer trading stamps to other forms of promotion.

Contests

96   One popular form of contest asks the consumer to write a jngle, a limerick, or a slogan. Another favorite is a bake-off using the manufacturer's product. Items submitted are judged and a reward given.

97   Another form is the sweepstakes. Here, the entrant's name is placed in a pool of names, and the winner's name is drawn out of the pool. Every person entering has an equal chance to win. One's chances of winning in a typical sweepstake event are small, since millions of names are usually sent in. Pepsi offered prizes ranging from $1 to $50. Kraft offered a "family reunion vacation." Publisher's Clearinghouse offers a new home. Sweepstakes may or may not require one to purchase a company's product.

98   Sweepstakes enhance a product's image and generate a high level of consumer

IS COUPONING A GOOD PRACTICE ECONOMICALLY?

Not everyone is agreed that the use of coupons is a good practice. Certainly the consumer who redeems coupons receives an immediate saving. But who pays for this? Does the producer, wholesaler, retailer, or the consumers who do not redeem coupons?

With which of the following statements do you agree, and with which do you disagree?

1. The cost of couponing does not justify its use.

2. Producers simply pass the cost of coupons on to others in the form of higher prices.

3. Wholesalers and retailers absorb the cost of couponing.

4. The savings made by consumers who use coupons justify their continued use.

5. The use of cents-off coupons is a good inflation fighter.

6. It is the consumers who do not redeem coupons who pay for the system.

7. Instead of issuing coupons, the seller should reduce the price of the goods.

8. If businesses did not spend money on couponing, they would spend it in other types of sales promotion.

9. Compared to the sums spent on advertising, the amount spent on coupons is minimal.

10. Consumers like coupons, and that alone justifies their use.

1. Are non–coupon users being discriminated against in pricing?

2. If couponing were discontinued, would consumer prices be lower?

interest. They offer a ready-made reason for setting up a point-of-purchase display. Most sweepstakes appeal to people of middle age who have children.

PUBLIC RELATIONS AS PROMOTION

99 Only recently has public relations been considered a part of the marketing mix. It is concerned with publicity and new-product developments.

100   The American Marketing Association defines PUBLICITY as *"any form of nonpaid commercially significant news or editorial comment about ideas, products, or institutions."* Publicity consists primarily of news stories and personal appearances. When a new firm is opening for business, publicity appears in the local newspaper. When a business is remodeling, building an addition, or moving to a new location, these also form the basis of stories in the local news media.

101   Authors, athletes, and other public figures are usually willing and available to make public appearances at department stores and other businesses to promote their activities. Publicity implies third-party endorsement.

102   Word-of-mouth publicity from satisfied customers is invaluable. Extra effort to give top-quality merchandise, fair treatment, and personal service will cause this publicity to be positive and will result in additional sales.

103   A company's public-relations department is usually not a part of its marketing organization. So public-relations activities related to marketing must be coordinated with other facets of public relations. Promotional efforts must be in line with the company's overall public-relations policy.

SUMMARY OF KEY CONCEPTS

Promotion refers to a company's efforts to influence people to buy.

Promotion is basically communication. Advertising is a one-way flow of communication. Personal selling is a two-way flow.

Personal selling usually involves an oral presentation by the seller to a prospective buyer.

There are five important stages in the personal-selling process.

Advertising attempts to reach large numbers through nonpersonal means.

As a tool of marketing, advertising serves to retain loyal customers, retrieve lost customers, and recruit new ones. As a social force, it has altered our living habits and has helped to raise living standards.

Economically, advertising has promoted the growth of industry, lowered unit costs, and served to identify families of products under one name or brand.

The more popular advertising media are newspapers, radio and television, magazines, and direct mail.

Sales promotion is basically a motivation activity. It is aimed at company personnel, intermediaries, and consumers.

Sales-promotion activities aimed at consumers include point-of-purchase displays, sampling, couponing, premiums, and contests.

Public relations is the fourth component of promotion. It includes some aspects of the other three.

Exercise 2: Basic Vocabulary Chart

Use your English-to-English dictionary to help you complete this chart. Put the chart on a separate sheet of paper so that you will have room to write all of the appropriate definitions and related words.

Word	Part of Speech	Meaning (as used in indicated paragraph)	Related Words	Synonyms
promotion (1)				
enhance (4)				
media (6)				
motivation (10)				
hierarchy (12)				
prospects (15)				
potential (15)				
drive (23)				
in the long run (*box, page 157*)				
hypnosis (24)				
(sales) pitch (24)				
ultimate (26)				

Word	Part of Speech	Meaning (as used in indicated paragraph)	Related Words	Synonyms
tact (29)				
diplomacy (29)				
volume (37)				
worthwhile (40)				
slogan (49)				
logo (50)				
deceptive (62)				
bargain (88)				
redeem (90)				
endorsement (101)				

Exercise 3: Recognizing the Correct Definition from Context

The following basic vocabulary words have more than one definition. Circle the letter of the appropriate definition for the word as it is used in the sample sentence.

1. The purpose of promotion is to <u>enhance</u> the firm's image or increase the sales of the firm's products.

   a. to heighten or increase, as in reputation, beauty, or quality.

   b. to raise the value of

2. <u>Promotion</u> is the third element in the marketing mix.

   a. advancement in rank or position

   b. a putting ahead to the next higher stage or grade

   c. effort to make a business or product successful

3. Closing a sale is an agent's <u>ultimate</u> goal.

   a. not susceptible of further analysis

   b. most distant, extreme

   c. the last of a series; final

4. A practical way to measure its effectiveness is through increased sales <u>volume</u>.

    a. a collection of sheets of paper bound together; a book

    b. a large quantity; a considerable amount

    c. quantity of sound or tone, loudness

5. Cashing in a coupon is a quick and easy wasy to get a <u>bargain</u>.

    a. a mutual agreement between persons, especially one to buy or sell goods

    b. to negotiate

    c. an aritcle bought or offered at a low price

6. Purpose, planning, enthusiasm, confidence, and <u>drive</u> are all ingredients in selling success.

    a. energy, aggressiveness

    b. a journey in a vehicle

    c. a large-scale, sustained attack

7. After a customer's confidence is won, the sales <u>pitch</u> begins.

    a. relative point, position, or degree

    b. a high-pressure sales talk (slang)

    c. the serving of a ball to a batter in baseball

8. In some businesses, salespeople are supplied with a list of <u>prospects</u>.

    a. outlooks for the future

    b. potential or likely customers

    c. anticipation, expectation

Exercise 4: Word Substitution with Basic Vocabulary

For each of the following sentences, choose one of the following words or phrases that has the same meaning as the underlined word or phrase. Write the answer in the blank.

motivation	potential	endorsement	redeem
enhance	deceptive	ultimate	drive

1. He paid ten dollars to <u>recover</u> the watch he had left at the pawn shop.

_____

2. Your idea has a lot of <u>possibility</u>, but we won't know how well it works until we actually try it.

   _____

3. Closing a sale is an agent's <u>final</u> goal.

   _____

4. His <u>incentive</u> for working consists of a good salary and many benefits.

   _____

5. The purpose of promotion is to <u>raise</u> the company's image <u>to a higher level</u>.

   _____

6. The size of the package is <u>misleading</u>: it actually contains less rather than more than the smaller box.

   _____

7. You need to put your <u>signature</u> on the back of a check before the bank will cash it.

   _____

8. In order to be a successful salesperson you need both enthusiasm and the <u>energy</u> to do the job.

   _____

Exercise 5: Guessing Word Meanings from Context

Try to guess the meanings of the underlined words in the following sentences from "Promotional Aspects of Marketing." Begin by underlining the words and phrases that give you the clues you need to make a good guess, then write your definition of the word on the line under the sentence. Do not look these words up in your dictionary until *after* you have guessed their meanings.

   Example: The presentation may be <u>informal</u> or tightly structured.

Since *informal* is placed in a structure that can indicate opposites (informal *or* tightly structured), we can assume that *informal* is the opposite of *tightly structured*.

Informal means "not tightly structured" or "loosely structured."

Notice that *or* in the preceding sentence is used to introduce a paraphrase rather than to indicate opposites. When *or* is used to introduce a paraphrase, it is usually preceded by a comma (,).

1. One useful approach is the "AIDA" persuasion process. This process involves four stages through which the <u>purchaser</u> passes mentally — attention, interest, desire, and action. After gaining the prospect's attention, the presentation must develop the buyer's interest.

2. The progress of the sales interview may <u>hinge on</u> the effectiveness of the salesperson's handling of objections.

3. Sales are not always closed at the end of the initial presentation. If more meetings are required, a date should be established for the first <u>follow-up interview</u>.

4. The follow-up contact is an important complement to the selling process. How well is the customer satisfied with the product or service? What postsale servicing is needed? And, of course, is another sale <u>in order</u>?

5. The main <u>task</u> in sales management consists of coordinating the selling efforts of individuals.

6. It is universally recognized that advertising <u>conveys</u> selling messages better than other techniques in certain situations.

7. Institutional advertising tries to create a favorable attitude toward the company offering to sell a good. It tries to build <u>goodwill</u> that will generate long-run rather than immediate sales.

8. Weyerhaeuser in its ads doesn't sell paper, it preaches conservation. Kellogg doesn't <u>peddle</u> cereal, it promotes nutrition.

    _____

9. From the advertiser's standpoint, the potential dollar sales should produce enough <u>gross-margin dollars</u>—the excess of sales over cost of goods sold—to pay the advertising costs.

    _____

10. Much advertising can be considered truthful. Still, there are too many <u>unscrupulous</u> advertisers who make misleading or half-true statements about their products.

    _____

11. Some people thought that television would destroy radio advertising. <u>To the contrary</u>, it has increased greatly.

    _____

Exercise 6: Guessing Word Meanings by Analysis

Prefixes	Meanings
post-	after
mis-	wrong
contro- (contra-)	against
re-	back, again
ad-	toward

Stems	Meanings
-ver-	turn
-cap-	head
-flex-	bend

Use the meanings of the stems and prefixes above to analyze the following words and guess their meanings:

1. *postsale*   When would a <u>postsale</u> call be made?

   _____

2. *misleading*   Advertising that is <u>misleading</u> causes the consumer to

   _____ .

3. *controversy*   What are the word parts of *controversy*? _____
   Does everyone agree with a controversial decision?

   _____ .

4. *flexible*   Materials that are <u>flexible</u> _____ easily.

   What is an example of a flexible material? _____

5. *per capita*   If there are two televisions <u>per capita</u> in a country, how

   many TVs does each person own? _____

SECOND READING

Carefully reread the chapter "Promotional Aspects of Marketing" from *Introduction to Modern Business* (pp. 152–181). As you read, revise your margin notes, checking to be sure that you have pointed out all of the main ideas. When you finish each section of the chapter, briefly summarize that section on a separate sheet of paper. These summaries will help you answer questions and prepare for essay exams.

POST–READING

REACTION QUESTIONS

1. What are the most common types of promotion used in your country?
2. What examples can you give of each of the six types of advertising mentioned in this chapter?
3. Make a list of the advertising slogans that you know.

4. Which medium contains the most advertising in your country?

5. How does advertising in your country differ from that in the United States?

Exercise 7: Short-Answer Comprehension Questions

The questions in this exercise are based on the main ideas found in this chapter. As you answer them check to see how many are answered by information that you underlined while you read through the chapter. If you underlined the important ideas in the chapter, most of them should be.

1. What is meant by *promotion?*

2. What aspects of marketing does promotion include?

3. Explain the steps in the personal-selling process.

4. What nonverbal clues does a customer give that he or she is ready to make a decision?

5. What techniques lead to success in selling?

6. Describe the different types of advertising.

7. What is the function of slogans and logos?

8. What are the advantages and disadvantages of each medium used for advertising?

9. What are some sales-promotion activities, and how does each work?

Exercise 8: Scanning for Details

On the first line below each question write the heading under which you think you will find the answer. Then, quickly scan the reading to find the answer and write it on the second line.

Example: What are the components of the promotion blend?

Heading: Figure 1

Answer: personal selling, advertising, sales promotion, and public relations

1. What is AIDA?

Heading: _____

Answer: _____

2. List three words the author suggests that a seller use to convince a buyer.

   Heading: _____

   Answer: _____

3. List five duties of a sales manager.

   Heading: _____

   Answer: _____

4. What are the three purposes of advertising?

   Heading: _____

   Answer: _____

5. For what four companies has Victor K. Kiam II worked?

   Heading: _____

   Answer: _____

6. What slogan did the Coca Cola company use in 1957?

   Heading: _____

   Answer: _____

7. What is an example of a logo?

   Heading: _____

   Answer: _____

8. What does FTC stand for?

   Heading: _____

   Answer: _____

9. What is the purpose of the Wheeler-Lea Act, which was passed in 1938?

   Heading: _____

   Answer: _____

10. How many daily newspapers are there in the United States?

    Heading: _____

    Answer: _____

11. How much money did NBC pay to sponsor the Rose Parade on January 1, 1983?

    Heading: _____

    Answer: _____

12. What percentage of the nation's adult population read magazines?

    Heading: _____

    Answer: _____

13. How many FM stations are there in the United States, according to this chapter?

    Heading: _____

    Answer: _____

14. How much of Florida's fruit crop was damaged by frost in 1982?

    Heading: _____

    Answer: _____

Exercise 9: Paraphrasing Practice

Paraphrase these sentences by following the directions after each.

1. Promotion refers to efforts to reach the customers in a target market and persuade them to act.

    a. Substitute a different phrase for <u>refers to</u>. (*consists of, means*)
    b. Substitute a synonym for <u>persuade</u>.

    _____

    _____

2. Promotion is communication, since the marketer is the sender of a sales message, and the customer is the receiver.

    a. Substitute <u>because</u> for <u>since</u>, and change the sentence to make it grammatically correct.

    _____

    _____

3. To progress in successful selling, one must want to succeed, exercise self-discipline, and develop good selling techniques.

    a. Use <u>so that</u> instead of <u>to</u> and change the sentence to make it grammatically correct.

    b. Substitute another word or phrase for <u>one</u>.

    _____

    _____

4. Both a reputation and income are determined by the sales record. Therefore, a successful sales representative pays special attention to the words he or she uses.

    a. Combine the two sentences into one.

    b. Substitute a different connective for <u>therefore</u>.

    _____

    _____

5. Only one out of three believes that advertisements really give a true picture of the product.

    a. Change <u>one out of three</u> to a phrase that means the same thing. (*one third of the people, 33.3 percent of the people*)

    b. Change <u>a true picture</u> to a synonymous phrase. (*an accurate description, an accurate view*)

    _____

    _____

6. Nine out of ten feel that advertisers should be required to prove their claims.

   a. Change <u>nine out of ten</u> to another phrase.

   b. Change <u>should be required</u> to another phrase. (*should have to, should be obliged to*)

   _____

   _____

7. For retailers, advertising ranks as the number-two expenditure, exceeded only by salaries.

   a. Change this sentence by using different words of comparison.

   _____

   _____

ANSWERING ESSAY QUESTIONS

In Unit 4 you learned four steps for writing a well-organized essay-question answer.

STEP 1: Write an introductory statement to begin your answer. Be sure that it mentions the topic and tells the reader what you will say about that topic.

STEP 2: Put your main supporting points in outline form under the introductory statement. Check to see that they are balanced and in order of importance.

STEP 3: Add a transition word or phrase next to each main supporting idea.

STEP 4: Write a concluding sentence that summarizes your main points. Check to be sure that you have not added any new ideas in your concluding sentence.

Exercise 10: Answering Essay Questions

Complete an outline for each of the following essay questions, and use the outlines to answer them.

1. Explain the advantages and disadvantages of each of the media used for advertising.

2. Decide which promotional activity is the most important, and defend your choice.

3. Explain why you think couponing is either here to stay or not here to stay.

SOME SUGGESTED TOPICS FOR FURTHER READING

advertising slogans

coupons

Abraham H. Maslow

the Federal Trade Commission

the Better Business Bureau

logos

false advertising

radio and advertising

television and advertising

newspapers and advertising

promotional activities

6

Reading Social Science

Becky King *by Andrew Wyeth, 1946*
Dallas Museum of Art, Gift of E. L. DeGolyer

Basic Vocabulary

will	sporadic	comply
deliberate	proponent	poll
unconscious	denounce	criteria
fatal	sustain	irreparable
coma	recourse	prognosis
promote	propose	

Exercise 1: Skimming

"Euthanasia" is the first half of a chapter called "The Right to Die" from a sociology book entitled Death: The Final Frontier by Dale Hardt. This book would probably not be the main textbook for a sociology class. Rather it would be a book you might use to find information for a research paper or a class report on the topic of euthanasia. If it were used as the textbook for a class, it would be a high-level seminar class concerned with the social issues related to death and dying.

Do each step, one at a time, answering the questions before you go on to the next step. (The chapter begins on page 198.)

STEP 1: Read the main title of the chapter and all of the headings. Notice how these relate to one another.

Besides euthanasia, what other topic is discussed in "The Right to Die"?

Why are euthanasia and this topic discussed in the same chapter? What is the relationship between the two?

STEP 2: Examine pictures, charts, and other illustrations in the chapter to get information about the chapter's contents.

The illustration on page 209 is an example of what?

STEP 3: Find the names of people, organizations, and so on (proper nouns), and try to determine who or what they are. There are many names in this chapter, and of course they are not all equally important. They should each be checked, however, because you may want to get more information on euthanasia by looking up some of these names in other sources.

   a. Identify each of the following famous people:

   1. Hitler _____

   2. Aristotle _____

   3. Cicero _____

   4. Hippocrates _____

   5. Pope Pius XII _____

b. Why are these people important to the issue of euthanasia?

   1. Karen Ann Quinlan _____

   2. Reverend Charles Francis Potter _____

   3. Cardinal Villot _____

   4. Chief Justice Richard J. Hughes _____

STEP 4: Look at all of the italicized words and phrases. Be aware of the author's reasons for italicizing them. The author of this chapter italicizes the names of books and a newspaper, important words that are being defined, and words used to emphasize an idea.

   a. What are the names of the books and newspaper mentioned in this chapter?

   b. What is the definition given for *indirect euthanasia?*

   c. What are the words that are italicized to emphasize an idea?

STEP 5: Look at the review questions and the bibliography at the end of the chapter to get more information about the chapter.

   Although this unit contains only half of the chapter entitled "The Right to Die," all of the notes at the end of that chapter and some of the bibliography are included in this excerpt.

   a. Which note in addition to note 1 comes from Richard Trubo's book *An Act of Mercy?*

   b. In which publications can you find more information about the Quinlan case?

   c. Which is the most recent publication in the bibliography?

STEP 6: Rapidly read the first and last paragraph of the chapter and the first sentence of each paragraph.

STEP 7: In a sentence or two, explain what you think this chapter is about. (You may answer orally or quickly write the answer that you would give orally.)

FIRST READING

Quickly read the half chapter "Euthanasia" from *Death: The Final Frontier*. As you read, make notes in the margins about the main ideas. After you have finished reading each paragraph or two, write a question that asks for the important information found there. For example, the main idea of paragraph 8 is summarized in the first sentence of the paragraph: "England, like the United States, was confronting the issue of euthanasia sporadically in the years to follow." The rest of the paragraph gives examples of how the country was confronting this issue. You can take this main-idea sentence and make it into the question "What was England doing to confront the issue of euthanasia?"

Forming questions that you can answer as you read will help you find and remember the important ideas in a chapter.

Euthanasia

Dale V. Hardt

Under the wide and starry sky,
Dig the grave and let me lie,
Glad did I live and gladly die,
    And I laid me down with a will.
This be the verse you grave for me:
Here he lies where he longed to be;
Home is the sailor, home from the sea,
    And the hunter home from the hill.

(Robert Louis Stevenson, *"Requiem"*)

1   We are well aware that people in almost all societies have a natural right to life as a consequence of being born. But, as a natural consequence of being born, do they also have a natural right to die? In his book *The Forseeable Future*, Sir George Thomson suggests that once all causes of senility are conquered, death will either be accidental or intentional. Intentional death may be thought of in terms of euthanasia or suicide.

2   Before confronting the issue of euthanasia, we must define it. Historically, the definition was responsive to a single concept: allowing an easy or good death by promoting death for reasons of mercy. The word euthanasia actually comes from the Greek *eu*, meaning *well* and *thanatos*, meaning *death*. However, the total concept is not really so simply defined. There is "promoting" death and then there is "allowing" death. Where does one concern begin and the other leave off? It is this gray area that concerns many. The problem of understanding the total concept is further muddled by remembrances of Hitler and his infamous "euthanasia centers," in which it is estimated some 275 thousand people died. Hence, use of the term euthanasia reflects mass genocide in the minds of many.

Dale V. Hardt, *Death, The Final Frontier*, © 1979, pp. 68–80, 89. Reprinted by permission of Prentice-Hall, Inc., Englewood Cliffs, N.J.

3   Genocide may be defined as the deliberate and systematic destruction of a racial, political, or cultural group. Euthanasia, while deliberate, is not systematic. In fact, because of the possible analogy between genocide and euthanasia, many authorities have suggested the use of other terms such as orthothanasia, agathanasia, benomortasia, dysthanasia, antidysthanasia, or mercy killing. For purposes of communication throughout the remainder of this discussion, let us define euthanasia as the allowance of death through the removal or withholding of treatments that prolong life. (Another term for this is *indirect euthanasia.*) Second, let us define an additional concern, mercy killing. In mercy killing, a deliberate action is taken causing death. This would include the administration of a fatal drug or an injection of air into the bloodstream that causes an air embolism resulting in death.

4   Further confusing the definitional game, for either of the above (euthanasia or mercy killing), we have to consider whether the patient is consciously choosing death or whether it is chosen for him while he is unconscious. Adding the terms voluntary and involuntary to the two previous terms may help clarify this confusion. Voluntary euthanasia can then be defined as the patient's granting of permission to allow for his death through removal or withholding of treatments that prolong life. Involuntary euthanasia implies the allowance of death *without* the patient's previous knowledge through removal or withholding of treatments that prolong life. Voluntary mercy killing can be described as the patient's granting of permission for deliberate action to be taken causing his death. Involuntary mercy killing can be described as a deliberate action taken without the patient's knowledge that hastens death. Indeed, some thin lines between the four definitions exist.

5   Looking at four examples of these definitions in practice may help alleviate any remaining confusion.

1. Mr. "X" asks his physician to remove him from the respirator if his condition worsens. (Voluntary Euthanasia)
2. Mr. "X" suddenly goes into a coma and is placed on the respirator. His relatives arrange to have him removed from the machine if his condition worsens. (Involuntary Euthanasia)
3. Mr. "X" asks his physician to administer a fatal drug if his condition worsens. (Voluntary Mercy Killing)
4. Mr. "X" suddenly goes into a coma. His family arranges for the physician to administer a fatal drug. (Involuntary Mercy Killing)

6   The concept of allowing or helping those in pain to die is founded in historical precedence. Trubo, in his research of euthanasia and mercy killing, found early use of the concept. On the Greek island of Cos, during the first

century B.C., the old and the ill would gather at a banquet held once a year. There they would drink a poisonous chemical to promote death. Obviously, society as a whole, at that time, agreed with this practice. Furthermore, Trubo points out the following:

> *A death potion was always kept in a public place in the Greek colony of Massila, to be used by those who could convince public officials that their death was justified. Aristotle advocated euthanasia for seriously deformed children. And Cicero wrote, "What reason is there for us to suffer? A door is open for us— death, eternal refuge where one is sensible of nothing."*[1]

Using our definition, Aristotle was actually promoting mercy killing, but the point is that euthanasia and mercy killing are not concerns confronted only by modern society. Obviously, they have been considered as far back as recorded history demonstrates.

7   Apparently, the euthanasia issue was of sporadic concern around 1906, when the editor of *Independent* wrote:

> *The renewal of interests in the old subject is due to the introduction of a bill into the Ohio Legislature providing that when an adult of sound mind has been fatally hurt or is so ill that recovery is impossible or is suffering extreme physical pain without hope of relief, his physician, if not a relative and if not interested in any way in the person's estate, may ask his patient in the presence of three witnesses if he or she is ready to die. If the answer is affirmative, then three other physicians are to be summoned in consultation, and if they agree that the case is hopeless, they are supposed to make arrangements to put the person out of pain and suffering with as little discomfort as possible.*[2]

While the editor explains that the bill was supported by a distinguished scholar and humanitarian, he also remarks that civilization at that time would not consider such legislation seriously. Hindsight shows us that he was wrong. The bill was referred to a committee for further consideration by a vote of seventy-eight to twenty-two. This margin indicated an increasing number of advocates for euthanasia.

8   England, like the United States, was confronting the issue of euthanasia sporadically in the years to follow. In 1931, Dr. Milland, the newly elected President of the Society of Medical Officers of Health of England, gave a Presidential address advocating the legalization of voluntary mercy killing. He proposed that adults who were mentally competent and suffering from an incurable or fatal disease that might cause a slow and painful death should be allowed to substitute a quick and painless one. It was the opinion of the editor of the issue in which the President's Address appeared that the great majority of people of the western nations, at least, are not ready for such an innovation. In retrospect, it appears that he was wrong because various organizations

supportive of euthanasia and mercy killing came into being shortly after this. While there are proponents of both euthanasia and mercy killing, as we have defined them, the former has gained the most support from various organizations. The first such organization was founded in England in 1935 under the name, the Voluntary Euthanasia Society.

9   Its American counterpart, the Euthanasia Society of America, was founded in 1938 by Reverend Charles Francis Potter. The Society was composed of lawyers, clergymen, doctors, and intellectuals who believed that the terminally ill had a "right" to die with dignity. After many years and numerous unsuccessful attempts at legislation, members of the Society realized that a massive educational campaign was necessary. In 1967 members of the Euthanasia Society established the Euthanasia Educational Fund for just that purpose. This name was changed to the Euthanasia Educational Council in 1972. In 1975 The Euthanasia Society of America was reactivated under a changed name, the Society for the Right to Die, in order to help legislators introduce bills. Hence, at the present time, both the Society for the Right to Die and the Euthanasia Educational Council exist for the respective purposes of legislation and education. A major belief of the Euthanasia Educational Council is that each person should have the right to die with dignity. To attain this, they believe in education leading to understanding and acceptance of death with the end result being the discovery of ways to humanize death. Such ways include withdrawal of life-support techniques and machinery and the use of medication to eliminate pain, even if the medication tends to shorten life. However, proponents of euthanasia do not necessarily believe that drugs or other means should be used to directly promote death.

10   Various physicians oppose euthanasia on the grounds that it is contrary to the oath of Hippocrates that all doctors must take. Others suggest that the Hippocratic Oath is outdated or easily misinterpreted. In 1948 the Hippocratic Oath was modified by the General Assembly of the World Medical Association. The following modification was later included in the International Code of Medical Ethics and was adopted in 1949 for subsequent use by physicians and medical schools:

Declaration of Geneva: I solemnly pledge myself to consecrate my life to the service of humanity. I will give to my teachers the respect and gratitude which is their due; I will practice my profession with conscience and dignity; the health of my patient will be my first consideration; I will respect the secrets which are confided in me; I will maintain by all means in my power the honor and noble traditions of the medical profession. My colleagues will be my brothers; I will not permit considerations of religion, nationality, race, party politics, or social standing to intervene between my duty and my patient. I will maintain the utmost respect for human life from the time of conception; even under threat, I will not use my medical knowledge contrary to the laws of humanity. I make these promises solemnly, freely, and upon my honor.[3]

Notice, however, that the declaration does not support or denounce euthansia *or* mercy killing. The question was not resolved by medical authorities at that time, and it remains unresolved even today.

11   Some nations, and even some states within the United States, have indicated movement toward legalization, or at least partial acceptance of euthanasia and mercy killing. Sweden allows voluntary euthanasia and voluntary mercy killing but not involuntary euthanasia or involuntary mercy killing. Hence, a physician can turn off or unplug life-sustaining machines but cannot administer a lethal poison. Interestingly though, he may place the poison in the hands of the patient for self-administration. Uruguay, extending the euthanasia concept of Sweden, allows mercy killing if it is administered as a result of patient request. The request is necessary to free the physician from any resulting prosecution. In such a case, the physician is said to have acted out of mercy and compassion. Norway's law is permissive because it is ambiguous. If a patient requests or consents to euthanasia and the physician heeds the request, the punishment is reduced below that outlined by Norwegian law. In effect, the physician is free from legal recourse. South Africa, in 1975, launched the South African Voluntary Euthanasia Society (S.A.V.E.S.). Their immediate goal is legislation of a euthanasia bill. Scottish law dictates that euthanasia is murder; however, no physician has ever been prosecuted for murder by euthanasia. English law, much like Scottish law, also considers euthanasia illegal. In fact, while permissiveness tends to be the rule, there appears to be no serious consideration of legalization. Rejected bills or motions in England include one proposed by the Voluntary Euthanasia Society in 1936, one discussed by the House of Lords and tabled before a vote was even taken in 1950, and one proposed by Lord Ragean of the House of Lords in 1969. Dignitaries and educators support, and have supported, these measures, but they still fail to pass into English law. Regardless of legalization, a precedent for euthanasia was set in 1957:

In 1957, a British Court found a doctor innocent of murder when he prescribed a pain-relieving drug which killed his patient. In that case, the jury was instructed by the presiding judge as follows: If the first purpose of medicine, the restoration of health, can no longer be achieved there is still much for a doctor to do, and he is entitled to do all that is proper and necessary to relieve pain and suffering, even if the measures he takes may incidentally shorten human life.[4]

12   In the United States a movement toward legal reform also occurred. Defeated bills or motions regarding euthanasia include a 1937 Nebraska attempt, a 1947 New York attempt, and a 1968 state of Washington attempt. Of these, the most

interesting defeat was the 1947 New York attempt. It began in 1945 with the Euthanasia Society sending letters to a group of physicians who had responded favorably to a Society poll. The letter asked each physician to join a medical committee for the legalization of euthanasia. Within a year, a committee of 1,776 physicians existed. A bill was drawn up that required the terminally ill patient to sign a petition for euthanasia and, along with an affidavit indicating terminal illness signed by his physician, the petition would be presented to a court of record. The court would appoint a three man commission of which two would be physicians. The commission would then investigate the case and present its finding to the court that would, in turn, make a final decision. Although support was obvious, the bill failed. Beginning in 1968, and each year thereafter, Dr. Walter W. Sackett Jr. has proposed a euthanasia bill in Florida. Dr. Sackett, a physician and member of the Florida House of Representatives, reported to a Special Committee on Aging that the United States should legalize the right to die when a person is irreversibly ill.

13   Since the Society for the Right to Die was reestablished out of the older Euthanasia Society of America in 1975, euthanasia bills have been introduced into the legislatures of at least fifteen states; among them are Oregon, Maryland, West Virginia, Idaho, Florida, Washington, Delaware, Wisconsin, Massachusetts, Illinois, Virginia, Rhode Island, Hawaii, and California. Legislators have noted increasing support for such a law in many of their states. In only one state, California, has such a bill been passed. Governor Brown signed into law, in October, 1976, a bill legalizing voluntary euthanasia. Referred to as a "right to die" bill, it allows any person, even those void of terminal illness at the time, to instruct the physician to cease life-support machines. Anyone in that state can sign a "living will," that must be witnessed by two people other than family members or the attending physician. (The "living will" concept will be discussed later in this chapter.) It remains in effect for a period of five years, and it may be renewed. Furthermore, it may be withdrawn at any time either verbally or in writing. In effect, physicians who comply with the living will and turn off or fail to use life-support devices may not be held liable for any crime or malpractice suit. Also, life insurance companies may not deny a person a policy because he or she has signed such a will.

14   No greater moral leader than Pope Pius XII has spoken on the issue at hand. In 1957, he asked ". . .does one have the right, or is one even under the obligation, to use modern artifical-respiration equipment in all cases, even those which, in the doctor's judgement, are completely hopeless?"[5] In answering his own questions, the Pope made it clear that the doctor reacts only to his patients' desires, either expressed or implied. As such, the physician should not provide care that is not desired by the patient or his guardian. Cardinal Villot, Vatican Secretary of State, summarized a letter to the International

Federation of Catholic Medical Associations in 1970 indicating that medicine is at the service of man. Man, on the other hand, is not an instrument for medical science.

15   Quite a few doctors (probably unknowingly) support the statements made by Pope Pius XII and Cardinal Villot. Dr. Sackett has been quoted as saying that he has let hundreds of patients die. In fact, he claims that ". . .seventy-five percent of the doctors he has known did."[6] It is probably safe to assume that as a result of today's technological advances, many people can be kept "alive" almost indefinitely. It is also safe to assume that euthanasia, withdrawing treatments or machines and allowing death, is more common than might be suspected *or* admitted. It comes as no surprise that many physicians are afraid to exercise judgement or comply with a patient's desires if one examines the fantastic increase in malpractice suits. Dr. R. H. Williams of the University of Washington reported in a study that about eighty percent of a group of physicians and about eighty percent of a lay group favored euthanasia as we have defined it. Interestingly, about eighteen percent of the physicians and thirty-five percent of the lay group actually favored mercy killing as we have defined it. In the same year, Sanders reported that of 156 responding Chicago, Illinois internists and surgeons, sixty-one percent affirmed that euthanasia is practiced. This might indicate that law and medical practices are far apart in moralistic understanding. However, when the question comes to court, the gap separating law and medicine closes. On August 9, 1967, a twenty-three-year-old man killed his mother by shooting her in the head. He was subsequently charged with murder and brought to court. He explained to the court that his mother was in great pain, that she was suffering from leukemia, and that she had attempted suicide already. He further explained that she had begged him to kill her. So he did. The murder (voluntary mercy killing?) was premeditated and intentional. The most lenient sentence he could legally be given was fourteen years in prison without probation. However, on January 24, 1969 he was found "Not Guilty" by reason of insanity. The jury also concluded that since he was no longer insane, he should be released. He was, and the case was ended.

16   Maguire, in his book, *Death By Choice*, offers a similar example in which a man was convicted of voluntary manslaughter for causing the death of his brother who was dying of cancer. He pleaded temporary insanity and claimed he was acting as a result of his brother's pleading. He was sentenced from three to five years in prison and fined five hundred dollars for his action.

17   On December 7, 1972 Dr. Vincent Montemarano allegedly injected a fatal overdose of potassium chloride into a cancer patient who had lapsed into a coma. On January 17, 1974 he was brought to trial. A licensed practical nurse maintained that Dr. Montemarano ordered her to fill a syringe with potassium chloride. She also testified that she saw the injection take place about ten

minutes before the patient was pronounced dead. Dr. Anthony Di Beneditto, Chairman of the Department of Surgery where the alleged mercy killing took place, testified that Dr. Montemarano confessed that he had given a dying patient potassium chloride to stop his heart. The defense never accepted the premise that an injection was made. In fact, both sides avoided reference to "mercy killing." Regardless, it was suggested by one newspaper reporter that many individuals believed it was a case of mercy killing. Over a hundred people in the courtroom and hundreds more waiting outside the courtroom awaited the verdict. As it was announced that Dr. Montemarano was not guilty, those in the courtroom broke into a loud and prolonged applause. This may be another indication of increasing attitudinal acceptance toward euthanasia and mercy killing.

18   In summarizing the preceding examples and the California bill, it can be said that, in general, the attitudes of people toward euthanasia *are* changing. In a 1973 survey regarding attitudes toward death, Dr. John W. Riley Jr., of the Office of Social Research of the Equitable Life Assurance Society, reported that only twenty-six percent of his national sample expressed the belief that doctors should use any means possible for keeping a patient alive. A more recent California poll suggested that almost nine out of every ten Californians polled believe that a terminal patient should have the right to refuse life-prolonging medication. Perhaps surprisingly, sixty-three percent support the right of an incurable patient to ask for and receive medication that would end his life.

19   Perhaps the time for reexamination of euthanasia and mercy killing is approaching. On April 15, 1975 twenty-one-year-old Karen Ann Quinlan lapsed into a coma. Breathing had stopped and artificial respiration techniques were employed to keep her alive until she reached a hospital. Although the cause of cessation of breathing had not been determined, interruption in the normal breathing process apparently caused anoxia (an insufficient supply of oxygen to parts of the body), resulting in a coma. She was placed on a respirator for assistance in breathing, at which time her own breathing did not resume. She remained on the respirator, in what her physician called an altered level of consciousness. Dr. Robert Morse, a neurologist in charge of her care, maintained that Karen Quinlan was not brain-dead. He referred to the Ad Hoc Committee of Harvard Medical School Criteria as the ordinary medical standard for determining brain death. Karen Ann Quinlan satisfied none of these criteria. She reportedly did not have a completely flat EEG, and she did exhibit involuntary muscle activity.

20   After three and a half months on the life-sustaining machine, Karen had not progressed. The original cause of her condition was still unknown. Her parents argued that the young woman was not really alive. Karen's parents consulted Father Trapasso, their family priest, and they were informed of the

Roman Catholic Church's position of not using extraordinary means to sustain life. With the Father's support, Karen's parents asked the physician to discontinue all extraordinary measures. Dr. Morse refused, indicating that his moral conscience would not allow him to agree to the cessation of the respirator.

21   On September 3, 1975, nearly five months after Karen went into a coma and was placed on the respirator, Mr. and Mrs. Quinlan filed a court action to have the machine unplugged. Her parents, religious in nature, claimed that it was God's will that their daughter be allowed to die. Their belief was that Karen was already dead and that it was only the machine that was keeping her alive. The legal papers filed by their attorney, Paul W. Armstrong, quoted doctors who had determined that Miss Quinlan suffered irreparable brain damage during her five months in a coma.

22   However, permission from the court to discontinue use of the machine was denied. On November 10, 1975 Judge Robert Muir, Jr. refused to allow the removal of the respirator that was keeping Karen Ann Quinlan alive. Legally and medically, Karen Ann Quinlan was still alive at that time. Alive also is the issue; who has the right, if anyone, to terminate life? Should euthanasia, either expressed or implied, be subject to legal control? The case continued. On December 17, 1975 the Quinlans were in the process of taking the case to the New Jersey Supreme Court. A hearing was scheduled for January 26, 1976. Some additional concerns came out of the Quinlan case at that time. Reacting to the court's decision of November 10, 1975, numerous religious and medical authorities made statements. Most of them supported the Judge's decision. However, Reverend William B. Smith, representing the Roman Catholic Archdiocese of New York, believed that the trusted judgement of medical authorities should be preferred to any legal decision. Dr. Max H. Parrot from Portland, Oregon commented that Judge Muir "recognized that such decisions are essentially medical rather than legal, and therefore the care and treatment of a patient and all decisions related thereto remain the responsibility of the treating physician."[7] Perhaps the most important reaction to the Quinlan court case came from Ralph Porzio, the lawyer for the doctors involved. He requested an international conference of the best medical and legal minds available to sit down and organize guidelines for solving future problems like those raised by the Quinlan case.

23   On March 31, 1976 the New Jersey Supreme Court ruled 7–0 in favor of allowing the removal of the respirator that had kept Karen Ann Quinlan alive for almost a year. Chief Justice Richard J. Hughes stipulated that doctors and a hospital ethics committee must agree that there was no reasonable possibility of her recovery before removal would be allowed. Once such an agreement was reached, criminal charges against the hospital or doctors would not be possible. Karen's father was appointed her personal guardian by the court. This meant that if the original doctors at the hospital did not agree with removal of

the respirator, he had the power to choose other doctors who would make the decision. However, the hospital ethics committee still had to agree with the doctors before removal was allowed. Neither the former court-appointed guardian nor the New Jersey attorney general appealed the Supreme Court decision.

24   Almost two months later, on May 24, 1976, Karen Ann Quinlan was moved to a private room where the respirator was removed. It was believed she would die almost immediately. She did not. While still in a coma, Miss Quinlan continued to breath on her own. There is, at this time, still no sign of recovery from her long coma. Most medical experts agree that she has probably suffered irreversible brain damage and could remain in a vegetative state indefinitely.

25   On June 10, 1976 Karen was moved to a nursing home where "extraordinary medical treatment" to keep her alive will not be used. It is unclear to this day what is meant by "extraordinary medical treatment."

26   Most people who argue against euthanasia suggest at one point or another that the physician can never be sure of what tomorrow's medicine may bring. What if the day after he lets Tommy die, a cure for cancer is found? What if the day after the court allowed Quinlan's respirator to be removed, a cure for "irreversible brain damage" was found? The question is one that can never be answered satisfactorily, mainly because these are rare cases. There are cases of those painfully dying from terminal cancer who, for no apparent reason, recover to outlive their doctors. Prognosis is fallible and diseases may go into unaccountable remission for no apparent reason. Yet, the percentages are behind the practice of medicine. Prognosis of some diseases or disorders can be very precise. However, the reality of the situation is that there *are* those cases where life is present but hope is not.

27   Randal Carmen, age seventeen, was kept alive on life-support machines for three weeks before he died. According to doctors, Randal spent three weeks on machines after his brain was dead. Repeated requests by his parents to end his life by removing the machines were ignored. The doctor maintained that everything within medical power must be done to maintain life saving procedures. Other than the prospect of life, should one not consider the excruciating pain that sometimes accompanies death? Should one not consider the dignity of the "person," or is his dignity secondary to the very technology that keeps him alive? Are physical signs of life more important than emotional or spiritual concerns? Do we keep the "body" alive at any cost? (For example, the estimated cost for keeping Karen Ann Quinlan alive for five months from April 15, 1975 to September 21, 1975 was one hundred thirty thousand dollars.) These are all questions that remain unanswered by medical or legal authorities. Yet each individual may have to confront them at some point in his life.

28   A second argument against euthanasia is that neither physicians nor courts have the right to "play God." This argument can no longer be taken seriously in today's advanced medical-technological world. If it is God's will that we are

concerned with, then medicine should be abolished to allow God's work to continue. If it is wrong to promote death and to put an end to suffering, likewise, it is wrong to delay death with medication or respirators. Very few people would abandon the advances that medical technology has made over the last few decades.

29   Recently, the movement toward "Death with Dignity" has intensified. During the 1970s, at least fifteen euthanasia bills were introduced in various states; one passed. Over seventy thousand members have enlisted support for the Euthanasia Educational Council. In 1967, Luis Kutner suggested a "Living Will" to the Euthanasia Educational Fund (now the Euthanasia Educational Council). Such wills have little legal foundation (except in California); however, there were one million of these wills distributed as of March 1976. While it is a legal document, it has not yet been tested in a court of law. It must be signed in the presence of two witnesses but does not have to be notarized. A copy should be kept on hand at all times. It is even recommended that copies be given to your doctor and next of kin so that your wishes are known. A copy of the document as it is today is shown on page 209.

30   It remains to be seen if these documents will be medically honored or if the courts will support the doctor's decision (other than in California where its use is legalized). Interestingly, courts are not usually called upon to support a doctor in his selection of which treatment is applicable to the patient. Whereas one treatment may cause a shorter but happier life, another may result in a longer, but more pain-filled life. The doctor makes these moral decisions every day. To remove this power of moral decision making from the physician is to assume that all of us want to live as long as possible regardless of the pain or circumstances. While many of us may want this, there are also many, if not more, who do not. This is evidenced by the advancement of the euthanasia movement in the United States and in other countries.

31   Just a few years ago, a "Patient's Bill of Rights" was approved by the American Hospital Association. It maintained that every patient had twelve basic rights. Among those pertaining to various aspects of euthanasia were:

1. The right to information concerning diagnosis, treatment, and prognosis
2. The right to advance information prior to consent for surgery or any other type of treatment
3. The right to refuse treatment

32   The third right listed above is extremely important for proponents of legalized euthanasia. The American Hospital Association claims that eighty-five percent of the nation's hospitals have accepted the Bill in principle; however, only thirty-five percent have used it in any form. Many people feel that the

My Living Will
To My Family, My Physician, My Lawyer
and All Others Whom It May Concern

Death is as much a reality as birth, growth, maturity and old age—it is the one certainty of life. If the time comes when I can no longer take part in decisions for my own future, let this statement stand as an expression of my wishes and directions, while I am still of sound mind.

If at such a time the situation should arise in which there is no reasonable expectation of my recovery from extreme physical or mental disability, I direct that I be allowed to die and not be kept alive by medications, artificial means or "heroic measures". I do, however, ask that medication be mercifully administered to me to alleviate suffering even though this may shorten my remaining life.

This statement is made after careful consideration and is in accordance with my strong convictions and beliefs. I want the wishes and directions here expressed carried out to the extent permitted by law. Insofar as they are not legally enforceable, I hope that those to whom this Will is addressed will regard themselves as morally bound by these provisions.

(Optional specific provisions to be made in this space — see other side)

DURABLE POWER OF ATTORNEY (optional)

I hereby designate _____ to serve as my attorney-in-fact for the purpose of making medical treatment decisions. This power of attorney shall remain effective in the event that I become incompetent or otherwise unable to make such decisions for myself.

Optional Notarization:

"Sworn and subscribed to

before me this _____ day

of _____, 19_____."

_____
Notary Public
(seal)

Signed_____

Date _____

Witness _____

_____
Address

Witness _____

_____
Address

Copies of this request have been given to _____

_____   _____

(Optional)   My Living Will is registered with Concern for Dying (No. _____)

Distributed by Concern for Dying, 250 West 57th Street, New York, NY 10107 (212) 246-6962

A Living Will[8]

Bill should either be posted where all can see it, or that it should be given to each patient as he enters the hospital.

33   Let us summarize the situation up to this point. About forty-two percent of the religions mentioned in the next chapter accept euthanasia as an individual decision to be made between the doctor, the patient, and the family. Slightly less (about thirty-five percent) are acceptant of mercy killing, usually depending upon the circumstances.

34   Summarily, we can suggest support for euthanasia for the following reasons:

1. To alleviate pain and suffering
2. To promote "meaning" to the state of life
3. Economic considerations
4. Use of hospital bed space, staff, and technological devices (that could be used by others)

While the last two reasons may not add much to the concept of "death with dignity," they are realistic concerns and must not be overlooked in any discussion for or against the practice of euthanasia. Likewise, there are reasons against euthanasia that are equally founded in logic. Those who oppose euthanasia usually do so citing the following:

1. The Oath of Hippocrates
2. Moral decision making by physicians and family
3. Religious considerations

Suicide

From this world-wearied flesh. Eyes, look your last!
Arms, take your last embrace! and, lips, O you
The doors of breath, seal with a righteous kiss
A dateless bargain to engrossing death!
Come, bitter conduct, come, unsavory guide!
Thou desperate pilot, now at once run on
The dashing rocks thy sea-sick weary bark!
Here's to my love! O true apothecary!
Thy drugs are quick. Thus with a kiss I die.

(William Shakespeare,
Romeo and Juliet,
Act V, Scene 3)

Again we have to ask if any individual has the right to take his own life. The law of any country allows killing as a legitimate activity depending upon circumstances. It may be acceptable to kill the enemy in a war; however, it is not acceptable to kill the "enemy" next door. It may also be acceptable to kill a convicted murderer; but again, not acceptable for the murderer to kill. This is all to say that in some cases the manner of death may be considered legitimate and socially and morally acceptable. Suicide, however, is rarely an acceptable form of dying.

[The chapter continues with a discussion of suicide.]

NOTES

1. Richard Trubo, *An Act of Mercy* (Los Angeles: Nash Publishing, 1973), p. 5.

2. "Euthanasia Once More," *Independent*, 60 (Feburary 1, 1906), 291.

3. G. E. W. Wolsten Holme and Maeve O'Connor, *Ethics In Medical Progress* (Boston: Little, Brown and Co., 1966), p. 222.

4. Trubo, *An Act of Mercy*, p. 37.

5. U.S. Congress, Senate, *Hearings Before The Special Committee on Aging*, 92d Cong., 2d sess., p. 149.

6. *Ibid.*, p. 148.

7. Peter Kihss, "Religious and Medical Leaders Back Court's Decision in the Quinlan Case," *New York Times*, November 11, 1975, p. 62, col. 1.

8. Reprinted with permission of Concern for Dying, 250 West 57th Street, New York, New York 10107.

9. Emile Durkheim, *Suicide*, trans. by John A. Spaulding and George Simpson (New York: The Free Press, 1951), p. 276.

10. H. L. P. Resnik, *Suicidal Behavior* (Boston: Little, Brown and Co., 1968), p. 196.

SELECTED BIBLIOGRAPHY

DURKHEIM, EMILE, *Suicide: Prevention and Intervention*. Boston: Beacon Press, 1951.

EPSTEIN, HELEN, "A Sin or a Right?" *New York Times*, September 8, 1974, sec. 6, p. 91.

EUTHANASIA EDUCATIONAL COUNCIL, *Euthanasia*. New York: December 1974.

EUTHANASIA EDUCATIONAL COUNCIL, *Euthanasia: An Annotated Bibliography*. New York: June 1974.

EUTHANASIA EDUCATIONAL COUNCIL, *"In Her Own Words."* New York.

EUTHANASIA EDUCATIONAL COUNCIL, *Euthanasia News.* New York. Vol. 1, no. 3 (May 1975); Vol. 1, no. 3 (August 1975); Vol. 1, no. 4 (November 1975).

"Euthanasia Once More," *Independent,* 60 (February 1, 1906), 291–292.

"Excerpts From Judge Muir's Decision in the Karen Quinlan Case," *New York Times,* November 11, 1975, p. 62, col. 4.

Exercise 2: Basic Vocabulary Chart

Use your English-to-English dictionary to help you complete this chart. Put the chart on a separate sheet of paper so that you will have room to write all of the appropriate definitions and related words.

Word	Part of Speech	Meaning (as used in indicated paragraph)	Related Words	Synonyms
deliberate (3)				
unconscious (4)				
fatal (5)				
coma (5)				
promote (6)				
sporadic (7)				
proponent (8)				
denounce (10)				
sustain (11)				
recourse (11)				
propose (12)				
comply (13)				
poll (18)				
criteria (19)				
irreparable (21)				
prognosis (26)				
will (29)				

Exercise 3: Recognizing the Correct Definition from Context

The following basic vocabulary words have more than one definition. Circle the letter of the appropriate definition for the word as it is used in the sample sentence.

1. Genocide may be defined as the <u>deliberate</u> and systematic destruction of a racial, political, or cultural group.

   a. slow and uneven; unhurried

   b. carefully weighed or considered; studied; intentional

   c. to consult or confer formally

2. Using our definition, Aristotle was actually promoting (<u>promote</u>) mercy killing, but the point is that euthanasia and mercy killing are not concerns confronted only by modern society.

   a. to advance in rank, postion, dignity, and so on (opposed to *demote*)

   b. to put ahead to the next higher grade or stage of a series of classes

   c. to help or encourage to exist or flourish; to further

3. The declaration does not support or <u>denounce</u> euthanasia or mercy killing.

   a. to censure or condemn openly or publicly

   b. to make a formal accusation against, as to the police or in a court

   c. to give formal notice of the termination or denial of (a treaty, pact, agreement, or the like)

4. A physician can turn off or unplug life-sustaining (<u>sustain</u>) machines but cannot administer a lethal poison.

   a. to undergo, experience, or suffer (injury, loss, and so forth)

   b. to provide for (an institution or the like) by furnishing means or funds

   c. to supply with a necessity of life

5. A more recent California <u>poll</u> suggested that almost one out of every ten Californians believe that a terminal patient should have the right to refuse life-prolonging medication.

   a. the voting at an election

   b. a sampling or collection of opinions on a subject, taken from either a selected or a random group of persons, as for the purpose of analysis

c. the head, especially the part of it on which the hair grows

6. Anyone in California can sign a "living will," which must be witnessed by two people other than family members or the attending physician.

a. the power of choosing one's own actions

b. a legal declaration of a person's wishes as to the disposition of his property or estate after his death

c. disposition, whether good or ill, toward another

Exercise 4: Word Substitution with Basic Vocabulary

For each of the following questions, choose one of the following words or phrases that has the same meaning as the underlined word or phrase. Write the answer in the blank.

intentional	suggested
without awareness, sensation, or cognition	obey, yield to
advocates	advocating
established rules for testing	unable to be remedied
condemn	supplying with a necessity

1. Euthanasia, while <u>deliberate</u>, is not systematic.

   _____

2. We have to consider whether the patient is consciously choosing death or whether it is chosen for him while he is <u>unconscious</u>.

   _____

3. Using our definition, Aristotle was actually <u>promoting</u> mercy killing, but the point is that euthanasia and mercy killing are not concerns confronted only by modern society.

   _____

4. While there are <u>proponents</u> of both euthanasia and mercy killing,

as we have defined them, the former has gained the most support from various organizations.

_____

5. The declaration does not support or <u>denounce</u> euthanasia or mercy killing.

_____

6. A physician can turn off or unplug <u>life-sustaining</u> machines but cannot administer a lethal poison.

_____

7. Rejected bills or motions in England include one <u>proposed</u> by the Voluntary Euthanasia Society in 1936.

_____

8. In effect, physicians who <u>comply</u> with the living will and turn off or fail to use life-support devices may not be held liable for any crime or malpractice suit.

_____

9. Karen Ann Quinlan satisfied none of the <u>criteria</u> for determining brain death.

_____

10. The doctors determined that Karen had suffered <u>irreparable</u> brain damage.

_____

READING PROBLEMS

Exercise 5: Connectives

Read the following sentences and underline the connective(s) in each. Circle the connective(s) at the end of the sentence that could be used to replace that (those) in the sentence. Do not consider punctuation.

Example: The word euthanasia actually comes from the Greek *eu*, meaning *well* and *thanatos*, meaning *death*. <u>However</u>, the total concept is not really so simply defined.

Although   Because   (But)

1. The problem of understanding the total concept is further muddled by remembrances of Hitler and his infamous "euthanasia centers," in which it is estimated some 275 thousand people died. Hence, use of the term euthanasia reflects mass genocide in the minds of many.

   So that   Because   Thus

2. While the editor explains that the bill was supported by a distinguished scholar and humanitarian, he also remarks that civilization at that time would not consider such legislation seriously.

   Although   Unless   Hence

3. Their immediate goal is legislation of a euthanasia bill. Scottish law dictates that euthanasia is murder; however, no physician has ever been prosecuted for murder by euthanasia.

   Nevertheless   Despite   Since

4. Cardinal Villot, Vatican Secretary of State, summarized a letter to the International Federation of Catholic Medical Associations in 1970 indicating that medicine is at the service of man. Man, on the other hand, is not an instrument for medical science.

   So that   Since   However

5. Both sides avoided reference to "mercy killing." Regardless, it was suggested by one newspaper reporter that many individuals believed it was a case of mercy killing.

   Nevertheless   Because   If

6. Prognosis is fallible and diseases may go into unaccountable remission for no apparent reason. Yet, the percentages are behind the practice of medicine.

   In addition   Still   Unless

7. If it is wrong to promote death and to put an end to suffering, likewise, it is wrong to delay death with medication or respirators.

   Therefore   So that   In the same way

8. It is recommended that copies be given to your doctor and next of kin so that your wishes are known.

   So   Because   Suppose

9. Summarily, we can suggest support for euthanasia for the following reasons.

   Finally   In addition   In sum

10. Whereas one treatment may cause a shorter but happier life, another may result in a longer, but more pain-filled life.

    So that   Despite   Although

Exercise 6: Guessing Word Meanings from Context

Try to guess the meanings of the underlined words in the following sentences from "*Euthanasia.*" Begin by underlining the words and phrases that give you the clues you need to make a good guess, then write your definition of the word on the line under the sentence. Do not look these words up in your dictionary until <u>after</u> you have guessed their meanings.

> **Example:** In mercy killing a deliberate action is taken causing death. This would include the administration of a <u>fatal</u> drug or an injection of air into the bloodstream that causes an air embolism resulting in death.
>
> Since we are talking about "killing" and the action taken is "causing death," when we talk about the administration of a <u>fatal</u> drug, we can assume that *fatal* means "deadly," or "something that kills."
>
> deadly, something that kills

1. Adding the terms *voluntary* and *involuntary* to the two previous terms may help <u>clarify</u> this confusion.

2. Looking at four examples of these definitions in practice may help <u>alleviate</u> any remaining confusion.

3. . . . When an adult of sound mind has been fatally hurt, his physician, if not a relative and if not interested in any way in the person's estate, may ask his patient in the presence of three witnesses if he or she is ready to die. If the answer is <u>affirmative</u>, then three other physicians are to be summoned in consultation, and if they agree that the case is hopeless, they are supposed to make arrangements to put the person out of pain and suffering with as little discomfort as possible.

4. The first such organization was founded in England in 1935 under the name, the Voluntary Euthanasia Society. Its American counterpart, the Euthanasia Society of America, was founded in 1938 by Reverend Charles Francis Potter.

_____

5. The Society was composed of lawyers, clergymen, doctors, and intellectuals who believed that the terminally ill had a "right" to die with dignity.

_____

6. Some physicians suggest that the Oath of Hippocrates is outdated or easily misinterpreted. In 1948 the Hippocratic Oath was modified by the General Assembly of the World Medical Association. The modification was adopted in 1949 for subsequent use by physicians and medical schools.

_____

7. Breathing had stopped and artificial respiration techniques were employed to keep her alive until she reached a hospital. Although the cause of cessation of breathing had not been determined, interruption in the normal breathing process apparently caused anoxia (an insufficient supply of oxygen to parts of the body), resulting in a coma.

_____

8. Chief Justice Richard J. Hughes stipulated that doctors and a hospital ethics committee must agree that there was no reasonable possibility of her recovery before removal would be allowed.

_____

9. These are all questions that remain unanswered by medical or legal authorities. Yet each individual may have to confront them at some point in his or her life.

_____

10. Just a few years ago a "Patient's Bill of Rights" was approved by the American Hospital Association. It maintained that every patient had twelve basic rights.

_____

Exercise 7: Guessing Word Meanings by Word Analysis

Prefixes	**Meanings**
pre- (prim-)	first, before
ad- (a-, ab-, ac-, af-, ag-, al-, an-, ap-, ar-)	to, toward, near
re-	again
inter-	between, among
mal-	bad, wrong
re- (retro-)	behind, back, backward
con- (co-, col-, com-)	with, together

Stems	**Meanings**
-spec- (-spic-)	look
-sequ- (-secut-)	follow
-gen-	become, produce, bear
-cide	killer or destroyer of, murder or killing of
-vene- (-vent-)	come
-voc- (-vok-)	call
-ced- (-cess-)	go, move, surrender
-spir-	breathe

Use the meanings of the preceding stems and prefixes to analyze the following words and guess their meanings.

1. *consequence*   What is the <u>consequence</u> of an action?

_____

2. *genocide*   Is <u>genocide</u> the killing of a group of people who are related in some way or a group of people who are unrelated? (Clue: The root *gen* is also found in *gene, genetic,* and *genealogy.*)

_____

3. *reactivate*   If *activate* means "to make active," what does <u>reactivate</u> mean?

_____

4. *intervene*   When two boys are fighting and the teacher <u>intervenes</u>, does he or she let them keep fighting or stop them from fighting?

_____

5. *precedence*   If one task has <u>precedence</u> over another, is it more or less important than the other?

_____

6. *malpractice*   What does it mean to say that a doctor is guilty of <u>malpractice</u>?

_____

7. *advocate*   Is an <u>advocate</u> of mercy killing for or against it?

_____

8. *respiration*   Is <u>respiration</u> the act of breathing in, or is it the complete breathing cycle?

_____

SECOND READING

Carefully read the half chapter "Euthanasia" from *Death: The Final Frontier* again (pp. 198–211). As you read, revise the notes in the margins; then use these notes to write brief summaries of each section.

POST–READING

REACTION QUESTIONS

1. What arguments given in this chapter either for or against euthanasia were new to you?

2. What do you think is the best argument against euthanasia and mercy killing?

3. What do you think is the best argument for euthanasia and mercy killing?

4. Can you think of arguments either for or against euthanasia or mercy killing that were not given in this chapter?

5. Do you think that a "living will" is a good idea? Why or why not?

6. Are euthanasia and mercy killing legal in your country?

Exercise 8: Short-Answer Comprehension Questions

The questions in this exercise are based on the main ideas found in the reading. As you answer the questions check to see how many are answered by the notes and summaries you wrote during your second reading. If you wrote down the important ideas in the chapter, most of them should be.

1. What examples are cited in this chapter to show that euthanasia has historical precedents?

2. At the time this textbook was written, what was the difference between the purposes of the Society for the Right to Die and the Euthanasia Educational Council?

3. What is the argument offered to counteract that of physicians who are against euthanasia because they think it is contrary to the Oath of Hippocrates?

4. What was the opinion about euthanasia given by Cardinal Villot in his 1970 letter to the International Federation of Catholic Medical Associations?

5. What statistics are cited to prove that the attitudes of people toward euthanasia are changing?

6. What does *extraordinary medical treatment* mean?

7. What seems to be the author's attitude toward the argument that the physician can never be sure what tomorrow's medicine may bring?

8. What is the main idea of paragraph 27?

9. What argument is given to counter the argument that neither physicians nor the courts have the right to "play God"?

10. What recent measures to allow people to die with dignity were mentioned in this chapter?

11. At the time this chapter was written, were "living wills" being honored by the medical profession and courts?

12. According to the Patient's Bill of Rights, what are a patient's rights in regard to euthanasia and mercy killing?

Exercise 9: Scanning for Details

Scan the reading for the answers to the following questions. Work as rapidly as you can. Remember to use headings to help you.

1. What is an example of voluntary mercy killing?
2. What was the first organization formed in support of euthanasia?
3. Who founded the Euthanasia Society of America?
4. When was the Hippocratic Oath modified?
5. Which countries are mentioned as having moved toward the legalization of euthanasia?
6. What is the full name of S.A.V.E.S.?
7. What was the original name of the Society for the Right to Die?
8. What percentage of the Californians polled believed that terminal patients should have the right to refuse life-prolonging medication?
9. When did Karen Ann Quinlan lapse into a coma?
10. When was the final decision made about the legality of removing Karen from the respirator?
11. At the time this chapter was written, what percentage of hospitals had ever used the Patient's Bill of Rights?

Exercise 10: Paraphrasing Practice

Paraphrase these sentences by following the directions after each.

1. Involuntary mercy killing can be described as a deliberate action taken without the patient's knowledge that hastens death.

   a. Substitute synonyms for underline deliberate and hasten.

b. Use a definition signal other than <u>can be described as.</u> (*can be defined as, is, is called*)

_____

_____

2. It was the opinion of the editor of the issue in which the President's Address appeared that the great majority of people of the western nations, at least, are not ready for such an innovation.

    a. Make the editor the subject of the sentence.

    b. Substitute a synonym for <u>innovation.</u>

_____

_____

3. The ways of humanizing death include withdrawal of life-support techniques and machinery and the use of medication to eliminate pain, even if the medication tends to shorten life.

    a. Use a connector other than <u>even if.</u> (*even when*)

    b. Change <u>the use</u> (of medication) and <u>withdrawal</u> to verbs.

_____

_____

4. Various physicians oppose euthanasia on the grounds that it is contrary to the Oath of Hippocrates.

    a. Substitute a synonym for <u>oppose.</u>

    b. Rewrite the part of the sentence that says <u>on the grounds that it is contrary to.</u> . . .

_____

_____

5. The question was not resolved by medical authorities at that time, and it remains unresolved even today.

    a. Substitute a synonym for <u>resolved.</u>

b. Use a present perfect verb in the part of the sentence that says it remains unresolved even today.

_____

_____

6. If a patient requests or consents to euthanasia and the physician heeds the request, the punishment is reduced below that outlined by Norwegian law.

   a. Use a connector other than if. (*When, suppose, in the case that*)
   b. Use synonyms for requests, consents to, and heeds.

_____

_____

7. Although support was obvious, the bill failed.

   a. Use a connector other than although. (*even though, despite the fact that*)
   b. Rewrite the part of the sentence that says support was obvious. (Begin the sentence with *There was.*)

_____

_____

8. The jury concluded that since he was no longer insane, he should be released.

   a. Use a connector other than since. (*because, as, therefore*)
   b. Substitute synonyms for concluded and released.

_____

_____

9. In summarizing the preceding examples and the California bill, it can be said that, in general, the attitudes of people toward euthanasia are changing.

   a. Use a phrase other than in summarizing. (*to summarize, as a summary of*)

b. Rewrite the part of the sentence that says, <u>it can be said that</u> <u>. . . .</u> (*we can say that, it can be concluded that*)

_____

_____

10. If it is wrong to promote death and to put an end to suffering, likewise, it is wrong to delay death with medication or respirators.

   a. Substitute a synonym for <u>put an end to</u>.

   b. Use a connector other than <u>likewise</u>. (*in the same way, also*)

_____

_____

MAKING INFERENCES

When a writer does not state an idea directly, but the reader understands that the idea follows logically from what the writer does say, the reader has made an <u>inference</u>. Readers must often make inferences because writers do not put all of their ideas on paper directly. To be a good reader, you must be sure that the inferences you make can be logically justified from what the writer says. Read the following sentences and decide what inferences might be made from the given facts.

   The red hat costs $ 12.00.

   The blue hat costs $ 14.00.

   The green hat costs $ 16.00.

   Ms. Light has decided to buy the red hat. (Why do you think she decided to buy it?)

You might infer that Ms. Light decided to buy the red hat because it is the cheapest or that she bought it because she prefers red to blue or green. Actually, she may have bought it because the other two were the wrong size or because the red one was a better style for her. There isn't enough information to make an accurate inference. In this case, you make unsupported assumptions no matter which inference you make.

   Practice in recognizing logical inferences is important for good reading. You need to be aware of the inferences you make while reading and learn to check them automatically for support. The next exercise is designed to give you practice in recognizing reasonable inferences. Practice this skill as you read the newspaper, listen to the news on television or the radio, and even as you talk to your friends. Always ask yourself, "What can I logically infer from this information without making assumptions that are not justified (supported) by the facts?"

Exercise 11: Recognizing Logical Inferences

Carefully read the sentences for each problem, then circle the letter of the inference that can be made logically from the information given in the original sentence(s).

1. Various physicians oppose euthanasia on the grounds that it is contrary to the Oath of Hippocrates that all doctors must take. Others suggest that the Hippocratic Oath is outdated or easily misinterpreted.

    a. The others mentioned in the quote support euthanasia because of the Hippocratic Oath.

    b. The others mentioned in the quote oppose euthanasia because of the Hippocratic Oath.

    c. The others mentioned in the quote don't think that the Hippocratic Oath is sufficient reason to oppose euthanasia.

2. Scottish law dictates that euthanasia is murder; however, no physician has ever been prosecuted for murder by euthanasia. English law, much like Scottish law, also considers euthanasia illegal. In fact, while permissiveness tends to be the rule, there appears to be no serious consideration of legalization.

    a. Scottish society actually permits euthanasia, even though it is not legal.

    b. Most Scottish people feel that euthanasia is murder.

    c. Euthanasia will probably soon be legalized in Scotland.

3. Cardinal Villot, Vatican Secretary of State, summarized a letter to the International Federation of Catholic Medical Associations in 1970 indicating that medicine is at the service of man. Man, on the other hand, is not an instrument for medical science.

    a. He thinks that doctors should learn more about medicine from patients who are kept alive artificially.

    b. He thinks that some doctors keep some patients alive partially so that they can learn more about medicine.

   c. He thinks that doctors must do everything they can to keep their patients alive.

4. Interestingly, about eighteen percent of the physicians and thirty-five percent of the lay group actually favored mercy killing as we have defined it. In the same year Sanders reported that of 156 responding Chicago internists and surgeons, sixty-one percent affirmed that euthanasia is practiced. This might indicate that law and medical practices are far apart in moralistic understanding. However, when the question comes to court, the gap separating law and medicine closes.

   a. Although euthanasia and mercy killing are actually illegal in many places, people who commit either are rarely convicted of murder.

   b. The laws concerned with euthanasia and mercy killing are strictly enforced, even though many people feel that they should not be illegal.

   c. More doctors oppose euthanasia and mercy killing than was originally believed.

5. Dr. Robert Morse, a neurologist in charge of her care, maintained that Karen Quinlan was not brain-dead. He referred to the Ad Hoc Committee of Harvard Medical School Critieria as the ordinary medical standard for determining brain death. Karen Ann Quinlan satisfied none of these criteria. She reportedly did not have a completely flat EEG, and she did exhibit involuntary muscle activity.

   a. Dr. Morse thinks that a patient must not be considered alive if that patient is not brain-dead.

   b. One of the criteria for being considered brain-dead is to exhibit involuntary muscle activity.

   c. A person considered brain dead has a completely flat EEG and no involuntary muscle activity.

PASSING ESSAY EXAMS: ANSWERING ESSAY QUESTIONS OF CONTRAST

The purpose of an essay of contrast is to show how two similar things are different. In order to explain how two things are different, you first need to organize your ideas in a graphic form so you can visualize the differences and the categories into which these differences fall.

   Let's take a very simple example to show how this works, and then we'll apply the idea to a more complicated example. Suppose you are trying to explain that you and your brother have different talents and abilities. You begin, as with any essay, by writing an introductory sentence: "My brother and I have different talents and abilities." (This introductory sentence can be improved once you know exactly what categories you will use to organize these talents and abilities.)

The next step (which takes the place of an outline) is to chart your talents and abilities.

Example 1:	You	Your Brother
	good with machines	
	good at many sports	

After you have charted your talents and abilities, you need to chart your brother's lack of ability in the same area.

Example 2:	You	Your Brother
	good with machines	no talent with machines
	good at sports	a little uncoordinated

Because we can assume that your brother, likewise, has abilities that you don't have, the next step is to chart his abilities and then to counter with your lack of talent in those areas.

Example 3:	You	Your Brother
	seem to be tone-deaf	has musical talent
	can't learn more than basic phrases	good at learning languages

This charting is much more effective than simply listing your abilities and your brother's abilities without matching them. The point is, after all, to contrast—to make the differences clear—and to do this, you want the contrasted items to be somewhat similar.

Once you have made a chart, you can write your introductory sentence mentioning the categories into which you place each ability. For example, a good introductory sentence for this essay would be, "My brother and I differ in our abilities to work with machines, to learn languages, to play sports, and to make music."

Using this kind of chart as an outline for the body of your essay, you can now write a paragraph of contrast. Here are some examples of the

connectors you can use to indicate each contrast. Notice the structure and punctuation of the sentence for each connector.

I am good with machines; <u>however</u>, my brother isn't.

<u>Although</u> I get along well with people, my brother prefers to be alone.

My brother has musical talent. <u>In contrast</u>, I seem to be tone-deaf.

<u>Whereas</u> my brother is very good at chess, I cannot understand the game.

<u>While</u> I am good at sports, my brother is a little uncoordinated.

<u>In contrast with</u> my brother, who learns language easily, I can't get beyond the most basic phrases.

Your essay of contrast should be completed with a concluding sentence that summarizes your main points and lets the reader know that you have finished.

You can do the same thing with the more complicated contrast of arguments for and against euthanasia. First, write an introductory sentence, then chart the information that you will use to explain and support your ideas. Begin the chart by listing the arguments for euthanasia, then fill in the arguments against euthanasia that are directly related. In examples 4 and 5, some of the arguments are left out; try to fill in the blanks.

Example 4:	*Arguments for euthanasia*	*Arguments against euthanasia*
	1. Alleviates pain and suffering.	1. _____
	2. _____	2. Can't put value on life.
	3. There are cases where life is present but no hope.	3. Physicians can never be sure what tomorrow's medicine will bring.

Next, look at the arguments against euthanasia and counter with related arguments for it.

Example 5:	*Arguments for Euthanasia*	*Arguments against Euthanasia*
	1. _____	1. Oath of Hippocrates.
	2. _____	2. Doctors shouldn't "play God."

Some arguments do not have counter arguments that are directly related to them. For example, proponents of euthanasia argue that it is wrong to use hospital space, staff, and technical devices for patients who are going to die anyway, because they could be used for other patients. There is not really an argument on the other side to counter this, so it can be discussed after all of the matching arguments are made.

For this essay, you need to label each argument *for* or *against*. To introduce the arguments for euthanasia you can say "An argument for euthanasia is . . .," "Proponents of euthanasia argue that . . .," "Advocates of euthanasia feel that . . .," or similar phrases. To introduce the arguments against euthanasia you can use "Those who are against euthanasia argue that . . .," "Opponents of euthanasia think that . . .," "Those who oppose euthanasia believe that . . .," or similar phrases. You will also need to use connectors of contrast (*however, but, whereas, while,* and so forth) to point out the differences between the ideas of opponents and proponents of euthanasia.

Exercise 12: Answering an Essay Question of Contrast

Using the charts in examples 4 and 5 as an outline for the body of your essay, write an answer to the question, "What are the arguments for and against euthanasia that are discussed in 'Euthanasia'?" Be sure to write an introductory sentence and to use appropriate connectors and signal words to make the body of your essay clear and cohesive. Finish your essay with a concluding sentence that summarizes your main points.

Exercise 13: Additional Essay Questions

---

1. Trace the attitudes toward euthanasia discussed in this chapter from the first century B.C. in Greece to the present.
2. Discuss the cases of euthanasia or mercy killing mentioned in "The Right to Die" and their effects on people's attitudes toward these practices.

SOME SUGGESTED TOPICS FOR FURTHER READING

Oath of Hippocrates

machines that prolong life

the Living Will
Society for the Right to Die
Euthanasia Educational Council
Karen Ann Quinlan
Patient's Bill of Rights
suicide

7

More Reading Social Science

Streetcar Terminal, Oklahoma City, 1939

Basic Vocabulary

racisim	exploitation	per se
prejudice	stigmatizing	congruence
variable	stereotype	de facto
antipathy	bias	efficacy
overt	hostile	catharsis
prototype	recipient	authoritarian
assess	ex post facto	

Exercise 1: Skimming Practice

The chapter you are going to read in this unit is taken from a sociology book called Race Relations by Harry Kitano. This chapter, entitled "Prejudice," is part of a unit called "Perspectives and Problems in Race Relations." Begin your reading of the chapter by following the seven skimming steps. Do each step, one at a time, answering the questions before you go on to the next step. (The chapter begins on page 236.)

STEP 1: Read the title of the chapter and all of the headings. Notice how these relate to one another.

    a. What are the five main subtitles listed under the general title "Prejudice"?

    b. What are the four main subheadings under the subtitle "Reducing Prejudice"?

    c. What are the examples of symbolic explanations that are discussed in this chapter?

STEP 2: Examine pictures, charts, and other illustrations in the chapter to get information about the chapter's contents.

STEP 3: Find the names of people, organizations, and so on (proper nouns), and try to determine who or what they are.

    a. What is the significance of (Rose, 1951: 5) in paragraph 3?

    b. Who are La Piere, De Fleur, and Westie?

    c. Who is Hobbes (paragraph 19)?

    d. Who is Marx (paragraph 28)?

    e. What is meant by the Middle Ages?

STEP 4: Look at all of the italicized words and phrases. Be aware of the author's reasons for italicizing them. Italics are used in this chapter for subheadings, titles of books, and definitions.

    a. What is the name of the book mentioned in this chapter?

    b. Quickly find the definition given in this chapter for *ethnocentrism*.

STEP 5: Look at review questions and the partial bibliography at the end of the chapter to get more information about the chapter.

    a. Where was the article "A Social Distance Scale" published?

    b. Does this bibliography consist only of published works?

STEP 6: Rapidly read the first and last paragraphs of the chapter and the first sentence of each paragraph.

STEP 7: In a sentence or two, explain what you think this chapter is about. (You may answer orally or quickly write the answer that you would give orally.)

Exercise 2: Scanning for Details

This time you will try scanning the chapter before you read it rather than after you read it. Because you know only generally where information is located (from the headings), you will have to use very specific clues to find details. You won't be able to find information that you remember having already read.

Scan the chapter to find the answers to the following questions. Work as rapidly as you can.

1. What does the *F* in *F*-scale stand for (represent)?
2. How did the La Piere experiment work?
3. What does GSR stand for?
4. What is TAT?
5. What are the Chinese cook, the Mexican bandito, the Italian gangster, the treacherous Japanese, and the Step n' Fetchit Negro examples of?
6. What does the term *self-fulfilling prophecy* mean?
7. What is a *scapegoat*?
8. Why is *The Authoritarian Personality* significant?
9. In what ways do people avoid propaganda?

FIRST READING

Quickly read the chapter "Prejudice" from *Race Relations*. As you read, make notes in the margin. When you finish reading each section, use your margin notes to form questions about the main points of the section. This question technique will help you (as it has helped many American students) to organize the ideas of the chapter in your mind for future use.

Prejudice

Harry H. L. Kitano

1   One point of view emphasizes that prejudice on the part of the individual is the basic "cause" of racism, and the logical cure is to change the individual's attitude. Behind every racist institution and structure lies a prejudiced mind, and behind every racist action lies a racist attitude.

2   Psychologists have been especially active in analyzing prejudice as the primary independent variable in racism and the number of research studies is large. Nevertheless, there are many unresolved aspects to prejudice, and no single theory can satisfactorily explain it. Furthermore, the linkages between prejudice, discrimination, and racism remain hypotheses that have still to be empirically demonstrated.

DEFINITIONS

3   There are many definitions of prejudice. It is "a set of attitudes which causes, supports, or justifies discrimination" (Rose, 1951: 5); ". . . an emotionally rigid attitude, or predisposition to respond to a certain stimulus in a certain way toward a group of people" (Simpson and Yinger, 1965: 10); ". . . an antipathy based upon a faulty and inflexible generalization" (Allport, 1958).

4   Collins, in summarizing the various definitions of prejudice, lists the following common features (1970: 249):

1. Prejudice is an intergroup phenomenon.
2. Prejudice is a negative orientation.
3. Prejudice is bad.
4. Prejudice is an attitude.

Harry H. L. Kitano, *Race Relations*, © 1974, pp. 17–36. Reprinted by permission of Prentice-Hall, Inc., Englewood Cliffs, N.J.

5   From this summary, racial prejudice can be viewed as an attitude towards an ethnic group that is directed in negative and often stereotypic terms, and is based on a social, not a scientific definition of race and groups. An individual is hated, depised, shunned, and avoided because of membership in a particular group.

6   Our definition of racial prejudice is "a prejudgment of others through negative racial signs." By negative racial signs, we refer primarily to stereotypes, and their primary effect in race relations is avoidance. Therefore, our total definition includes the prejudgment (an attitude), the mechanism or technique that maintains or justifies the attitude (stereotyping), and its primary effect on intergroup relations (avoidance).

MEASURING PREJUDICE

7   Since prejudice is defined as an attitude, researchers have been able to follow the general models of attitudinal research to assess this variable. The basic assumption that attitudes are accurate predictors of behavior remains debatable; nevertheless, without this theoretical linkage, attitudinal research is quite meaningless.

8   Collins lists and criticizes some of the more common means of measuring prejudice (1970: 253–54).

The Self–Report

9   The usefulness of the self-report is limited primarily because of problems of validity. Can a person's response to a paper-and-pencil test measure his actual behavior in interracial situations? Generally, the self-report is gathered through an attitudinal scale. A person responds to a question such as, "By nature the Negro and the white man are equal"; and it is presumed that the prejudices of a person are revealed through his responses. The *F*(fascism)-scale drawn from *The Authoritarian Personality* (Adorno et al., 1950) and the Bogardus social-distance scale (1933) are examples of the paper-and-pencil self-report.

10   The self-report can be used to survey a respondent's attitudes toward an ethnic group. The experimenter can then introduce an independent variable by exposing the subject to new information or knowledge about the group, and follow it up with another self-report. The expected change between the first and second reports would illustrate the attitudinal change.

Observations of Overt Behavior

11   There has been little research linking overt behavior to prejudice. The major limitation is the problem of identifying the appropriate behaviors to be

measured and their association with significant attitudes. For example, although a person may hold "liberal attitudes" towards ethnic minorities, it is difficult for a researcher to observe his actual behavior in interracial situations. Perhaps the most valid technique would be for a researcher to live with a family for a period of time, but the time and cost problems present a major barrier. In contrast, the self-report attitudinal scale is easy to administer to large samples.

12   The La Piere experiment (1934) is one of the prototypes of the measurement of overt behavior. In this study, an Oriental couple traveled around the country, first writing for hotel reservations (high refusal) and then actually showing up (low refusal).

13   Recent work on nonverbal communication such as proxemics (Hall, 1963; Mehrabian, 1967) introduces behavioral techniques in the measurement of prejudice. Proxemics refers to the degree of closeness, directness, or intimacy of nonverbal interaction between two communicators. The major variables are distance (how far apart the communicators choose to be), eye contact (the percentage of time the communicators look into each other's eyes), and body relaxation (the amount of leaning forward or backward by the communicators). Negative racial feelings were supposed to be shown by remaining at a greater distance, less eye contact, and the tendency to lean away from rather than toward the other party.

14   Even these behavioral techniques, although objective, reliable, and quantifiable, can be misleading. For example, many Japanese deliberately avoid eye contact. They consider it rude to look directly into another person's eyes, and therefore their avoidance may be unrelated to racial prejudice. A knowledge of various cultural styles is important because similar behaviors may entail different motivations.

The De Fleur–Westie Study

15   A laboratory experiment by De Fleur and Westie (1958) linked attitudes and behavior. Subjects who had already taken a written test of attitudes were shown some colored photographic slides of a well-dressed, good-looking Negro man with a well-dressed white woman. Other slides showed a white man with a Negro woman. The subjects were then asked if they would be willing to be photographed with a Negro person of the opposite sex; they were then given a standard photograph release agreement. It was specified that the signature was necessary so that the photograph could be given public exposure. The subjects were to sign the release; those who refused to sign were considered to be prejudiced.

16   The findings indicated some consistency between behavior and attitudes. By both measurement techniques, eighteen subjects were classified as prejudiced and fourteen as unprejudiced. However, the remaining fourteen, or

nearly a third of the sample, behaved "inconsistently"—that is, they were classified as prejudiced under one measure and unprejudiced under the other.

Physiological Reactions

17   Another technique for assessing prejudice employs physiological measures. The galvanic skin response (GSR) has been used to assess prejudice (Cooper and Singer, 1956; Cooper and Siegel, 1956; De Fleur and Westie, 1958). The technique assesses only extreme responses, and not the direction of the attitude. However, with increased sophistication and continued use, this technique may become a valuable indicator.

Projective Techniques

18 . The projective test is a device whereby the subject is asked to respond to an unstructured stimulus such as a set of pictures (TAT) or to ink blots (Rorschach). Its use in the assessment of racial attitudes has been limited, and it remains somewhat unreliable, difficult to interpret, and expensive. The major advantage of this method is its indirectness; the unstructured responses and the lack of obvious "racist" stimuli reveal information that is relatively easy to conceal with a direct approach.

EXPLANATIONS OF PREJUDICE

19 Most explanations of prejudice are related to the scientific discipline of the observer.

> *Some theories of prejudice emphasize the historical aspect; they may regard slavery and Reconstruction as important variables in explaining the current Negro problem. Some theories lean toward an economic exploitation approach, emphasizing the functional nature of prejudice in maintaining an exploited group either for its labor or for its resources. A case may be made for urbanization, for industrialization, for the effects of materialism, depersonalization, and the mass culture; another point of view . . . emphasizes mobility in our society, either upward or downward.*
>
> *Broader theories, based on Hobbesian perspectives, find the roots of prejudice in the unsavory nature of man himself. Some theories emphasize prejudice as one outcome of the frustration-aggression model; others emphasize inadequate socialization and the development of the authoritarian personality; while others stress the importance of stereotypes. Each perspective can probably be partially validated with empirical data. But no one theory can explain every aspect of prejudice (Daniels and Kitano, 1970: 16–17).*

20   Simpson and Yinger (1965) mention that early studies were limited in their usefulness because they attempted to find simple, one-factor explanations. It would be difficult to defend a single causal factor or prejudice when we know that:

1. Groups differ in the direction and amount of prejudice they exhibit.

2. Individuals differ in the direction and amount of prejudice they exhibit.

3. Target groups change over time, and the *kinds* of target groups may also change.

21   One of the main tasks of the social scientist is to identify the process by which prejudice is acquired, developed, maintained, and transmitted. Hopefully, with this understanding the process can be reversed and prejudice can be reduced, controlled, or eliminated.

CLASSIFICATION OF CAUSES

22 There are various kinds of explanations for prejudice. Simpson and Yinger (1965) divide and discriminate by: (1) personality functions, (2) weapons in group conflict, (3) cultural factors, and (4) consequences on both the minority and majority groups.

23   Collins (1970) uses a two-level analysis schema on the causes of prejudice: societal and individual. Societal explanations trace the development of prejudice in a given social system, culture, or group, and have been the focus of historians, sociologists, anthropologists, and social psychologists. Individual explanations look for the causes of prejudice in the individual personality and have been the chief domain of psychologists, psychiatrists, and social workers.

24   There are four categories that encompass most of the explanations on how prejudice develops. We are omitting those views that explain prejudice as an inherited instinct, since our basic assumption is that prejudice is learned. The categories form simple guidelines, and they overlap somewhat: (1) exploitation, (2) ignorance, (3) racism-ethnocentrism, and (4) symbolic.

Exploitation Explanations

25   According to these theories, one group dominates another sexually, economically, and socially. The "inferior" group must be kept in its place so that the "superior" group can achieve and enjoy the advantages of better employment and social status. The inferior group pays higher rents, is charged higher prices, is denied the use of public facilities, and is paid lower wages.

This system has been called "a mask for privilege," and it describes how the economically advantaged are able to use and exclude rising groups from full participation in American life.

26   Slavery is an obvious and dramatic example of the exploitation of one group by another. There are several hypothesized conditions which can lead to this use of other human beings. First, the culture must have one primary goal, the maximization of profit. Second, societal organizations such as the business and educational establishments must also support this primary goal. Third, there must be a large labor force for the unpopular and menial jobs. Fourth, the inferior group must be considered heathen or subhuman and therefore deserving of unequal treatment. Finally, their skin color is also an important factor.

27   Nonwhite groups have felt the relationship between prejudice and economic exploitation. In California, the Chinese were wanted for labor, later the Japanese, then the Mexicans and the Filipinos. None of these groups was readily accepted into the larger society, and the minute their labors were no longer needed (or they desired to look for other than the menial agricultural positions), they faced heightened prejudice and discrimination.

28 *The Marxian Perspective*   Marxist writers have proffered the strongest explanation for prejudice as a tool in economic exploitation. Cox (1948) views racial prejudice as an attitude propagated among the public by an exploiting class for the purpose of labeling an inferior class. The inferiority is related to their supposed subhuman nature so that by stigmatizing a group as parahuman or inferior, the capitalist can exploit this group and their resources.

29   Under capitalism, labor is just another factor of production to be used in maximizing profit. It can be bought or sold on a dehumanized basis so that the importance of individuality and the family is minimized. Human beings are treated as commodities, little different from land and capital. Therefore, in capitalistic countries, the industrialists must proletarianize the masses; and in dealing with colonial, or nonwhite labor, they can go one stage further by denying them even the status of white proletariats.

30   As Mason states, ". . . the inhabitants of distant or outlying territories could be exploited even more ruthlessly than those at home, and with even less opportunity of revolt, while the domestic labor could be encouraged to take part, up to a point, in the exploitation" (1970: 62).

31   Race hostility and prejudice in the Marxist perspective are not the central issues of capitalism and imperialism. The central issue is class conflict. White people, in order to bolster their positions in the class structure, have been brought to look at nonwhites as a lower class. The correlation between racism and the development of capitalism, however, is one of cause and effect; therefore, the prediction is that race prejudice would disappear with the collapse of capitalism.

32   Broad theories such as the Marxist perspective are difficult to evaluate. Prejudice is relative—it is not an absolute in that one country or culture has it and another does not. All countries contain varying degrees of racism; it is not a trait peculiar only to capitalistic countries.

Ignorance

33   Explanations of prejudice based on ignorance cover a wide range. Ignorance can result from a simple lack of information and knowledge, from preset attitudes, false beliefs, selective perceptions and experiences, and from superficial knowledge of groups. Stereotypes and images projected through the mass media such as books, radio, magazines, newspapers, television, and the movies play on the ignorance of large numbers. Each of these factors keeps the ignorance and stereotypes of the past alive for new generations.

34   The simplest explanation is that prejudice results from pure ignorance. Asians are generally unknown in the eastern and southern states; the northern states have not had much contact with Mexican Americans; and there are rural areas that have had almost no contact with any ethnic group. Under these conditions, information about groups is garnered from whatever existing sources; and the influence and power of the mass media become extremely important.

35   For example there was a recent report of the stereotype of the "sneaky, tricky Jap" in Georgia. There are few Japanese in that state, and intergroup contacts are minimal, but a war movie had been shown on a popular TV time slot, and the World War II stereotype lingered in the minds of many viewers.

36   The problem is not solely regional. Segregation and separation reinforces a growing insulation between groups. Although there may be some contact in integrated work and school situations, there is seldom any meaningful social and emotional communication across ethnic and racial lines, and people remain generally ignorant of other groups. The mass media provide the only ethnic contact and exposure for many, and this is limited to stereotypes of the Chinese cook, the Mexican bandito, the Italian gangster, the treacherous Japanese, and the "Step n' Fetchit" Negro.

37 ***Selective Perceptions and Experiences***   Another series of events often shapes prejudice. When stereotypes of a group are already given wide credence, selective perceptions and experiences can validate the attitude. The term "self-fulfilling prophecy" is an apt one; for example, if a group is labeled loud and pushy, an experience with a member of that group who fits the stereotype reinforces the prejudice. Evidence concerning those who do not fit the label is usually ignored; and making exceptions such as "but he doesn't act like one of them" does nothing to upset the basic prejudice.

38   A particularly negative experience with a member of an ethnic group is

also used to reinforce prejudice. Individuals can "remember when," and these negative feelings remain in spite of numerous other intervening experiences and the passage of time.

39   The problem of selective perceptions is a constant one and remains a special barrier in attitudinal change. An emotional preset or bias works in such a manner that the viewer selects those incidents in a movie or those examples in a book that reinforce his prejudices and conveniently ignores the rest of the exposure.

40   Another technique that is related to selective perceptions is to place the blame for minority problems on the minorities themselves. It is referred to as the "earned reputation" approach by Rose (1951). This perspective shifts the responsibility from the dominant to the minority group. "It's their fault," "if only they would change, the problem of prejudice and discrimination will disappear," are statements that enable the majority to ignore the plight of ethnic groups.

41   A hypothesis by Rokeach, Smith, and Evans (1960) contends that a prejudiced person does not reject a person of another race, religion, or nationality because of ethnic membership per se but rather because he perceives that the other differs from him in important beliefs and values. The question he asks might be, "Can I be friends with that person" rather than "I don't like his color." Stein et al. (1971) devised an experiment that supported Rokeach's theory that the major portion of prejudice was based on belief congruence. They concluded that if different races encountered one another on the basis of equal status, which then led to shared beliefs, then racial prejudice could be substantially reduced. The basic assumption behind the belief congruence approach appears to involve an oversimplification of the problem. Perhaps the qualification, "other things being equal" (e.g., social class, values, goals, power, status, vulnerability) would be necessary; and such conditions are often themselves determined by ethnic group membership.

Ethnocentrism–Racism

42   Simpson and Yinger (1965) feel that the underlying attitude in the use of prejudice as a weapon in group conflict is *ethnocentrism*, the belief that one's own group is unique and "right." They see the phenomenon as almost universal.

43   As an individual is socialized to the beliefs and behaviors of his own family and society, he begins to feel that what he and his group do is "natural" and so begins to judge others from this standpoint. In this sense, ethnocentrism is almost inevitable since the very standards one uses to judge others are part of the culture he has absorbed. Those who deviate are then viewed as "unnatural" and can become the target of prejudice.

44   The family plays an important part in this process. The way one's family conducts itself is "normal." The food, the conversation, and the life style become

a part of a standard, and other families who differ may be judged strange, foreign, or alien.

45   Ethnocentrism is a part of the "identity" of an individual, and may be linked to other variables such as pride, belonging, standards, and the like. In this sense it is normal, and one may hypothesize that some measure of pride in one's own family and culture is a positive strength. It turns into a negative prejudice only when it becomes overly rigid and intolerant of the behavior of others.

46   One of the more damaging aspects of racism is the "reverse" ethnocentrism often observed in ethnic groups. An individual may lack even a minimal sense of pride in his own family and culture because of his constant exposure to American models. Therefore, rather than being proud of his family, or his ethnic background, the individual may deny his family, or "lie" about his background so that his immigrant parents are now fluent and acculturated, or he may attempt to pass as a member of the majority culture. This obviously destroys any healthy sense of identity for many ethnic group members. However, there is current evidence (e.g., "black is beautiful") that styles are changing.

47   Ethnocentrism mainly serves the group in power. The European colonists' self-esteem led them to think of Western civilization as the "best," and to lack respect for the achievements of Asian, African, and South American cultures. Prejudice provides the rationalization for those who want to maintain the equilibrium between the "dominant" and the "inferior."

48 *Structural Opposition*   Prejudice may also be conceptualized as a product of structural opposition. Prejudice is a part of the "we-they" phenomenon, and the very formation of one unity in contrast to another leads to certain conditions. As Daniels and Kitano say, "[we prefer] . . . an interpretation in which a man is a member of a group of a certain kind by virtue of his nonmembership in other groups. A person belongs to a tribe or its segment, and membership is activated when there is opposition to this tribe. Therefore a man sees himself as a member of a group only in opposition to other groups, and he sees a member of another group as a member of a social unity, however much that unit may be split into opposing segments" (1970: 19). Social groups form because in response to stimuli, people choose to associate with certain persons and not with others. A football team is not really an entity until there is an opponent; once the opposition is present, prejudice between the "enemies" can be predicted.

49   Although race and color prejudice are the current divisive issues, other conflicts were more central in previous eras. Religious differences were major problems of the Middle Ages, and the world was divided between "superior" and "inferior" religions. Great amounts of prejudice are also found in class and national conflicts.

Symbolic Explanations

50   Another group of theories views prejudice as a symptom, a symbol, or a byproduct stemming from other concerns. Psychological symptom theories are most often associated with Freudian psychoanalytic thought. The basic assumption in Freudian theory is that all behavior is psychically determined and that prejudice, as a symptom, is a reflection of deeper intrapsychic phenomena.

51 *Prejudice as a Displacement of Hostility—Scapegoating*   Social psychological theory has emphasized frustration-aggression as one of the critical variables behind prejudice. The blockage of goal-directed behavior, whether by other people, by natural forces, or by one's own lack of skill or unrealistic expectations, is a frustrating experience and creates hostile impulses. In many instances this hostility cannot be directed against the primary source of the frustration; it may be too powerful and it may retaliate; in other cases, the source of frustration cannot be easily identified. In any case, the individual may then direct his hostile impulses against a more convenient target, or a scapegoat. Less powerful but readily identifiable racial groups can become the unwilling recipients of such hostility. The studies of Dollard and Miller (1939) and their colleagues typify this point of view. The very ineffectiveness of the frustration-hostility-scapegoat cycle can lead to the further development of prejudice. The frustrated individual may feel somewhat guilty about his displaced hostility, and the effectiveness of the outlet may be open to question. Therefore as guilt and anxiety develop, there may be further displacement and hostility towards the scapegoat, which serves to reinforce the vicious cycle.

52 *Displacement*   Displacement is the process whereby the hostility is directed towards a target that cannot realistically be shown to be the cause of one's difficulties. A classical example of displacement is the case of German anti-Semitism described by Dollard and Miller (1939).

53   From 1914 to 1933, the Germans developed a policy of overt anti-Semitism. Rather than channeling their hostilities directly toward the all-powerful Allies who had defeated them in war, dictated the Treaty of Versailles, and forced them to relinquish their colonies, the Germans vented their frustrations against the Jews. The subsequent depression, the ruinous inflation, and the collapse of their economic system was blamed on the Jews, and anti-Semitism was one of Hitler's planks in his rise to power.

54   There is some evidence that the choice of a scapegoat is not a purely random factor. Some are attacked, but not others. The attack is not always against the weakest, but often against those who are stronger and potentially more dangerous.

55   Both the frustration-aggression and displacement explanations analyze prejudice as an indirect rather than a direct phenomenon. Therefore, any attempt

to solve the problem without an attack on the "real causes" may be futile. The theories, although plausible on an ex post facto basis, are difficult to validate because of the relativity of such concepts as frustration and aggression and because of the difficulty of operationalizing the terms adequately. Nevertheless, these views do not see prejudice as a simple, linear phenomenon, but one involving different levels and orders.

56 ***Rationalization***   Rationalization is similar to the "earned reputation" approach. In both the actor attempts to justify actions that he knows to be wrong with the explanation that the victim "deserves what he gets" or "gets what is coming to him." By this process, prejudicial attitudes can be justified, and restrictive acts and outright violence can be rationalized.

57   Neutralization is a common technique that is used to dehumanize the intended victim. By defining the victim as less than human (animals are a favorite label, especially dogs, rats, and pigs), the actor can permit himself to do what he had previously inhibited himself from doing. Labelling and categorization play an important part in the dehumanization process.

58   The process is an extremely common one and may be more closely related to discrimination (action) than to prejudice (attitude). The ease with which other human beings can be bombed, burned, and destroyed simply by labelling them "the enemy" is frightening, especially when such behavior is often cloaked in self-righteousness, morality, patriotism, and heroism. Further, there is often a lack of prejudice by those who destroy ("I don't hate them"; "I was just doing my duty") which further removes the act from a sense of emotion, participation, and reality.

59 ***Prejudice Caused by a "Sick" Personality***   Another explanation of prejudice views the problem as a result of improper socialization and the development of a "sick" personality. The most well-known view from this perspective is found in *The Authoritarian Personality* (1950), which was the joint product of a group of psychologists headed by Adorno, Frenkel-Brunswik, Levinson, and Sanford, who were based primarily in Berkeley several years after the end of World War II. The study focused on the relationship between personality structure and prejudice, especially anit-Semitism.

60   Although the authors leaned heavily on Freud's structure of the personality, they were guided by academic psychology when dicussing the more directly observable and measurable aspects of personality. Their findings encouraged the view that the prejudiced person was closer to a pathological personality than the normal person. For example, the authoritarian was pessimistic, cynical, anti-intellectual, distrustful, suspicious, dogmatic, and lacking in poise and appearance. On the other hand, those low in prejudice were flexible, tolerant, autonomous, self-reliant, and possessed realistic goal orientations.

61   There have been many criticisms of the interpretations in *The Authoritarian Personality*. Its methodological weaknesses include biased sampling procedures, no control for education and group membership, and the dubious coding procedures of the qualitative material. The interpretations are open to question, and replications of various subscales have brought out conflicting and contradictory material.

62   Nevertheless, *The Authoritarian Personality* was a valuable addition to the study of race relations. It brought together many of the scattered works of the previous era, provided a series of empirical tools for analyzing prejudice, encouraged research, and served as an impetus for a legion of studies in this vital area.

Social Change

63   A more sociological perspective mentioned by Park (1950) relates the "cause" of prejudice to social change. The more rapid the social change, the higher the degree of prejudice. Conversely, the more static a society, the lesser the degree of prejudice. We add that the higher the diversity of groups, the higher the probability of prejudice.

64   Prejudice, from this perspective is essentially a conservative tool. It is used to retain a social distance and to preserve the social order. In a rigid and static class-caste system, the internal organizations and patterns of communication are established, and most people know their place in the society. Therefore, there are few constant challenges to status and power, and prejudice is hypothesized to be low.

65   In a rapidly changing culture with multiple and diverse groups there are constant challenges to status. The need to retain social distance becomes higher, and prejudice is hypothesized as one consequence of this state. The great amount of prejudice in our rapidly changing, multi-group culture demonstrates the validity of this perception.

66   The view of prejudice as a resultant of changing social forces is intriguing but almost impossible to evaluate. Japan's rapid change into an industrial giant may not have been accompanied by a high rise in prejudice since her social institutions (e.g., family "ie" system) are so stable. Thus other variables must be taken into account.

67   In summary, the "causes" of prejudice are multiple, varied, and interactive. We assume that it is learned and that it has both positive and negative functions. However, race prejudice is primarily a negative phenomenon because it is a prejudgment, a stereotyping, and a condemnation of a whole race. As such, it creates barriers between entire groups and fosters conditions that can lead to more destructive intergroup actions. Therefore, although it is unrealistic to think it can ever be completely eliminated, we should give the highest priority

to programs aimed at reducing it through fostering healthier intergroup and interpersonal patterns.

REDUCING PREJUDICE

68 Prejudice-reducing programs are closely linked to hypothesized causes. Since these differ so widely, it is important that the programs be based on the theories, otherwise the attempts will appear diffuse and unrelated.

Lessening Exploitation: Equal-Status Contact

69   One of the most common prescriptions for eliminating prejudice is to get rid of the capitalistic system. The basic assumption is that the exploitation and the competitiveness under free enterprise is directly related to prejudicial attitudes. Although this assumption is difficult to validate empirically, it is logical to speculate whether there are any "prejudice-free" societies under other forms of government. As far as we know, there are none. But since the term "prejudice-free" is relative rather than absolute, some societies are considered to be less racially prejudiced than others. South Africa is generally considered to have one of the most highly prejudiced systems, whereas Brazil and the state of Hawaii have among the lowest prejudiced systems.

70   Bettelheim and Janowitz (1964), along with Dicks (1959), suggest solutions to intergroup conflict through social and economic changes that would reduce the feelings of fear and deprivation by controlling certain sources of prejudice such as unemployment and by guaranteeing security such as extending social welfare. These solutions remain long range rather than immediate and are difficult to assess.

71   Some advocate increased contact as a means of lessening interethnic fears and anxieties. The contact method has at times proved effective where members of different groups have equal economic and social status. By destroying old stereotypes, the person feels compelled to change his beliefs and attitudes toward the outgroup. He feels uneasy when his feelings and beliefs toward the outgroup are inconsistent, and he tries to bring them into congruence (Rosenberg, 1956).

72   But contact can work both ways. It may confirm stereotypes by actually forcing the outgroup to behave according to the stereotype. For example, a prejudiced person with unfavorable stereotypes of an outgroup may react negatively towards that group, which in turn will induce a member of the outgroup to behave in congruence with the prejudiced person's stereotype. Rosenthal's study (1964) indicated that teacher attitudes toward minority-group children

as being "really not educable" had been an important cause in their low academic achievement.

73   Contact itself may be rather specific. A study by Secord and Backman (1964) shows that contact with certain minority-group members in particular situations destroys only those stereotypes formed in that situation. For example, interaction with minority-group members as neighbors eventually leads to greater acceptance of those members, but only in that particular role. Another example can be found in the greater acceptance and willingness to work with members of minority groups if there is direct contact on the job. However other prejudiced attitudes may remain scarcely changed.

74   Studies of occupational contact have shown that reduction of prejudice does not go beyond the work situation. Reed's (1947) and Minard's (1952) studies have indicated that wider community norms have often made off-the-job friendships extremely difficult or impossible. Another factor that may preclude reduction of prejudice beyond the work situation is distance of housing between coworkers due to segregated neighborhoods. Mandelbaum's study (1952) of the air force, where residential segregation does not prevail among personnel, supports this assumption.

75   Many studies indicate that contact per se is not sufficient in reducing racial prejudice. Cole, Steinberg, and Burkheimer (1968) found that token integration and passive, uninvolved contact did little to reduce the prejudice and hostility of white students toward blacks.

76   Contact methods in reducing prejudice by unlearning attitudes and re-evaluating the outgroup are successful under the following conditions. First, the behavior of the member of the outgroup who comes into contact with the prejudiced person must not conform to the stereotype, and the outgroup member's beliefs must be congruent with those of the prejudiced person. Second, the duration of the relationship must be long and the sample large enough so that the prejudiced person cannot attribute his change in attitude to the specific contact situation or to individual exceptions to the rule. Third, the prejudiced person must be able to perceive those behaviors that are inconsistent with his fixed, stereotyped perceptions of the outgroup (Collins, 1970: 317).

The Shared-Coping Approach

77   This approach supplements the previously discussed approaches by explaining when and how prejudice is reduced through intergroup contact. It proposes that prejudice can be reduced through intergroup contact involving shared goals and shared-coping to achieve these goals, which in part foster cooperation and interdependence.

78   The shared goal promotes cohesiveness of the group (whether it be a fund-raising party or survival in a lifeboat), requires group interdependence, and

promotes a common fate for all involved. Shared-coping and cooperation is thus deemed necessary to achieve these goals, for it reinforces the unlearning mechanisms and reduces misperception.

79   Feshbach and Singer (1957) found that the creation of superordinate goals produces a new in-group composed of minority and majority members, and that reduction of prejudice proceeds by having both groups work toward the superordinate goals.

80   Shared-coping experiences also tend to reduce ethnic prejudice through the development of intergroup friendships. These friendships tend to foster greater acceptance of other members of a minority group and of the group as a whole. It also encourages the prejudiced person to be more receptive to favorable information concerning the minority group; it also tends to close the social distance in other contact situations since the role of a friend is quite varied. Finally, intergroup friendship forces the prejudiced person to bring into congruence and consistency the views that he holds of his friend to those that he holds of the outgroup.

81   Studies indicate that the more acquaintance one has with members of an outgroup, the more favorable the attitude towards the entire group in general (Orata, 1927; Diggins, 1927; Gray and Thompson, 1953). A study by Stouffer and his colleagues (1949) shows how the interaction between shared goals and shared-coping during World War II between black and white soldiers reduced prejudice. The research was initiated when units were mixed racially due to the extreme shortage of white infantry replacements; black volunteers were then recruited into replacement platoons previously restricted to all-white companies. Those who had closer cooperative intergroup contact with black soldiers were less prejudiced than those who did not.

82   We believe that the studies indicate some success in reducing prejudice under certain proscribed conditions such as equal status contact. The findings support the attempts to eliminate discriminatory barriers in housing, education, and jobs in order that minorities may eventually have the opportunity to meet their white peers on an equal level.

Ignorance

83   If ignorance is one of the main reasons for prejudice, then the preferred solution would be to provide information. Prejudice can be reduced by re-socializing those who have been exposed to misinformation and thus have made overgeneralizations, formed misconceptions, and made incorrect causal attributions. Therefore, evidence conveying information contrary to this misinformation could reduce prejudice. Two major vehicles useful for conveying such evidence would be propaganda and education.

Propaganda

84   Although propaganda under certain conditions has been found effective in reducing prejudice, studies have shown that people tend to avoid propaganda (Lazarsfeld, 1944). Even if not avoided entirely, people tend to receive different implications from the propaganda from what was intended. Cooper and Johoda (1947) describe four such mechanisms for propaganda evasion.

1. Although the message may be initially understood and followed, people finally miss the main appeal of the message.

2. People may understand the message but proclaim it invalid or as not revealing ther entire picture, or they may rationalize by stating that a few prejudices are permissible.

3. Studies have shown that propaganda aimed at increasing tolerance has instead increased or reinforced prejudice (Bettelheim and Janowitz, 1964). It is believed that those who have strongly cemented prejudiced attitudes often selectively perceive and interpret information and facts to fit their views.

4. Often the person to whom the appeal is being made lacks the education to understand it.

85   Propaganda has been found successful when projected to captive audiences (especially through motion pictures) and when prejudiced attitudes are initially low. But its effectiveness remains questionable when applied to those already highly prejudiced. Protolerance campaigns in the past have been ineffective because of the great amount of avoidance and evasion.

Education

86   Many studies indicate that those who have more education tend to be less prejudiced (Bettelheim and Janowitz, 1964; Harding et al., 1954). However, the variables of income, social status, and intelligence that usually accompany higher education tend to cloud the efficacy of education per se in reducing prejudice.

87   In other studies, however, higher education has led to more prejudice toward ethnic groups. McNeill's study (1960) showed that prejudice actually increased from the tenth to the twelfth grade; Sims and Patrick (1936) showed that attitudes of prejudice increased among northern students attending a southern university, whereas there was a reduction in the prejudice of southern students attending a northern university, which indicates that geographical location is also an important variable. However, Stember's study (1961) did

conclude that less rigid ethnic attitudes were more prevalent among those with higher education than those with less.

88   The kind of education one is exposed to in elementary school may also be a crucial variable in prejudice reduction. A study conducted by Litcher and Johnson (1969) investigating the effects of curriculum materials on racial attitudes found a marked positive change of attitude of white elementary school students toward Negroes after a multiethnic reader was used.

89   Special education programs directly aimed at reducing prejudice have often been successful, but the specific agents responsible for attitude change still remain unknown. Probably the most ambitious and controversial program involving the educational system has been that of school busing. The logic of different racial and class groups working together in school seems valid, especially since de facto segregation will probably limit effective contact at any other time. But so many other issues have entered into the argument that there is little room for calm discussion. The notion that busing is a "sociological experiment" is a defensible one, but interestingly enough, the term is often used disparagingly to imply that it is unworthy of consideration. But unless children get together at some time in their lives, their sole means of communication and interaction may remain at the stereotyped level.

The Symptom Theory Approach

90   Suggestions offered by those who believe in symptom theories, which claim that the cause of prejudice is maintained by psychological conflict, tend to solve the problem of prejudice by reconstructing the psychological conflicts that underlie prejudice. However, according to Ashmore (Collins, 1970: 298), direct methods to reduce prejudice will not work if one adheres to the symptom theories because of the following reasons:

1. Prejudice functions as a crutch for people to solve inner conflict, tension, and anxiety. Therefore, if prejudice is used in this manner, one encounters high resistance to change of attitudes.
2. Efforts to reduce prejudice may, in fact, increase its intensity since they may increase the psychological conflicts within the individual.
3. If the symptom (prejudice) is removed, but the actual personal conflict that caused it is not removed, the person will in fact find another target on which to vent his hostility.

91   Therefore Ashmore suggests the following indirect methods as a more successful means for reducing prejudice:

Psychotherapy

92   Perhaps the most effective method of reducing prejudice would be to work on the individual's basic personality structure while attempting to integrate the personality and eliminate the hostility toward target groups. There has been conflicting evidence of the efficacy of this method. Pearl (1955) found psychotherapy to actually increase rejection of target groups, whereas Allport (1958) has found that therapy reduces it.

93   However, in view of the high expense, time consumption, and questionable efficacy of individual psychotherapy, more attention has been given to group therapy. Studies by Haimowitz and Haimowitz (1950) revealed actual reduction in prejudice by using the Rogerian Group therapy of evaluating change in intergroup attitudes and measuring actual reduction of social distance. But because of the biased nature of their sample of twenty-four highly educated and ethnically mixed people, broad generalizations could not be drawn from their results. As Ashmore points out, one cannot be certain whether "intergroup contact" or group therapy itself improved personality structure and was responsible for reducing social distance. Pearl's studies (1954, 1955) showed that some aspects of group therapy reduced ethnocentric attitudes. Rubin's study (1967) in sensitivity training revealed that improved self-concepts and more self-acceptance increased acceptance of outgroups. This study also involved an ethnically mixed sample of whites and blacks so that the change of attitude could also be partially explained by intergroup contact.

94   The effectiveness of group therapy is probably high, although studies have not yet revealed how it actually does reduce prejudice. Is it, in fact, the group therapy itself or the intergroup contact that is responsible? The independent effects of these two factors must be further analyzed before the effectiveness of group therapy can be assessed.

95   More recent variations of the group approach include "t" groups, encounter sessions, and interracial confrontations. Because of their recency and the lack of research data, there is little experimental evidence to demonstrate the effectiveness of these approaches.

Insight

96   Self-insight training has been found effective in several experiments. Katz, Sarnoff, and McClintock (1956) used this technique by reasoning that if prejudice is an attitude that one uses for ego defense, then one can reduce prejudice through insight into its true nature. This insight, which would bring about reorganization of the personality, would make one less dependent on ego-defense mechanisms.

97   Subsequent studies have also found self-insight procedures to be effective

in reducing prejudice, although the role of the reorganized personality has been questioned. Stotland, Katz, and Patchen (1959) found self-insight methods most effective when motivated by an appeal to a consistent pattern in attitude, behavior, and values. This result brings into question the precise mechanisms of attitude change.

98   How effective this self-insight training will be on the average citizen also remains in doubt, for all subjects in past research have been college students. It is felt that college students are more concerned about self-consistency and are also more skilled in language and logic than the general population, which would produce a bias in the research.

Catharsis

99   The basic assumption of catharsis is that verbal release of hostility reduces aggression. This assumption has been challenged by the research of Bandura and Walters (1963) and by Berkowitz (1962). Overt release of hostility may actually increase prejudice by reinforcing the expression of hostility and may even increase prejudice in other directions.

Alternative Means of Reducing Tension

100   Release of tension through one activity may result in decreasing tension in another sphere. Bettelheim and Janowitz (1964) report that under normal conditions, tensions could be handled with greater ease if people could engage in mutually gratifying sexual relations. Pleasing as this alternative may seem, its probability of success remains very tenuous.

Change in Child–Rearing Practices

101   Changes in child-rearing practices have been encouraged by proponents of the authoritarian personality explanation of prejudice as the only permanent way of reducing prejudice. This method would concentrate on eliminating personality conflict before it develops by teaching parents to be more understanding and less capricious and authoritarian in their control over their child. This approach, which was especially popular several decades ago, appears simplistic and naive today. Nevertheless it would be difficult to argue against encouraging the development of healthy children through better socialization techniques.

102   There is one consistent omission in the study of prejudice which is both welcome and unwelcome at the same time. The majority of studies concentrate on the dominant white group; this is appropriate since their power remains the most important consideration. Nevertheless there is very little about the development and maintenance of prejudice among the ethnics. Is the function

and process of prejudice the same in the minority groups? How does one change the attitudes of the minority? The study of prejudice up to now has been primarily from and about the white majority point of view.

103   In summary, the techniques for the reduction of prejudice are as broad and varied as the "causes." The evidence of the effectiveness of various approaches remains indefinite, and research evidence presents conflicting results. However, there is some agreement that prejudice can be reduced under the broad conditions of equal-status contact, where people work together under cooperative conditions; where role positions are equal and complementary; where past experiences have not been too damaging; where the people have knowledge about the other group so that feedback is positive and negative stereotypes do not develop. But, as we emphasize, such conditions are quite difficult to achieve in modern-day America.

104   There is one grave concern about the problem of prejudice in our complicated social system. A nonprejudiced leader cannot do much in reshaping an institution in terms of racism; perhaps his power is essentially negative in that he can prevent certain things from happening. Conversely, an extremely prejudiced person can wield a great deal of influence over racist practices. To think of the actions of extremely prejudiced individuals in positions of great power is frightening.[1]

105   We would also emphasize that very few researchers today would defend the position that prejudice is the sole or the main cause of racist behavior. However, it remains as one important factor among a complex of other factors that contribute to the problem.

BIBLIOGRAPHY

ADORNO, T. W., ELSE FRENKEL-BRUNSWIK, D. J. LEVINSON, and R.N. SANFORD (1950). *The Authoritarian Personality*. New York: Harper & Row, Publishers.

ALLPORT, G. W. (1958). *The Nature of Prejudice*. New York: Doubleday & Company, Inc.

ASHMORE, R. D. (1969). "Intergroup Contact as a Prejudice-reduction Technique: An Experimental Examination of the Shared-coping Approach and

---

[1] Our national experiences built upon the prejudices of anti-Communism remain too recent for objective evaluation. Nevertheless it would appear that a high proportion of critical, rational decisions of national policy were built upon prejudiced viewpoints about the nature of the "enemy."

Four Alternative Explanations." Unpublished Ph.D. dissertation. Los Angeles: University of California.

BANDURA, A. and R. H. WALTERS (1963). *Social Learning and Personality Development*. New York: Holt, Rinehart & Winston, Inc.

BANTON, MICHAEL (1967). *Race Relations*. London: Tavistock Publications.

BERKOWITZ, L. (1962). *Aggression: A Social Psychological Analysis*. New York: McGraw-Hill Book Company.

BETTELHEIM, B. and M. JANOWITZ (1964). *Social Change and Prejudice*. New York: The Free Press.

BOGARDUS, E. S. (1933). "A Social Distance Scale." *Sociology and Social Research*, 17: 265–71.

BURNSTEIN, E. and A. V. McRAE (1962). "Some Effects of Shared Threat and Prejudice in Racially Mixed Groups." *Journal of Abnormal and Social Psychology*, 64: 257–63.

CAMPBELL, E. Q. (1958). "Some Social Psychological Correlates of Direction in Attitude Change." *Social Forces*, 36: 335–40.

Exercise 3: Basic Vocabulary Chart

Use your English-to-English dictionary to help you complete this chart. Put the chart on a separate sheet of paper so that you will have room to write all of the appropriate definitions and related words. Provide the meaning of the word as it is used in the indicated paragraph.

Word	Part of Speech	Meaning (as used in indicated paragraph)	Related Words	Synonyms
racism (1)				
prejudice (1)				
variable (2)				
antipathy (3)				
overt (11)				
prototype (12)				

Word	Part of Speech	Meaning (as used in indicated paragraph)	Related Words	Synonyms
assess (17)				
exploitation (24)				
stigmatizing (28)				
stereotype (35)				
bias (39)				
hostile (51)				
recipient (51)				
ex post facto (55)				
per se (75)				
congruence (80)				
de facto (89)				
efficacy (92)				
catharsis (99)				
authoritarian (101)				

Exercise 4: Word Substitution with Basic Vocabulary

For each of the following sentences, choose one of the following words or phrases that has the same meaning as the underlined word or phrase. Write the answer in the blank.

aversion	observable	race prejudice
preconceptions	appraise	brands
antagonistic	dictatorial	

1. <u>Racism</u> often prevents people from getting the jobs they need to live the kind of life they desire.

   _____

2. Most people have a great deal of <u>antipathy</u> toward the practice of genocide.

   _____

3. The prejudices of some people are more <u>overt</u> than those of others.

   _____

4. Before asking for money for car repairs, we must first <u>assess</u> the damage that the accident caused.

   _____

5. When the military <u>stigmatizes</u> the enemy as subhuman, it is easier for a soldier to kill his fellow human beings.

   _____

6. Our <u>biases</u> often cause us to perceive only those incidents that reinforce our prejudices.

   _____

7. People can usually sense when others have <u>hostile</u> feelings toward them, even when those feelings are not expressed overtly.

   _____

8. His <u>authoritarian</u> approach to problems causes many people to refuse to work for him.

   _____

SYNONYMS

Synonyms are words that have generally the same meaning. Sometimes one can be substituted for another, but often they have slightly different meanings and therefore must be used in different situations. For example *slim* and *skinny* have the same general meaning, but *slim* is a more complimentary word. When you say that someone is *skinny*, you are really saying that you think the person is *too* thin, rather than that he or she looks good that way.

Despite the need to be very careful when you use synonyms in your writing and speaking, it is useful to learn synonyms as a means of expanding your vocabulary. In addition, it is good to be able to recognize synonyms as you read, because writers use synonyms to make their writing more interesting.

Exercise 5: Recognizing Synonyms

Match the words on the left with their synonyms on the right. When you have finished, look up the answers to the ones you did not know.

1. stigmatize _____
d 2. bias _____
h 3. recipient _____
4. congruent _____
e 5. catharsis _____
b 6. authoritarian _____
c 7. per se _____
a 8. hostile _____

a. malevolent
b. commanding
c. intrinsically
d. slant
e. purification
f. conforming
g. blemish
h. beneficiary

Exercise 6: Guessing Word Meanings from Context

Try to guess the meanings of the underlined words in the following sentences from "Prejudice." Begin by underlining the words and phrases that give you the clues you need to make a good guess, then write your definition of the word on the line under the sentence. Do not look these words up in your dictionary until *after* you have guessed their meanings.

Example: Marxist writers have <u>proffered</u> the strongest explanation for prejudice as a tool in economic exploitation.

The cue word in this sentence is *explanation*. What does a person do with an explanation? One can *give* an explanation, or *offer* one. The word *proffer* means to *offer or suggest*.

1. Human beings are treated as <u>commodities</u>, little different from land and capital.

   _____

2. The term "<u>self-fulfilling prophecy</u>" is an apt one; for example, if a group is labeled loud and pushy, an experience with a member of that group who fits the stereotype reinforces the prejudice.

   _____

3. The food, the conversation, and the life style become a part of a

standard, and other families who differ may be judged strange, foreign, or <u>alien</u>.

_____

4. By defining the victim as less than human (animals are a favorite label, especially dogs, rats, and pigs), the actor can permit himself to do what he had previously <u>inhibited</u> himself from doing.

_____

5. He feels uneasy when his feelings and beliefs toward the outgroup are inconsistent, and he tries to bring them into <u>congruence</u>.

_____

6. But contact can work both ways. It may <u>confirm</u> stereotypes by actually forcing the outgroup to behave according to the stereotype.

_____

7. Many studies indicate that those who have more education tend to be less prejudiced. However, the variables of income, social status, and intelligence that usually accompany higher education tend to cloud the <u>efficacy</u> of education alone in reducing prejudice.

_____

Exercise 7: Guessing Word Meanings by Word Analysis

Prefixes	Meanings
pre- (prim-)	first, before
inter-	between, among
para-	beyond, aside from
co-	with, together, jointly
multi-	many

Stems	Meanings
-dic-	say, speak
-cred-	believe
-uni-	one
-equi-	equal

Use the meanings of the preceding stems and prefixes to analyze the following words and guess their meanings. Circle the letter of the best answer.

1. *interracial*   If something is interracial, it is:

    a. between races.

    b. within a race.

    c. against a race.

2. *parahuman*   Something that is parahuman is:

    a. better than human.

    b. consisting of two persons.

    c. less than human.

3. *credence*   If a story has credence, it is:

    a. not easy to believe.

    b. easy to believe.

    c. hard to understand.

4. *universal*   A universal idea is one that is:

    a. believed all over the world.

    b. believed in only one part of the world.

    c. difficult to explain to people from other countries.

5. *multiethnic*   A neighborhood that is multiethnic includes:

    a. only one ethnic group.

    b. two ethnic groups.

    c. several different ethnic groups.

6. *predictor*   The cover of a book is not always a good predictor of what

    it contains. In other words, _____

    _____.

NOTE TAKING

Good note taking consists of reading carefully enough to decide what the main ideas and the important supporting points are in each paragraph. Headings should be used to help with note taking. Be sure that all questions you can form by using the headings are answered in your notes.

In addition to main ideas and support for those ideas, it is a good idea to write down your reaction to what you read in your notes. These reactions should be kept separate from the text material, however. You can put notes from the textbook on one side of the page, and put your reaction to this information on the other side of the page. For example, suppose you are reading some information that brings questions to your mind. You will read on to find the answers, but if the text does not give you a good answer to your question, you should write that question in your notebook on the page across from the page on which you wrote the main and supporting ideas of the reading. If you disagree with an idea that the author expresses, you should explain why on the opposite page. Finally, you may want to write your own examples that support the main ideas of the text. By reacting to the text as you read it, you will find that you will remember the important information.

SECOND READING

Read the chapter "Prejudice" from *Race Relations* again carefully. As you read, try to find the main ideas in each paragraph or paragraphs and underline them. Also, look for the supporting information that explains the main idea. As you finish reading each complete section, write notes from your reading on a separate sheet of paper.

POST–READING

REACTION QUESTIONS

1. Which method of measuring prejudice appears to be the most effective?

2. Which of the causes of prejudice given in this chapter seem reasonable to you? Why do you think these are possible causes?

3. Which of the ideas mentioned for reducing prejudice do you think could actually work?

4. What kinds of prejudice have you seen in your country?

5. Is there anything being done in your country to reduce the damage caused by prejudice?

6. When you closely examine your own ideas and behavior, what prejudices do you find?

Exercise 8: Short-Answer Comprehension Questions

The questions in this exercise are based on some of the main ideas and important supporting information in the chapter. Use your notes on the chapter to answer as many questions as you can. Skim the chapter to find the answers that were not in your notes.

1. What elements do all the definitions of prejudice have in common?

2. What is the author's definition of prejudice?

3. What are the disadvantages of the *self-report?*

4. Why can behavioral techniques be misleading as a method of measuring prejudice?

5. What is the problem with using physiological responses to measure prejudice?

6. What are the advantages and disadvantages of the projective technique?

7. What makes it difficult to defend a single causal factor for prejudice?

8. According to the exploitation theory, what are the conditions that can lead to slavery?

9. According to Marxist theory, what is the main reason for prejudice?

10. What are the factors that cause the ignorance that leads to prejudice?

11. How does ethnocentrism contribute to prejudice?

12. What is *reverse ethnocentrism?*

13. What is *scapegoating?*

14. What is the main idea of the book *The Authoritarian Personality?*

15. According to sociological theory, how is social change related to prejudice?

16. Under what conditions are contact methods successful in reducing prejudice?

17. In what ways do people avoid the effects of propaganda?

18. According to those who believe in symptom theories, what is the cause of prejudice?

19. Does the author of this chapter believe that any of the techniques for reducing prejudice are completely effective?

UNDERSTANDING PARAPHRASING

Exercise 9: Paraphrasing Practice

Paraphrase these sentences by following the directions after each.

1. There are many definitions of prejudice.

    a. Begin your sentence with <u>Prejudice</u> and use a definition marker. (*can be defined, is defined*)

    _____

    _____

2. An individual is hated, despised, shunned, and avoided because of membership in a particular group.

    a. Substitute synonyms for <u>individual</u> and <u>shunned</u>.

    b. Use *because* rather than <u>because of</u> and change the remainder of the sentence to make it grammatically correct.

    _____

    _____

3. There has been little research linking overt behavior to prejudice.

    a. Make <u>little research</u> the subject of the sentence.

    b. Use a phrase other than <u>linking</u>. (*showing the relationship between, connecting*).

    _____

    _____

4. Another technique for assessing prejudice employs physiological measures.

    a. Substitute synonyms for <u>assessing</u> and <u>employs</u>.

b. Substitute a different connective for <u>another</u>. (*in addition, also*)

_____

_____

5. Slavery is an obvious and dramatic example of the exploitation of one group by another.

   a. Make the noun <u>example</u> into the verb of the sentence. (*exemplify*)

   b. Make <u>obvious</u> and <u>dramatic</u> into adverbs rather than adjectives.

_____

_____

6. As an individual is socialized to the beliefs and behaviors of his own family, and society, he begins to feel that what he and his group do is "natural" and so begins to judge others from this standpoint.

   a. Substitute other connectives for <u>as</u> and <u>so</u>.

   b. Substitute synonyms for <u>individual</u> and <u>standpoint</u>.

_____

_____

7. Rather than channeling their hostilities directly toward the all-powerful allies who had defeated them in war, dictated the Treaty of Versailles, and forced them to relinquish their colonies, the Germans vented their frustrations against the Jews.

   a. Find a substitute phrase for <u>channeling their hostilities</u>. (*being hostile*)

   b. Substitute another phrase for <u>Rather than</u>. (*Instead of*)

_____

_____

UNDERSTANDING INFERENCES

The Scientific Method

1. Curiosity (question).
2. Hypothesis (guess).
3. Gather facts to test (experiment).
4. Organization of the facts confirms (or doesn't confirm) the hypothesis.
5. Facts lead to a conclusion that either satisfies the original question or alters the original question.

The scientific method is based on the idea that a scientist gathers information, makes an hypothesis about that information (a guess about the conclusions that can be drawn from the information), then tests that hypothesis by gathering more facts from experiments. Sometimes the facts that a scientist gathers disprove the hypothesis, and sometimes the facts convince the scientist that the hypothesis is probably true. There is, however, always an element of doubt. Part of being a scientist is always to question so-called facts in order to further test their validity.

When you read about science, you will find that ideas are often stated with reservation. A scientist will tell you that something "appears" to be true, rather than "is" true, except for proven facts, of course. A science text will give the theories or hypotheses that seem to explain a situation, but then explain the problems involved with this interpretation. For example, the author of the chapter you have just read introduces information about the "self-report" by saying, "The usefulness of the self-report is limited primarily because of problems of validity." The key words in this statement are *limited* and *validity*. The author means that the "self-report" is not all bad, but that it must be used with caution; it is not completely accurate.

Let's look at another example. In the following statement the author is discussing the self-report as a means of measuring prejudice. "A person responds to a question such as, 'By nature the Negro and the white man are equal'; and *it is presumed that* the prejudices of a person are revealed through his response." With this statement, the author is telling the reader that the theory behind this measure of prejudice is that people's responses do reveal their prejudices, but the phrase *it is presumed that* tells us that this is only a theory, and not a proven fact. The author is being cautious, and as a reader of science you need to recognize this.

Exercise 10: Phrases of Reservation

An author can use many phrases to indicate reservation about an idea being expressed. Words and phrases such as *limitations, is supposed to, misleading, unreliable, biased, dubious, contradictory,* and *difficult to evaluate* all indicate that the author has doubts about the information being presented. In the following sentences, underline the phrase or phrases that put doubt into the mind of the reader.

1. The major limitation is the problem of identifying the appropriate behaviors to be measured and their associations with significant attitudes.

2. Negative racial feelings were supposed to be shown by remaining at a greater distance, less eye contact, and the tendency to lean away from rather than toward the other party.

3. Even these behaviorial techniques, although objective, reliable, and quantifiable, can be misleading.

4. Its use in the assessment of racial attitudes has been limited and it remains somewhat unreliable, difficult to interpret, and expensive.

5. Simpson and Yinger (1965) mention that earlier studies were limited in their usefulness because they attempted to find simple, one-factor explanations.

6. Broad theories such as the Marxist perspective are difficult to evaluate. Prejudice is relative—it is not an absolute in that one country or culture has it and another does not.

7. The basic assumption behind the belief congruence approach appears to involve an oversimplification of the problem.

8. The theories, although plausible on an ex post facto basis, are difficult to validate because of the relativity of such concepts as frustration and aggression and because of the difficulty of operationalizing the terms adequately.

9. There has been conflicting evidence of the efficacy of this method.

10. How effective this self-insight training will be on the average citizen also remains in doubt, for all subjects in past research have been college students.

USING CONNECTIVES TO LOCATE ARGUMENTS

You have just completed an exercise designed to help you recognize when a science writer is indicating reservation about a theory; in other words, the writer is telling you that it is just a theory and not a proven fact. Now we will focus on one kind of cue word that not only shows reservation but also points out the arguments against the theory: the connective we have called *unexpected result* or *contrast*. An unexpected result, or in this case an argument against a theory, is pointed out before the "cause" by the use of the connectives *although, even though, despite,* or *in spite of*.

> Example 1:   Although propaganda under certain conditions has been effective in reducing prejudice, studies have shown that people tend to avoid propaganda.

The *although* comes before the idea that is being discussed (the cause)— "propaganda has been effective in reducing prejudice"—but it signals the argument against this idea that appears in the other clause of the sentence— "people tend to avoid propaganda."

An argument is pointed out by "however," "but," and "nevertheless" just before the clause that gives the argument.

> Example 2:   Propaganda has been found successful when projected to captive audiences (especially through motion pictures) and when prejudiced attitudes are initially low, but its effectiveness remains questionable when applied to those already highly prejudiced.

We could rewrite the first example by using *but* instead of *although*, and the meaning would remain the same.

> Example 3:   Propaganda under certain conditions has been found effective in reducing prejudice, but people tend to avoid propaganda.

These connectives are very useful for quickly locating arguments. As you take notes while reading, you can use these connectives to find the arguments and organize the ideas in a **chart** with ideas on one side and arguments against those ideas on the other:

Idea	Arguments against the Idea

Exercise 11: Locating Arguments

The section "Reducing Prejudice" in the chapter you have just read consists of explanations of suggested ways to reduce prejudice and arguments against these suggestions. Use connectives as clues to locate the arguments, then fill in the missing parts of the following chart.

Suggestions	Connective	Argument against Suggestion
Example: Get rid of the capitalistic system	although	difficult to evaluate empirically
1. increased contact	_____	_____
2. specific contact	_____	_____
3. providing information with propaganda	although but	_____ _____
4. education	however but	_____ _____
5. school busing; different racial and class groups working together in school	but but	_____ _____
6. direct methods related to symptom theory	_____	_____
7. group therapy	but although	_____ _____
8. self-insight procedures	although	_____

Exercise 12: Essay Questions

Answer the following essay questions as clearly and completely as you can. The underlined word in each sentence is the essay-exam clue word that tells you what to do with the information in the chapter. To *discuss* means to describe, giving the details and explaining the pros and cons of the subject being discussed.

  1. <u>Discuss</u> the various ways of measuring prejudice mentioned in this chapter.

2. <u>Discuss</u> the explanations of prejudice given in this chapter. Explain why you think that some explanations are more reasonable than others.

3. <u>Discuss</u> the methods of reducing prejudice mentioned in this chapter. Which one do you think is the most effective? Why?

SOME SUGGESTED TOPICS FOR FURTHER READING

prejudice

race relations

<u>The Authoritarian Personality</u>

proxemics

exploitation

stigmatizing

stereotypes

ethnocentrism

scapegoating

Sigmund Freud

propaganda

psychotherapy

aggression

social distance

8

Reading
An Experiment Report

Photo: AFL-CIO News

American unionists support Solidarity
December, 1981

Basic Vocabulary

prohibition	intoxication	initiative
ban	discredit	militia
strike	dismissal	tipsy
survey	confiscated	informants
sober	provocation	black market
disciplinarily	categorical	

Exercise 1: Skimming Practice

The article you are going to read comes from an interdisciplinary quarterly called *Contemporary Drug Problems*. It is from the Fall 1982 issue, which also contains other experiment reports and short articles about alcohol and other drugs that are abused.

Begin your reading of this article by using the seven skimming steps. As you complete each step, answer the questions that follow it. (The article begins on page 274.)

STEP 1: Read the main title of the chapter and all of the headings. Notice how they relate to one another.

    a. What are the main divisions of this report?

STEP 2: Examine pictures, charts, and other illustrations in the chapter to get information about the chapter's contents.

    a. What is the purpose of table 1 on page 280?

    b. What was the most positive effect of the prohibition, according to table 2?

    c. What is the source of the data given in table 3?

STEP 3: Find the names of people, organizations, and so forth (proper names) in the chapter, and try to determine who or what they are.

    a. Who are Antoni Bielewicz and Jacek Moskalewicz?

    b. What is the Representative Committee?

    c. What is the Voivode?

    d. What are *Gazeta Poznańska*, *Trybuna Ludu*, and *Wieczór Wybrzeża?*

    e. What is the Solidarity Union?

    f. What are Wolów, Poznań, and Gdańsk names of?

    g. Who is E. Gierek?

STEP 4: Look at all of the italicized words and phrases. Be aware of the author's reasons for italicizing theme.

    a. The authors of this article use italicized words for only one reason. What is that reason?

STEP 5: Look at the review questions and bibliography at the end of the article to get more information about the article.

(There are no questions and no bibliography.)

STEP 6: Rapidly read the first and last paragraphs of the chapter and the first sentence of each paragraph.

STEP 7: In a sentence or two, explain what you think this article is about. (You may answer orally or quickly write the answer.)

FIRST READING

Quickly read the experiment report "Temporary Prohibition: The Gdańsk Experience, 1980" from *Contemporary Drug Problems*. You will notice that this report consists of four basic parts—four kinds of information that the authors want the reader to have. As you read, make notes in the margins about the main ideas and mark each section with one of the following labels.

    1. Conclusions from experiment

    2. Results of experiment

    3. Purpose of experiment

    4. Procedure for experiment

These four basic parts will be discussed later in the unit.

Temporary prohibition: The Gdańsk experience, August 1980

Antoni Bielewicz
Jacek Moskalewicz

INTRODUCTION

1 The prohibition experiences in Poland are not as rich as those of the USA or Scandinavian countries, where alcohol prohibition was in force over a large period of time. Though under both prewar and postwar anti-alcohol laws, the establishment of dry areas in Poland was possible, local authorities have rarely used that right. It was used to some extent in the district of Wolów in the late fifties. The ban on the sale of vodka in catering outlets resulted in some reduction in alcohol consumption in the district. The lack of vodka in catering outlets was not fully compensated for by buying alcohol in shops.

2   Since that time prohibition has not been introduced in Poland, the exceptions being one-day bans on alcohol sales and services issued by the Council of Ministers on days regarded as particularly festive (*e.g.*, May Day, elections). The next prohibition that lasted more than one or two days was introduced in the summer of 1980 during the mass workes' protest, which brought about substantial sociopolitical changes.

3   Our study on the prohibition introduced during the strikes was carried out in Gdańsk several months later. Although started several weeks later than in other parts of Poland, the strikes in Gdańsk played a crucial part in reaching the agreements between the authorities and the workers. The strikes in Gdańsk

AUTHORS' NOTE: This paper was first presented at the meeting of the Alcohol Epidemiology Section of the International Council on Alcohol and Addictions, Helsinki, June 1982. Accounts of the place of alcohol policy in subsequent Polish history can be found in J. Moskalewicz "Alcohol as a Public Issue: Recent Developments in Alcohol Control in Poland," 10 *Contemporary Drug Problems* 11–21 (1981); and I. Wald and J. Moskalewicz, "Alcohol Policy in the Crisis Situation," *British Journal of Addiction* (forthcoming).

Reprinted with permission of Federal Legal Publications, Inc., 157 Chambers Street, New York, NY 10007, from *Contemporary Drug Problems*, Fall 1982, pp. 367–381.

lasted from August 14 to 31. The prohibition was in force for almost the entire period, first in the striking factories and then in the whole province of Gdańsk.

4   To render a picture of the effects of the strike prohibition, we have used several sources of information: an informally conducted survey of about 300 inhabitants of Gdańsk; nondirective interviews with the representatives of the local administration and strike committees; and analysis of documents.

THE DECISION ON PROHIBITION

5   The idea to introduce prohibition within the factories emerged as early as the first day of the strike. In the Gdańsk shipyard, the issue was introduced by management's accusation that the strike had been organized by people who were not quite sober. At the workers' meeting on August 14, the head of the personnel department announced that one-fourth of the strikers were drunk. It was then that the motion to introduce a ban on drinking alcohol in the shipyard was first raised. There were voices, too, to proclaim prohibition in the whole province of Gdańsk. Immediately after the meeting, the Strike Committee went on inspection, which revealed two instances of drinking alcohol by the shipyard workers. The two workers were immediately removed from the shipyard and, after the strike, dismissed disciplinarily. A few hours later, the Strike Committee got a message that a young woman had been raped somewhere in the shipyard. The committee representatives checked the information immediately in the shipyard hospital. It turned out, according to the physician on duty as well as the patient, that no rape had taken place. An alarming fact, however, was that the woman was very drunk.

6   Attempts to discredit the strike as well as the above-mentioned instances of breaking of discipline by the workers brought about the Strike Committee's decision to introduce "an absolute ban on bringing in and drinking alcohol as well as remaining in a state of intoxication within the premises of factories." Like most decisions made in the first days of the strike, there was no direct consultation on this decision with the workers. For breaking the ban, there were very severe punishments: immediate removal from the shipyard followed by disciplinary dismissal.

7   In the Gdańsk oil refinery, the alcohol issue was raised at the beginning of the strike, too. It was known by then that vodka was being brought into the plants on strike. Owing to the particular character of the oil refinery, alcohol might have proved very dangerous. The Gdańsk refinery plants are spread over an area of 260 hectares, so the possibilities of bringing in alcohol were great. There was a danger of a fire being started by someone under the influence of alcohol. Here is what one of the members of the Representative Committee (the counterpart of Strike Committees in other factories) said in this regard:

"A drink, a smoke and fire's there. One drunken frolic and the whole strike will end in failure." An absolute ban on bringing in and drinking alcohol as well as remaining in a state of intoxication within the premises of the refinery was proclaimed as early as the second day of the strike, although no attempts at bringing alcohol in or instances of drinking among the workers had then been observed. Sanctions for breaking the ban were as severe as those in the shipyard.

8   The prohibition proclaimed in factories was strictly observed and controlled by the strike order-keeping forces. Parcels received by workers were checked. Even single bottles of beer were confiscated. Over the whole period of strikes in the refinery, only one case of breaking the ban was recorded. The drunken worker was dismissed disciplinarily. Several weeks after the strike, due to his sustained efforts, he was given the job back at lower pay.

9   Around August 20, an attempt to bring 14 bottles of spirits into the shipyard ended in failure. Eight bottles were broken at the gate, while the rest of them were sent to the shipyard hospital. Although the person trying to bring the spirits in was a close associate of the Strike Committee, sanctions as envisaged were applied against him (removal from the shipyard, disciplinary dismissal). Interviews with the members of the Strike Committee suggest that a provocation was suspected—that the incident was an attempt to cause disorder in the shipyard.

10   Several days following the proclamation of the prohibition in factories, on August 18, a ban on the sale and serving of alcoholic beverages was introduced in eight major cities of the Gdańsk Province. On August 21, the ban was extended to cover the whole province. According to the account given by the members of the Strike Committee of the Gdańsk shipyard, the day before the ban was introduced initial talks with the local authorities had taken place at the Provincial Government Office. A delegation from the shipyard had insisted on a proclamation of prohibition, but their demand had not then been accepted. The Voivode (head of the Provincial Government) feared the possible negative effects of the decision, suspecting that it might further increase tension in the city.

11   During the talks going on simultaneously concerning the supply of 50 thousand liters of gasoline to be used by the ambulance service and other city services, the members of the Representative Committee of the Gdańsk refinery agreed to release the gasoline on the condition that alcohol sales were stopped. In a letter to the Voivode on August 18, the demand was expressed in categorical terms: "On behalf of the workers of all plants on strike and themselves, the Representative Committee of the Gdańsk Refinery demands categorically that all vodka stores and departments be closed down for the duration of the strike, for obvious reasons." The response came immediately. About an hour later,

the director of the Gdańsk refinery received a telex signed by the Voivode: "In reply to the refinery workers' demand concerning the prohibition of alcohol sales, I inform [you] that I have issued a ban on the sale of beverages of over 2 percent alcohol content, both retail and in catering outlets." Indeed, the same day the Provincial Office released the following telex: "From August 18th until further notice the sale of alcoholic beverages (including beer) in all retail and catering outlets is forbidden. . . ."

12 As the above shows, restrictions introduced by the provincial administration ranged far beyond the workers' demands. The Representative Committee of the Gdańsk refinery demanded the closing down of all vodka stores; the administration banned the sale of all alcoholic beverages in all stores and catering outlets. Also, the account of the events as presented by the Provincial Office differed considerably from the workers' version. According to the interviews with the representatives of the administration, anti-alcohol demands were raised when the decision on the prohibition had already been made. The prohibition, according to the Voivode of Gdańsk,

> *was surely our initiative. What we had in view was the need to keep order. That was a part of the plan of action to have the city prepared in case the events took a course like during riots in December 1970. . . . The danger was that in such circumstances the social margin . . . would take advantage of the unrest to start extreme actions; that hooligan acts would take place.*

13 The decision was made at the provincial "top level," in no consultation, however, with the central authorities in Warsaw. The head of the Department of Trade and Services stated that he had been summoned by "the three bosses" (the First Secretary of the Provincial Committee of the Polish United Workers' Party, the Voivode, and the Vice-Voivode) and told to carry out the decision. Thus, as in the factories, the decision on the prohibition had not been a matter of consultation or discussion in wider circles. This shows the importance attached to a prompt introduction of the prohibition.

14 The decision to introduce the prohibition provides an example of the independent and efficient action on the part of the provincial authorities that largely contributed to the fact that the conflict ended in agreement and did not turn into a sharp confrontation. The prohibition was not merely a technical means to keep the peace during the strikes. It was a move of considerable political significance, too. Both parties expressed their willingness to solve the conflict by peaceful means; they wanted to be perceived as social peace agents.

15 In Polish political life, alcohol has often been used as an argument to discredit the opposing forces. Way back in June 1956, the press repeatedly reported on "drunk individuals" taking the lead in the workers' demonstrations.

An unsigned article that appeared in *Gazeta Poznańska* (the Poznań daily paper) on July 1, 1956, read:

> *I have been listening all night to interrogations of people arrested by the security forces, suspected of bloody riots and robbery. . . . They mostly were very young people . . . people, most of whom when interrogated (12 hours after the disturbances had been suppressed) were still partly intoxicated with alcohol. . . . I have heard statements by old gangsters, criminals who on June 28th left a broken down prison. . . . Here I am, sitting face to face with Zygmunt C.: his looks wild, the smell of alcohol in the air.*

16   Similar arguments appearing in the press accompanied subsequent social conflicts. For example, in 1968 the Warsaw *Trybuna Ludu* of March 12 reported that the student leaders called for help with "groups of dirty hooligans that usually stand by the kiosks with beer." In December 1970, the accusation that demonstrations were dominated by a drunken mob was very frequently heard. Even when E. Gierek came to power, the press did not stop presenting events in this way. The front page of *Glos Szczeciński* (the newspaper in Szczecin) on December 19, 1970, talked about a delicatessen having been broken into, "from which alcohol was stolen and a food store which also was plundered mostly of alcoholic beverages. Drunken scum of all sorts started for other public buildings, *e.g.*, the Militia headquarters."

17   Reviewing press articles of the years of previous unrest (1956, 1968, 1970, and 1976) makes it easier to understand why the Gdańsk workers in 1980 demanded that prohibition be proclaimed during the conflict. It seems that the need to keep the peace in the city was of secondary importance. The introduction of the prohibition first of all made it impossible to once again use the alcohol issue as a political weapon. To justify the demand for prohibition, the Chairman of the Works Committee of the Solidarity Union at the Gdańsk refinery said: "People recalled the year 1970. The press at that time wrote constantly that it was not a protest of the working class but what they called tipsy individuals."

18   The demand to ban the sale of alcohol was one of the first workers' demands formulated in categorical terms. It was the first specific test of power in an area that seemed politically neutral. The test took place when the Strike Committees had not yet been recognized by the authorities.

19   It is worth noting that the previously mentioned telex from the Voivode about the introduction of the prohibition was addressed to the director of the refinery and not to the Representative Committee. It also is interesting in this context that the information on that first agreement was not passed on to the central authorities until several days later. It was not announced immediately in the local press, either.

THE SOCIAL PERCEPTION AND
ACCEPTANCE OF THE PROHIBITION

20 Despite the lack of announcement in the mass media, the information about the prohibition spread rapidly among the inhabitants of Gdańsk. Over 80 percent of our survey informants learned about it in the first week of the strike. They learned mostly from informal sources: relatives, colleagues, friends—43.2 percent; strike bulletins, leaflets, factory radio circuits—19.8 percent. Other subjects learned about the ban in shops (while trying to buy alcohol, from notices, seeing shelves with alcohol curtained, closed-down departments, etc.). Most of the respondents thought the idea to introduce prohibition came from the workers. This probably accounts for the wide acceptance of the prohibition. When asked whether the prohibition had been necessary, only 2 percent of the respondents gave a negative answer, while 85 percent definitely supported the move.

21 Justifications given were generally the same as presented by those who had made the decision. Almost all the respondents maintained that the prohibition had helped to keep the peace, that it had been necessary in order to prevent public disorder; two-thirds of the respondents recalled the experience of December 1970 and about one-third said that the possibility of provocation was thus limited.

22 Although the Gdańsk prohibition did not forbid drinking, more than three-fourths of the respondents thought alcohol should not have been drunk at all during that time. Instances of breaking this social norm were relatively rare. During the two weeks of the prohibition, nearly 80 percent of the subjects did not drink alcohol at all. Of those who did drink at that time, most took alcohol once at the occasion of traditional family celebrations (namedays, birthdays, weddings). Almost three-fourths of the respondents did not see any drunk people in the streets during the strikes, though the militia were not particularly active in preventing public drunkenness. On the contrary, the militia almost disappeared from the streets in order not to provoke unnecessary conflicts.

23 The observance of the ban on the sale of alcohol in shops and restaurants was not monitored and the regulation by the Voivode did not include any sanctions against shop assistants or waiters. Still, both direct interviews and questionnaires showed a firm attitude of shop assistants, who—according to our respondents—definitely refused to sell alcohol. According to our informants, the same was true in restaurants. Even in the best hotels alcohol was not served—not even to foreign journalists, hotel guests, government representatives, or the Inter-Factory Strike Committee's advisers.

24 In view of the common acceptance of the prohibition, it is interesting to see how the subjects answered the question: "To what extent did the below-listed restrictions or limitations make daily life of the inhabitants of Gdańsk

difficult during the strikes?" (See table 1.) In the case of alcohol, there was a relatively large divergence of opinion. Sixty percent of the subjects maintained that the lack of alcohol during the strikes did not affect the city life at all. However, every fourth respondent felt deprived by not being able to buy alcohol. Among the eight factors that made the daily life of the inhabitants difficult, the prohibition was ranked fourth. In light of these findings, we can presume that the prohibition was accepted not from the purely moral point of view (disapproval of alcohol, as such), but rather for instrumental reasons (the need to keep the peace, avoid provocation) and as a gesture symbolizing the public's support of the strike.

TABLE 1   The Effect of Various Limitations on Life in Gdańsk During the Strikes

Nature of Limitation	Degree of Difficulty (Percentage of Responses*)			
	Large	Small	None	No Opinion
No telephone communication	72.4	11.5	10.5	5.6
Transport disruptions	40.9	36.0	20.6	2.4
Lack of newspapers	25.8	39.7	29.6	4.9
Lack of alcohol	25.0	13.0	59.9	2.1
Shortages in supply of basic foodstuffs	19.2	35.9	41.5	3.5
Lack of cigarettes	14.1	28.9	48.9	8.1
Lack of coffee	13.0	33.3	34.7	18.9
Limited entertainment	10.8	24.1	55.6	9.4

Totals may vary from 100% due to rounding.

EFFECTS OF THE PROHIBITION

25 The prohibition, like every alcohol control measure as well as drinking itself, brought about a range of effects, both positive and negative. According to the respondents, the introduction of the prohibition played a considerable part in maintaining order and social discipline during the strikes. Nearly 90 percent of the subjects were of this opinion. The decision was of great political significance, too—it prevented the strikes from turning into street riots. This opinion was expressed by three-fourths of the respondents. These and other positive aspects of the prohibition are shown in table 2.

TABLE 2   Positive Effects of the Prohibition

Nature of Consequence	Advantage (Percentage of Responses)			
	Large	Small	None	No Opinion
Maintaining discipline during the strikes	86.8	7.3	4.2	1.7
Preventing the strikes from turning into street riots	74.9	12.5	9.1	3.5
Reducing the number of accidents	62.0	25.8	5.9	6.3
Reducing the number of rows, riots, etc.	83.6	12.2	1.4	2.8
Calling the public's attention to the problem of alcohol in Poland	53.5	24.8	14.0	7.7

26   Complementary to the survey findings was the opinion expressed by the Voivode of Gdańsk: "There was great discipline among people. The city life went on so that visitors were saying: 'Nothing is happening here. . . .' A drop in the number of crimes was noted, although the militia activity in the town was reduced to a minimum. The point was to make them less visible."

27   The lack of alcohol clearly affected the work of the ambulance service as well as statistics from sobering-up Wybrzeża stations. *Wieczór Wybrzeża* [The Coast Evening] twice reported on the work of the ambulance service running quietly throughout the strike period (August 20, and August 25, 1980). Similar opinion was expressed by Maria Olszańska in her 1980 article in *Problemy Alkoholizmu* [Alcoholism Issues]. Sobering-up stations noted a considerable decline in attendance. During the 16 days of the prohibition, the sobering-up station in Gdańsk admitted 226 clients—less than half the number admitted during the 16 days preceding the prohibition, and about one-third the number admitted during the 16 days following the prohibition in September. In the first week of the prohibition, only 40 persons were admitted to the sobering-up station in Gdańsk; that is, one-sixth the number admitted in the week preceding the prohibition. An increased attendance in the second week of the prohibition may have reflected illicit supplies of alcohol beginning to come from other regions. The extension of prohibition over a longer period of time would probably have resulted in the development of an alcohol black market to meet the unsatisfied demand.

28   The illicit sale of alcohol at a time when alcohol was lacking did not surprise our respondents. Only 13.2 percent of them maintained that the prohibition

had not affected the spread of unlicensed trade. Every eighth subject witnessed instances of vodka being sold in the streets, gateways, etc.

29   Black-market alcohol came mostly from other provinces. In the strike period, the militia seized 10 transports of alcohol coming to Gdańsk. Amounts of alcohol seized were not too large; in some instances, however, several cases of vodka were involved. Black-market prices of vodka were two to three times as high as the official ones. Shops and catering outlets played a minor part as sources of alcohol, and only 9 percent of the respondents thought that the prohibition substantially stimulated the illegal sale of alcohol in shops.

30   Among the negative effects of the prohibition, 60 percent of the respondents mentioned difficulties in organizing traditional family celebrations. No permissions to buy alcohol were given during the prohibition, even on the occasion of wedding or baptism ceremonies. Nevertheless, there were only two cases where previously announced weddings were called off. It seems that alcohol was somehow arranged for most celebrations of this kind. However, their tone differed considerably from the usual, regardless of whether there was alcohol or not, and in what quantities: the events that were taking place in the town affected the atmosphere and course of such celebrations. Alcohol was a minor or insignificant factor.

31   When the prohibition was repealed, the consumption of alcoholic beverages in the Gdańsk province increased and surpassed the usual level. Presumably, for many people, redoubled drinking was a kind of compensation for the dry period. According to our survey findings, 41.9 percent of the subjects took alcohol during the first week after the ban on the sale of alcohol had been lifted, of which half did it as soon as the first or second day. Increased alcohol consumption corresponded with increased attendance in sobering-up stations. On the first day, the sobering-up station in Gdańsk, which has 41 beds, admitted 54 intoxicated persons. The increased influx of clients lasted for about two weeks; that is, until the second Sunday after the strike. As compared to the analogous period of the year before, admittance during those 11 days was 34 percent higher. On the following days, the situation was back to normal. The brief rise in alcohol consumption did not particularly affect its overall level in the third quarter of 1980. (See table 3.)

32   Lower than usual consumption during the three months in question cannot be explained by the ban on the sale of alcohol. The 16 days of the prohibition constituted 17 percent of the three-month period, whereas alcohol consumption in that quarter was 30.7 percent lower than the average three-month consumption in 1980. It seems, then, that the prohibition had a considerable impact on the attitudes toward alcohol among the inhabitants of Gdańsk, thus moderating the level of consumption, particularly in the latter part of September. Responses to the survey question, "To what extent did the prohibition contribute to calling

TABLE 3 Sales of Alcoholic Beverages of Over
4.5 Percent Alcohol Content in 1980

Quarter	Thousand Liters of 100% Alcohol	Percentage of Annual Total*
First	1,955.3	25.6
Second	2,357.8	30.3
Third	1,348.8	17.3
Fourth	2,119.2	27.2

The total varies from 100% due to rounding.
Source: Data of the Gdańsk Provincial Office.

the public's attention to the problem of alcohol in Poland?", support that hypothesis; 53.5 percent of the respondents regarded that contribution as substantial, while only 14 percent did not see the relationship. (See table 2.)

33   Over the following several months, the positive effects of the prohibition during the strikes as well as the fact that alcohol had become a political issue resulted in a frequent use of this new alcohol control measure by both the government and Solidarity. In these months prohibition, local or country-wide, was introduced several times. The result was the depreciation of the gesture; subsequent bans were no longer accepted and observed so commonly, and their negative effects became more visible.

FINAL REMARKS

34 The temporary prohibition in Gdańsk proved to be a very effective alcohol control measure. Its influence in maintaining discipline and order in a period of serious social tensions is unquestionable. The lack of drunken comportment in the strikes reduced considerably the risk of force being used in that social conflict.

35   The significance of this prohibition goes far beyond the direct instrumental functions of any alcohol control measure. Its introduction made it impossible to use alcohol as a political weapon in discrediting the workers' movement. It must also be stressed that the demand to introduce prohibition was the first workers' demand formulated in categorical terms to be accepted by the authorities. The part this first "agreement" played in determining the further "rules of the game" in that social conflict cannot be ignored.

Exercise 2: Basic Vocabulary Chart

Use your English-to-English dictionary to help you complete this chart. Put
the chart on a separate sheet of paper so that you will have room to write
all of the appropriate definitions and related words. Provide the meaning
of the word as it is used in the indicated paragraph.

Word	Part of Speech	Meaning (as used in indicated paragraph)	Related Words	Synonyms
prohibition (1)				
ban (1)				
strike (3)				
survey (4)				
sober (5)				
disciplinarily (5)				
intoxication (6)				
discredit (6)				
dismissal (6)				
confiscated (8)				
provocation (9)				
categorical (11)				
initiative (12)				
militia (16)				
tipsy (17)				
informants (23)				
black market (29)				

Exercise 3: Word Substitution with Basic Vocabulary

For each of the following sentences, choose one of the following words or
phrases that has the same meaning as the underlined word or phrase. Write
the answer in the blank.

dry	prohibited	confiscated
tipsy	informants	sober
dismissed	discredit	sanction
confrontations		

1. Smoking is <u>forbidden</u> in areas that contain flammable substances.

   _____

2. It was possible to have areas in Poland <u>where alcohol was prohibited</u>.

   _____ areas in Poland

3. Mr. Greg was <u>a little drunk</u> when the police removed him from the car and led him into the police station.

   _____

4. The scientists found fifty people to act as <u>sources of information</u>.

   _____

5. All of the alcohol found in public places was <u>appropriated by the authorities</u>.

   _____

6. There were very few people at the party who were <u>not intoxicated</u>.

   _____

7. It is not clear what the <u>punishment</u> is for this crime.

   _____

8. The employee was <u>let go</u> because his work was not up to the standard.

   _____

9. Very few <u>fights</u> took place between the police and the strikers because of the prohibition.

   _____

10. The job of the lawyer was to try to <u>prove that</u> the witness <u>was not telling the truth</u>.

    To _____ the witness

Exercise 4: Recognizing Synonyms

Match the words on the left with their synonyms on the right. When you have finished, look up the answers to the ones you did not know.

1. informant _____	a. forbid
2. ban _____	b. begin
3. prohibit _____	c. seize
4. survey _____	d. cease working
5. dismiss _____	e. discharge
6. discredit _____	f. outlaw
7. confiscate _____	g. inspect
8. sober _____	h. refuse to believe
9. strike _____	i. respondent
10. initiate _____	j. self-controlled

READING PROBLEMS

Exercise 5: References

Read the following sentences from "Temporary Prohibition: The Gdańsk Experience, August 1980." References are underlined. On the lines under the sentences, write the word or phrase to which each reference refers.

> Example: At the workers' meeting on August 14, the head of the personnel department announced that one fourth of the strikers were drunk. It was <u>then</u> that the motion to introduce a ban on drinking alcohol in the shipyard was first raised.
>
>   then ____August 14____

1. A few hours later, the Strike Committee got a message that a young woman had been raped somewhere in the shipyard. The committee representatives checked <u>the information</u> immediately in the shipyard hospital.

   the information _____

2. A delegation from the shipyard had insisted on a proclamation of prohibition, but their demand had not then been accepted. The

Voivode feared the possible negative effects of <u>the decision</u>, suspecting that it might further increase tension in the city.

the decision _____

3. In Polish political life, alcohol has often been used as an argument to discredit the opposing forces. Way back in June 1956, the press repeatedly reported on "drunk individuals" taking the lead in workers' demonstrations. Even when E. Gierek came to power, the press did not stop presenting events <u>in this way</u>.

in this way _____

4. Most of the respondents thought the idea to introduce prohibition came from the workers. <u>This</u> probably accounts for the wide acceptance of the prohibition.

This _____

5. Both direct interviews and questionnaires showed a firm attitude of shop assistants, who—according to our respondents—definitely refused to sell alcohol. According to our informants, <u>the same</u> was true in restaurants.

the same _____

6. Sixty percent of the subjects maintained that the lack of alcohol during the strikes did not affect the city life at all. However, every fourth respondent felt deprived by not being able to buy alcohol. Among the eight factors that made the daily life of the inhabitants difficult, the prohibition was ranked fourth. In light of <u>these findings</u>, we can presume that the prohibition was accepted not from the purely moral point of view, but rather for instrumental reasons.

these findings _____

7. According to the respondents, the introduction of the prohibition played a considerable part in maintaining order and discipline during the strikes. The decision was of great political significance, too—it prevented the strikes from turning into street riots. <u>These</u> and other positive aspects of the prohibition are shown in table 2.

These _____

8. Among the negative effects of the prohibition, 60 percent of the respondents mentioned difficulties in organizing traditional family

celebrations. No permissions to buy alcohol were given during the prohibition, even on the occasion of wedding or baptism ceremonies. Nevertheless, there were only two cases where previously announced weddings were called off. It seems that alcohol was somehow arranged for most celebrations <u>of this kind</u>.

of this kind _____

Exercise 6: Scanning for Details

Scan the article (pp. 274–283) to find the answers to the following questions. Work as rapidly as you can.

1. Where was this paper first presented?
2. What are May Day and elections examples of in this article?
3. What happened in Poland from August 14, 1980, to August 31, 1980?
4. How many people were surveyed in this study?
5. How large an area do the Gdańsk refinery plants cover?
6. When did someone attempt to bring some alcohol into the shipyard?
7. What percentage of alcohol did the banned beverages contain?
8. How long did the prohibition last?

Exercise 7: Guessing Word Meanings from Context

Try to guess the meanings of the underlined words in the following sentences from "Temporary Prohibition: The Gdańsk Experience, August 1980." Begin by underlining the words and phrases that give you the clues you need to make a good guess, then write your definition of the word on the line under the sentence. Do not look these words up in your dictionary until *after* you have guessed their meanings.

Example: Immediately after the meeting, the Strike Committee went on inspection, which <u>revealed</u> two instances of drinking alcohol by the shipyard workers.

to make clear, or to point out _____

Since an inspection *revealed* this information, and we know that *inspection* means "to look carefully into something," *reveal* must mean "to make clear" or "to point out."

1. Here is what one of the members of the Representative Committee (the counterpart of Strike Committees in other factories) said in this regard.

2. The prohibition proclaimed in factories was strictly observed and controlled by the strike order-keeping forces. Parcels received by workers were checked. Even single bottles of beer were confiscated.

3. Around August 20, an attempt to bring 14 bottles of spirits into the shipyard ended in failure.

4. The account of the events as presented by the Provincial Office differed considerably from the worker's version.

5. Most of the respondents thought the idea to introduce prohibition came from the workers. This probably accounts for the wide acceptance of the prohibition.

6. Although the Gdańsk prohibition did not forbid drinking, more than three-fourths of the respondents thought alcohol should not have been drunk at all during that time. Instances of breaking this social norm were relatively rare. During the two weeks of the prohibition, nearly 80 percent of the subjects did not drink alcohol at all.

7. In view of the common acceptance of the prohibition, it is interesting to see how the subjects answered the question: "To what extent did the below-listed restrictions or limitations make daily life of the inhabitants of Gdańsk difficult during the strikes?"

8. In the first week of the prohibition, only 40 persons were admitted to the sobering-up station in Gdańsk; that is, one-sixth the number

admitted in the week preceding the prohibition. An increased attendance in the second week of the prohibition may have reflected <u>illicit</u> supplies of alcohol beginning to come from other regions.

---

9. Alcohol was a <u>minor</u> or insignificant factor.

---

10. When the prohibition was repealed, the consumption of alcoholic beverages in the Gdańsk province increased and <u>surpassed</u> the usual level.

ELEMENTS OF A JOURNAL REPORT

A journal report usually consists of several basic parts, no matter if it is a report of an experiment in electrical engineering or the results of a sociological study. First, the <u>purpose</u> of the study or experiment is stated. The writer tells the reader why the information was gathered and perhaps the hypothesis that he or she wanted to test. Second, the <u>procedure</u> that was used to conduct the experiment or study is explained. If it is an experiment, the writer describes the equipment or apparatus used and the step-by-step process that was followed. If it is a sociological study, like the article you are about to read, the writer explains how the information was gathered (surveys, interviews, observation of behavior, and so on) and who the informants were.

Next, the writer explains the <u>results</u> of these surveys, interviews or experiments. He or she will describe what happened during the experiment or what the answers were to questions asked. This information will usually be illustrated with charts, tables, or graphs, and will be expressed as statistics.

Finally, the writer draws <u>conclusions</u> from the results. What do these statistics imply? What has the writer learned? Perhaps the study disproved rather than proved the writer's hypothesis. The author's thoughts are discussed in the "Final Remarks" or "Conclusions" section of the report.

The writer may mix these four parts. For example, in the article in this unit, the authors give statistics and comment immediately on their assumptions based on the statistics. To let the reader know that they are stating conclusions and assumptions, the authors introduce their statements with the following phrases:

"It seems then. . ."
"As the above shows. . ."
"This shows that. . ."
"It seems that. . ."
"In the light of these findings. . ."
". . .cannot be explained by. . ."

The authors of this article also use special phrases to help the reader follow the process of their thinking. They introduce ideas with the following phrases:

"It is worth noting. . ."
"It is interesting in this context. . ."
"It is interesting to see. . ."

As you read the article again, be aware of the structure of the report and the special phrases that the authors use to make their ideas more clear to the reader.

SECOND READING

Read the article *Contemporary Drug Problems* carefully. As you read, try to find the main idea in each paragraph and underline it. Also, look for supporting information that explains the main idea. As you finish reading each section, write notes from your reading on a separate sheet of paper.

POST–READING

REACTION QUESTIONS

1. Which results of the prohibition were surprising to you?
2. What did not happen as a result of the prohibition that you would have expected to happen?
3. How do the results of this prohibition in Gdańsk differ from the results that you think would occur from a similar prohibition in your city?

4. What was the purpose of this study?

5. How might the information learned from this study be used in the future?

Exercise 8: Understanding the Findings

Use the statistics and tables in this article to quickly answer the following questions. (Tables are located on pages 280, 281, and 283.)

1. How many people were surveyed in the study discussed in this article?

2. How many people in the survey felt that the prohibition was unnecessary?

3. What percentage of those surveyed didn't drink any alcohol during the prohibition?

4. Which limitation on life during the strikes presented the least amount of difficulty, according to those surveyed?

5. How many informants felt that prohibition played a large part in maintaining order and social discipline during the strike?

6. How many people were admitted to the Gdańsk sobering-up station on the first day after the ban had been lifted?

7. How many respondents felt that there was no relationship between the prohibition and calling the public's attention to the problem of alcohol in Poland?

RECOGNIZING THE CHRONOLOGICAL ORDER OF EVENTS

In order to draw logical conclusions from statistics and events, especially cause-result conclusions, it is necessary to determine the order in which events took place. This may not be the same as the order in which these events are discussed in a report. The reader needs to notice times, dates, and such time indicators as *then, after that, the following day, the first day, a few hours later,* and so on. These clues will help the reader order events, and thereby come to logical conclusions about those events.

Exercise 9: Recognizing the Chronological Order of Events

The following events were reported in the article you have just read. They are, however, out of order. Put these events in the sequence in which they actually occurred by numbering them 1–6.

____ A ban on bringing in and drinking alcohol as well as remaining in a state of intoxication within the premises of the oil refinery was proclaimed.

____ A ban on the sale and serving of alcoholic beverages was introduced in eight major cities of Gdańsk Province.

____ Gdańsk shipyard management claimed that the strike was organized by people who were not sober.

____ The Strike Committee decided to introduce a ban on bringing in and drinking alcohol and being intoxicated on the premises of factories.

____ Someone tried to bring 14 bottles of alcohol into the shipyard.

____ The ban on selling and serving alcoholic beverages was extended to cover the whole of Gdańsk.

Exercise 10: Finding Support for the Writers' Conclusions

The authors of this article come to several conclusions based on the statistics they gathered. They usually state their conclusion in the first sentence of a paragraph, then give support for that statement in the rest of the paragraph.

The sentences that follow are conclusions that the authors come to in this article. After each conclusion list the support given by the authors for that conclusion.

1. The introduction of the prohibition played a considerable part in maintaining order and social discipline during the strikes.

_____

_____

_____

_____

2. The lack of alcohol clearly affected the work of the ambulance service.

_____

_____

_____

3. Lack of alcohol clearly affected statistics from sobering-up Wybrzeża stations.

_____

_____

_____

4. When the prohibition was repealed, the consumption of alcoholic beverages in the Gdańsk Province increased and surpassed the usual level.

_____

_____

_____

5. Lower than usual consumption during the three months in question cannot be explained by the ban on the sale of alcohol._____

_____

_____

Exercise 11: Paraphrasing Practice

Paraphrase the following sentences by following the directions after each one.

1. Since that time prohibition has not been introduced in Poland, the exceptions being one-day bans on alcohol sales and services issued by the Council of Ministers on days regarded as particularly festive.

a. Use *except* rather than <u>the exception being</u>, and change the structure of the sentence to make it correct.

b. Remove <u>regarded as</u> and substitute another phrase. (*thought of as, considered*)

_____

_____

2. Although started several weeks later than in other parts of Poland, the strikes in Gdańsk played a crucial part in reaching the agreements between the authorities and the workers.

a. Use a different connector for <u>although</u>.

b. Use <u>the strikes</u> as the subject of the sentence.

_____

_____

3. Like most decisions made in the first days of the strike, there was no direct consultation on this decision with the workers.

a. Substitute another word or phrase for <u>like</u>.

b. Make <u>the workers</u> the subject of the sentence.

_____

_____

4. Owing to the particular character of the oil refinery, alcohol might have proved very dangerous.

a. Substitute another word or phrase for <u>owing to</u>. (*due to, because of*)

b. Substitute another word for <u>dangerous</u>.

_____

_____

5. Several weeks after the strike, due to his sustained efforts, he was given the job back at lower pay.

    a. Substitute another word or phrase for <u>due to</u>.

    b. Rephrase the part of the sentence that reads <u>he was given the job back</u>. (Make it active rather than passive, or change the subject to <u>the job</u>.)

_____

_____

6. Also, the account of the events as presented by the Provincial Office differed considerably from the workers' version.

    a. Use a different phrase for <u>differed from</u>.

    b. Substitute a different word or phrase for <u>version</u>.

_____

_____

7. Reviewing press articles of the years of previous unrest makes it easier to understand why the Gdańsk workers in 1980 demanded that prohibition be proclaimed during the conflict.

    a. Begin the sentence with <u>It is easier</u>.

    b. Change *Reviewing press articles* to *If one reviews press articles*.

_____

_____

8. In the case of alcohol, there was a relatively large divergence of opinion.

    a. Use another word for <u>divergence</u>.

    b. Substitute a different phrase for <u>In the case of alcohol</u>. (*as far as alcohol is concerned, regarding alcohol*)

_____

_____

9. In the light of these findings, we can presume that the prohibition was accepted not from the purely moral point of view, but rather for instrumental reasons.

a. Use a different phrase for <u>In the light of these findings</u>.

b. Rephrase the part of the sentence that reads <u>but rather for instru-mental reasons</u>. (Use the word *instead*.)

_____

_____

_____

Exercise 12: Essay Questions

Answer the following essay questions as clearly and completely as you can. The underlined word in each sentence is the essay-exam clue word that tells you what to do with the information in the article. To <u>discuss</u> means to describe, giving details and explaining the pros and cons of the subject under consideration. To <u>trace</u> means to put information in chronological order.

1. <u>Discuss</u> both the negative and positive effects of the temporary prohibition.

2. <u>Trace</u> the important events that occurred from the idea to ban alcohol use within the factories to the repeal of this ban.

SUGGESTED TOPICS FOR FURTHER READING

prohibition	Polish politics
alcoholism	effects of alcohol on behavior
strikes	Solidarity
labor unions	substance abuse

Appendix:
Affixes and Stems

PREFIXES

Prefix	Usual Meaning	Examples
a- (an-)	not, without, lacking	amoral, atheist
anti-	against	antiabortion
auto-	self	automatic, autobiography
bi-	two, twice	bilingual
by-	close, incidental	byproduct
circum-	around	circumstance
co- (col-) com- (con-)	with, together	coauthor
contra-	against	contradict
cor-	with, together	correspond
counter-	contrary, opposite, complimentary	counterproductive
de-	reduce, lower, down	decrease
dis-	away, not, fail to	disappear, disorganized
ex-	out, from	exit
extra-	very, outside the scope of	extracurricular
hyper-	above, excessive, beyond	hypertension
hypo-	under, less than, lower	hypodermic
il- (ir-, im-)	not	immoral
im- (in-)	in, into, on, inside	immerse
inter-	between, among	international
intra- (intro-)	within, inside	introspection
macro-	large	macrocosm
mal-	bad, wrong	malfunction
mega-	large, powerful	megaphone
micro-	small	microphone
mid-	middle, halfway	midweek
mini-	very small or short	minimum
mis-	bad, wrong, not	miscalculate
mono-	single, one	monopoly
multi-	many	multipurpose
non-	not	nonproductive
poly-	many	polygamy

Prefix	Usual Meaning	Examples
post-	after, behind	postgraduate
pseudo-	false, unreal, sham	pseudonym
re-	again	reorganize
re- (retro-)	behind, back, backward	retroactive
semi-	half, partially	semiretired
sub- (suc-) suf- (sug-) sup- (sus-)	under, below, lower, lesser	substandard
super- (supra-)	above, over, higher or greater than	supersonic
trans-	across	transport
tri-	three	tricycle
un-	not, opposite, reverse	undo
under-	lower, inferior, below	underlie
uni-	one, single	unify, unicycle

STEMS

Stem	Usual Meaning	Examples
-ali- (-alter-)	another, other	alternative
-anthrop-	human	anthropology
-arch-	chief, leader	monarchy
-aud-	listen, hear	audition
-auto-	self	autonomous
-ben- (-bon-)	good	benefactor
-bibl-	book	bibliography
-bio-	life	biology
-capit- (-capt-)	head, chief	capital
-ced- (-cess-)	go, move, surrender	proceed
-cent-	hundred	century
-chron-	time	chronic
-corp-	body	corporation
-cosm-	world, order	microcosm
-cycl-	cycle, wheel	bicycle

Stem	Usual Meaning	Examples
-dem-	people	democratic
-dic-	say, tell	dictate
-duc-	lead	conduct
-fact-	do	manufacture
-fed- (-fid-)	faith, trust	confident
-fin-	end	finish
-fort-	strong	fortify
-geo-	earth	geography
-gram- (-graph-)	write	autograph
-hetero-	different	heterodox
-homo-	self, same	homogeneous
-hydro-	water	hydroelectric
-man-	hand	manual
-medi-	middle	medium
-metr-	measure	thermometer
-miss- (-mit-)	send	transmit
-mort-	death	mortal
-nov-	new	renovate
-ology-	study of	biology
-ortho-	correct, true, straight	orthodox
-para-	resembling, beside	paramedical
-pathy-	feeling	sympathy
-ped- (-pod-)	foot	bipedal
-port-	carry	import
-psych-	mind	psychology
-sequ- (-secut-)	follow	consecutive
-soph-	wisdom	sophisticated
-spec- (-spic-)	look	spectator
-tele-	long distance	telephone
-tract-	pull	tractor
-vene- (-vent-)	come	convene
-ver-	true	verify
-vers- (-vert-)	turn	converse
-voc- (-vok-)	call	vocal

SUFFIXES

Suffix	Usual Meaning	Examples
-ability	capacity for, ability to	educability
-able (-ble, -ible)	capable of being	learnable, edible
-al	possessing the quality of	comical
-ance (-ence)	state, condition of, quality of	tolerance, indifference
-ate	to make	translate
-ation (-tion)	condition or act of	translation, devotion
-dom	state or condition	wisdom
-ee	recipient of an action	employee
-en	to make	widen
-er (-or)	person or thing who/that	farmer
-ess	female	lioness
-ful	characterized by, having the quality of	eventful
-fy	to make	satisfy
-hood	state, condition	statehood
-ic (-ical)	quality or condition of	magical
-ine	like, with the quality of	marine
-ious (-ous)	like, full of	religious
-ish	like, somewhat, partly	sheepish
-ism (-ist)	action, state, condition	communism
-ist	person who	communist
-ization	act or state of	mechanization
-ize	to make	socialize
-less	without, lacking	penniless
-ly	like, in the manner of	quickly
-ness	state, condition	happiness
-ogy (-ology)	science, study of	biology
-oid	like, resembling	schizoid
-ory	having the quality of	sensory
-ous (-ose, -ious, -uous)	like, full of, having the quality of	comatose
-proof	resistant to	waterproof
-ship	quality, state of, office, skill	leadership

Suffix	Usual Meaning	Examples
-tion	state, condition, act of	addiction
-ward	in the direction of	backward
-wise	in the direction or manner of	sidewise
-y	having the quality of	healthy